Pocket SAN FRANCISCO

TOP SIGHTS • LOCAL LIFE • MADE EASY

Alison Bing

In This Book

QuickStart Guide

Your keys to understanding the city – we help you decide what to do and how to do it

Need to Know
Tips for a smooth trip

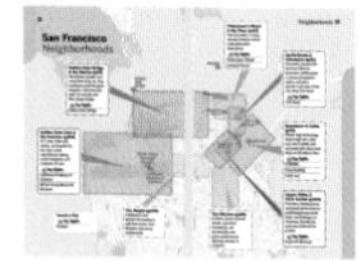

Neighborhoods
What's where

Explore San Francisco

The best things to see and do, neighborhood by neighborhood

Top Sights
Make the most of your visit

Local Life
The insider's city

The Best of San Francisco

The city's highlights in handy lists to help you plan

Best Walks
See the city on foot

San Francisco's Best...
The best experiences

Survival Guide

Tips and tricks for a seamless, hassle-free city experience

Getting Around
Travel like a local

Essential Information
Including where to stay

Our selection of the city's best places to eat, drink and experience:

- Sights
- Eating
- Drinking
- Entertainment
- Shopping

These symbols give you the vital information for each listing:

- Telephone Numbers
- Opening Hours
- Parking
- Internet Access
- Wi-Fi Access
- Vegetarian Selection
- Family-Friendly
- Pet-Friendly
- Bus
- Ferry
- Metro
- Muni
- Subway
- Tram
- Train

Find each listing quickly on maps for each neighborhood:

Lonely Planet's San Francisco

Lonely Planet Pocket Guides are designed to get you straight to the heart of the city.

Inside you'll find all the must-see sights, plus tips to make your visit to each one really memorable. We've split the city into easy-to-navigate neighborhoods and provided clear maps so you'll find your way around with ease. Our expert authors have searched out the best of the city: walks, food, nightlife and shopping, to name a few. Because you want to explore, our 'Local Life' pages will take you to some of the most exciting areas to experience the real San Francisco.

And of course you'll find all the practical tips you need for a smooth trip: itineraries for short visits, how to get around, and how much to tip the guy who serves you a drink at the end of a long day's exploration.

It's your guarantee of a really great experience.

Our Promise

You can trust our travel information because Lonely Planet authors visit the places we write about, each and every edition. We never accept freebies for positive coverage, so you can rely on us to tell it like it is.

QuickStart Guide 7

Explore San Francisco 21

Worth a Trip:

The Best of San Francisco 179

San Francisco's Best Walks

San Francisco's Best...

Survival Guide 203

QuickStart Guide

Welcome to San Francisco

Fisherman's Wharf sea lions and Telegraph Hill parrots agree: this town is totally wild. Somewhere between urban farms and legendary surf beaches you'll find San Franciscans in their natural habitat, going crazy for California cuisine and Pride parades. Come as you are, and ditch your inhibitions – you won't be needing those in San Francisco.

Classic Victorians around Alamo Square (p150) in the Haight
RICHARD CUMMINS/LONELY PLANET IMAGES ©

San Francisco Top Sights

Golden Gate Bridge (p24)

Other bridges are marvels – this one's magic. When afternoon fog rolls in, poof! It disappears. Mornings the span appears reddish against blue skies, a trick assisted by 25 daredevil painters, who apply 1000 gallons (3785L) of paint weekly.

SABRINA DALBESIO/LONELY PLANET IMAGES ©

Cable Cars (p80)

Leap onto the baseboard and grab a leather strap – you're in for the ultimate urban carnival ride. When vertiginous climbs yield sudden glimpses of the Golden Gate, public transit never seemed so poetic.

LEE FOSTER/LONELY PLANET IMAGES ©

San Francisco Museum of Modern Art (p76)

Vaseline and video are only the beginning at SFMOMA, where Matthew Barney debuted and new-media art appeared before anyone knew what to call it. Now the museum is doubling in size, with 1100 new works. Watch this space.

ROBERTO GEROMETTA/LONELY PLANET IMAGES ©

MH de Young Memorial Museum (p164)

The sleek, copper-clad de Young is oxidizing green to match the park, but its eclectic, globetrotting collection is a standout. Creative breakthroughs await at every turn: 1950s Beat collage, 1980s Jean Paul Gaultier bras, 1890s Oceanic masks.

Ferry Building (p78)

The towering achievement here isn't the 19th-century clock tower – it's the 21st-century food, innovated in the Bay Area. Award-winning chefs serve signature dishes with sparkling bay views, and local producers supply constant culinary inspiration.

ANGUS OBORN/LONELY PLANET IMAGES ©

Fisherman's Wharf (p36)

Sea lions are living the dream at Pier 39: lolling on yacht docks, canoodling with harems and enjoying seafood feasts. The city's unofficial mascots have goofed off dockside for decades, inspiring humans to follow suit along the wharf.

STEPHEN SAKS/LONELY PLANET IMAGES ©

Alcatraz (p50)

No prisoner escaped this notorious island prison alive (at least, not officially), but once the door clangs behind you in D-Block solitary, the 1.25-mile swim through rip tides seems worth a shot. Good thing you've got a ferry scheduled.

LEE FOSTER/LONELY PLANET IMAGES ©

Lombard Street (p40)

Eight hairpin turns down Lombard St get all the attention on postcards, but just up this street are secret stairway walks and million-dollar Golden Gate Bridge views dedicated to a penniless poet at Sterling Park.

SHANIA SHEGEDYN/LONELY PLANET IMAGES ©

California Academy of Sciences (p162)

Renzo Piano's 2008 structure – with an electric-eel forest and rooftop wildflower meadow – houses the Academy, known for its pioneering research and rare wildlife since 1853.

KRIS DAVIDSON/LONELY PLANET IMAGES ©

RICK GERHARTER/LONELY PLANET IMAGES ©

Asian Art Museum (p106)

When San Francisco's Pacific Ocean panoramas are lost in fog, you can still see all the way across Asia in this 17,000-piece collection of masterworks spanning 6000 years, from Pakistan to Japan.

ANTHONY PIDGEON/LONELY PLANET IMAGES ©

Coit Tower (p54)

Wild parrots may mock your progress up Telegraph Hill's garden-lined Filbert staircase, but they can't keep the bay vistas to themselves. Tower-top panoramas and controversial 1930s murals reward climbs to Coit Tower.

San Francisco Local Life

Insider tips to help you find the real city

The city with its head perpetually in the clouds is also surprisingly down to earth. Dive into San Francisco's neighborhoods to observe its outlandish ideas in action, from graffiti-art-gallery alleyways to certified green nightclubs.

The History-Making Castro (p144)

- Gay history landmarks
- GLBT community organizations
- SF's favorite movie palace

The center of the gay world knows how to throw a Pride party, but the Castro's historic triumphs in civil rights, free speech and HIV/AIDS treatment were hard-won. America's first GLBT history museum tells the epic story, and you can join the next chapter, unfolding at Castro community institutions.

Mission Murals (p128)

- Mural-lined alleyways
- Groundbreaking graffiti

When 1970s *muralistas* disagreed with US foreign policy they took to the streets, paintbrushes in hand. Thanks to neighborhood support, you can still see original Balmy Alley works dating from 1971. Today some 400 murals bring meaning to the mean streets of the Mission, incorporating graffiti graphics from SF's homegrown skate culture.

Shops, Sushi & Shows in Japantown (p124)

- Legendary jazz
- Cutting-edge style and decor
- Japanese spa

Godzilla himself couldn't scare Japantown; this tiny neighborhood has faced exclusion and internment since 1860, and emerged with civil rights, talent and style intact. Japantown's latest superhero power is reinvention – traditional Japanese baths and sushi are still here, but so are Japanese bossa nova and SF-psychedelic ninja shoes.

SoMa Nightlife (p84)

- Warehouse dance scene
- Gay/lesbian/bi/trans clubs
- All-ages club nights

Go costumed, retro, or underground in SoMa, San Francisco's party central since the 1970s. Some things have changed: now certified-green clubs generate electricity on the dance floor, and DJ sets range from mash-up to dance-goth. The bathhouses may be gone, but retro club anthems

Street mural in the Castro district

induce crowd euphoria, and Sunday gay dance scenes reign supreme.

Upper Polk Bars & Boutiques (p72)

- Boho boutiques
- Kitsch cocktails
- Live music

San Francisco's original postwar gay-club strip, between California and Vallejo Sts, still has a wild streak. Urban legendary nights now begin with a cocktail in the long shadow of Sasquatch, while Bohemian shopping sprees yield one-off glamour: jointed marionette necklaces, silkscreened organic cotton sunhats and wallets made of SF street maps.

Freedom Day Parade

Other great places to experience the city like a local:

- San Francisco Giants games (p98)
- Hayes Valley Farm (p112)
- La Raza Skatepark (p133)
- Fort Mason (p28)
- Nob Hill (p64)
- Kayo Books (p121)
- Ina Coolbrith Park (p44)
- Humphry Slocombe (p138)
- Rincon Annex Post Office (p90)

San Francisco Day Planner

Day One

Grab a leather strap on the **Powell & Hyde cable car** (p81), and hold on – you're in for hills and thrills. Hop off at Vallejo to take stairway walks to literary locations: hilltop **Ina Coolbrith Park** (p44) leads to shady Macondray Lane from Armistead Maupin's *Tales of the City*; **Jack Kerouac's Love Shack** (p43), where he wrote *On the Road* in the attic; and on to **Lombard Street** (p40) and **Sterling Park** (p41), where **Golden Gate Bridge** (p24) views inspired SF's original 'King of Bohemia', George Sterling.

Pause for pizza at **Za** (p45) before you cover the waterfront, where you can explore newly restored underwater murals and mosaics at **Aquatic Park Bathhouse** (p43), save the world from Space Invaders at **Musée Mecanique** (p37), and enter underwater stealth mode inside **USS Pampanito** (p37). Afterwards, watch sea lions salute the setting sun at **Pier 39** (p37).

End the evening with shivers on a night tour of **Alcatraz** (p50). Afterwards, at the **Ferry Building** (p78), celebrate your great San Francisco escape with bubbly and oysters at **Hog Island** (p79) and Dungeness crab noodles at **Slanted Door** (p79).

Day Two

Discover your inner San Franciscan, starting with eye-opening coffee and political slogans at **Coffee to the People** (p153). Next, drag yourself into **Piedmont Boutique** (p157) for a feather boa, get a glam-rocker makeover at **Wasteland** (p156) or score a laid-back surfer look at **Aqua Surf Shop** (p158). Head into the park to see carnivorous plants enjoying their insect breakfasts at **Conservatory of Flowers** (p168) and dahlias wet with dew in the **Dahlia Garden** (p169).

Take a walk on wild side in the rainforest dome of the **California Academy of Sciences** (p162), then enjoy an organic lunch prepared by top chefs at the Academy Café. Follow Andy Goldworthy's artful sidewalk fault-lines to find sublime Oceanic masks and tower-top views at the **Mh De Young Memorial Museum** (p164), then enjoy an iron pot of tea amid miniature forests at the **Japanese Tea Garden** (p168). Bliss out in the secret redwood grove at **Strybing Arboretum & Botanical Gardens** (p168).

Hop the N Judah to dinner at **Outerlands** (p171), followed by a starlit stroll along **Ocean Beach** (p168) and a toast with microbrews and moonlight over the Pacific at the **Beach Chalet Brewery** (p173).

Short on time?

We've arranged San Francisco's must-sees into day-by-day itineraries to make sure you see the very best of the city in the time you have available.

Day Three

Start at **Balmy Alley** (p129), where the Mission muralist movement began, then join the cult of cappuccino at **Ritual Coffee Roasters** (p138) and browse beach-shack decor at **Gravel & Gold** (p141) and **Viracocha** (p140). Adopt a pirate accent searching for treasures at **826 Valencia** (p133), and enter **Clarion Alley** (p129) to see the latest in the Mission's graffiti-art show.

Assemble a picnic of local artisan foods at **Bi-Rite** (p142) to enjoy in **Mission Dolores Park** (p132), then stop by **Mission Dolores** (p132) to pay respects to its Native American builders and SF's namesake saint. Gallery hop from **Creativity Explored** (p133) to **Ratio 3** (p182), then head over Market St to globe-trot through the **Asian Art Museum** (p106). Score last-minute **San Francisco Symphony** (p117) or **Opera** (p119) tickets, and troll Hayes St Victorian storefronts until curtain-time.

Drift from great performances into **Jardinière** (p112), where star chef Traci des Jardins whips up decadent, sustainable California cuisine. Afterwards, it's time for a Dead Reckoning – one of the historic rum drinks served at pirate-themed **Smuggler's Cove** (p115).

Day Four

Hit SF's high points, starting with truffled eggs at **Boulette's Larder** (p93). Gold-rush through historic Jackson Square and up **Filbert St Steps** (p55), but take a breather for dizzying views over the bay. Wild parrots cheer your arrival at **Coit Tower** (p54), where you'll glimpse uplifting murals and views of the **Golden Gate Bridge** (p24). Roll down to boho North Beach to **Caffe Trieste** (p65), where Francis Ford Coppola wrote *The Godfather*, and enjoy a contemplative moment in the Poet's Chair at **City Lights** (p68). Stumble over sidewalk poetry in **Jack Kerouac Alley** (p58) to pagoda-roofed Grant Ave, and up to temple-lined **Waverly Place** (p58).

Take lunch to another level with dumplings at **City View** (p61), then reach new artistic heights in the rooftop sculpture garden at the **San Francisco Museum of Modern Art** (p76). Pop into the **Contemporary Jewish Museum** (p88) for think-piece art in illuminated galleries.

At Union Square, score last-minute half-price tickets to **American Conservatory Theater** (p97), and dine on urban-farm-fresh fare at **Sons & Daughters** (p91).

Need to Know

For more information, see Survival Guide (p203).

Currency
US dollar ($)

Language
English

Visas
The US Visa Waiver program allows nationals of 27 countries to enter the US without a visa; see p212.

Money
ATMs widely available; credit cards accepted at most hotels, stores and restaurants. Farmers markets, food trucks and some bars are cash only.

Cell Phones
Most US cell phones besides the iPhone operate on CDMA, not the European standard GSM; check compatibility with your phone service provider.

Time
Pacific Standard Time (GMT/UTC minus eight hours)

Plugs & Adaptors
Most plugs have two flat pins, some appliances have two flat pins plus a round pin; electrical current is 120V.

Tipping
At restaurants, 15% (bad service) to 25% (exceptional service). In bars $1-2 per drink, $2 per bag to hotel porters, 10% or $1 minimum per taxi ride.

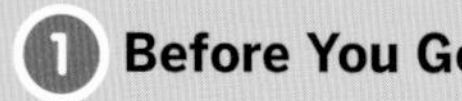

1 Before You Go

Your Daily Budget

Budget Less Than $100
- Dorm beds $25–$30
- Food-truck dishes $5–$10
- Mission galleries & murals free
- Live music at Hotel Utah $5–$12

Midrange $100–$250
- Motel/downtown hotel $80–$180
- Ferry Building meal $15–$35
- SFMOMA $18
- MUNI Passport $14

Top End More Than $250
- Boutique hotel $150–$380
- Chef's tasting menu $65–$140
- City Pass (MUNI + five attractions) $69
- Alcatraz night tour $33

Useful Websites

Lonely Planet (www.lonelyplanet.com/San Francisco) Expert local advice.

Bay Citizen (www.baycitizen.org) SF news, culture and community.

SFGate (www.sfgate.com) *San Francisco Chronicle* news, events, restaurants.

Advance Planning

Two months before Book hotels for May to September; walk to build stamina for hills.

Three weeks before Book Alcatraz and Precita Eyes Mission Mural tours, dinners at Frances or Coi.

One week before Look for tickets to American Conservatory Theater, San Francisco Symphony or Opera.

2 Arriving in San Francisco

Service from three airports makes reaching San Francisco quick and convenient. BART offers easy access to downtown San Francisco from SFO and Oakland airports; from San Jose airport, shuttles connect to Caltrain. Amtrak trains are a low-emissions, scenic option for domestic travel to San Francisco.

From San Francisco Airport (SFO)

Destination	Best Transport
Downtown/Mission	BART
Rest of SF	Taxi/door-to-door shuttle

From Oakland Airport (OAK)

Destination	Best Transport
Downtown/Mission	BART
Rest of SF	Taxi/door-to-door shuttle

At the Airports

San Francisco Airport All terminals have ATMs, and there is a currency exchange in the International terminal. Information kiosks and white courtesy phones are located on the lower (Arrivals) levels of all three terminals. To reach the airport health clinic, use the white courtesy phone. Luggage storage is available in the travel agency area of the main hall of the International Terminal.

Oakland Airport ATMs are available throughout the airport. Taxis, door-to-door shared vans, and AirBART shuttles leave curbside.

3 Getting Around

Small, hilly San Francisco is walkable, with public transportation and occasional taxis for backup. For transit options, departures and arrivals, check www.511.org or call ☎511. A detailed *Muni Street & Transit Map* is available free online and at the Powell Muni kiosk ($3).

Cable Cars

Frequent, slow and scenic, from 6am to 1am daily; joyride from downtown to Chinatown, North Beach and Fisherman's Wharf. Single rides cost $6; for frequent use, get a Muni passport.

Muni Streetcar

Lines connect Downtown with Golden Gate Park, the Mission, and the Castro. Historic F line streetcars run from Fisherman's Wharf down Market Street to the Castro. Fares are $2.

Muni Bus

Reasonably fast, but schedules vary wildly by line; infrequent after 9pm. Fares are $2.

BART

High-speed transit from downtown to Civic Center, the Mission, Oakland/Berkeley, SFO and Millbrae, where it connects with CalTrain. Fares run $2–8.

Taxi

Fares run about $2.25 per mile; meters start at $3.50.

San Francisco Neighborhoods

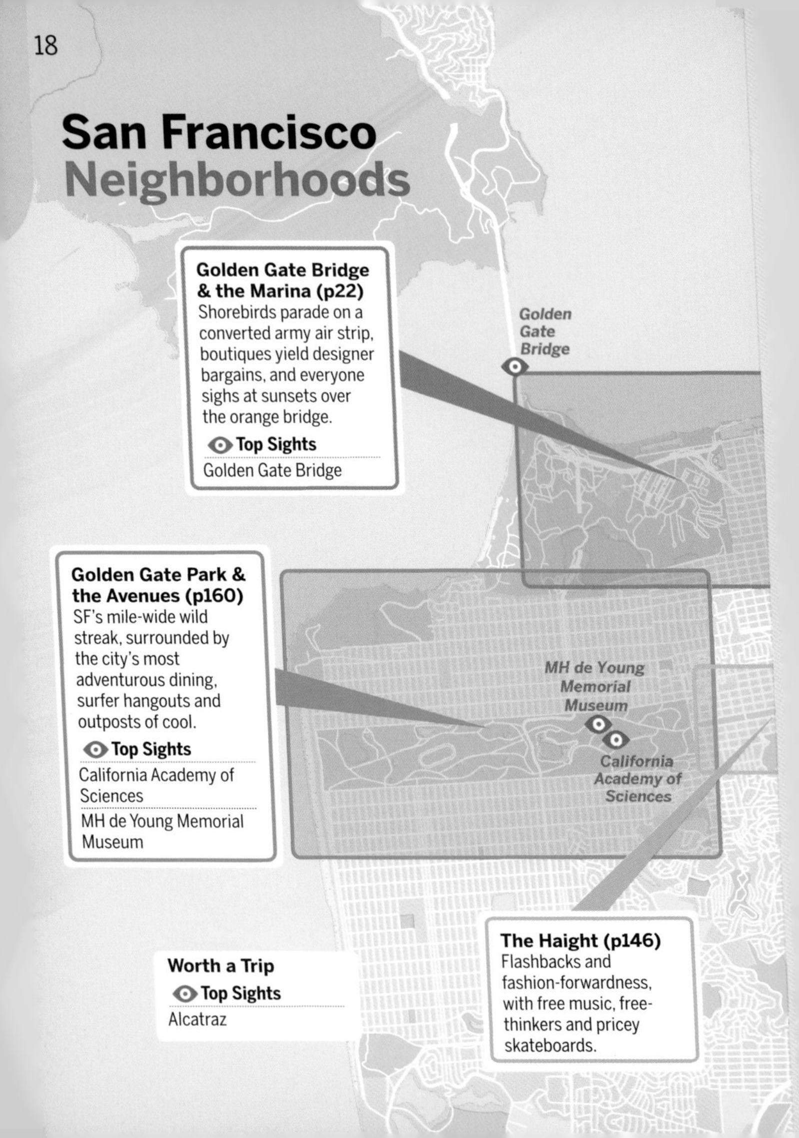

Golden Gate Bridge & the Marina (p22)
Shorebirds parade on a converted army air strip, boutiques yield designer bargains, and everyone sighs at sunsets over the orange bridge.

Top Sights

Golden Gate Bridge

Golden Gate Park & the Avenues (p160)
SF's mile-wide wild streak, surrounded by the city's most adventurous dining, surfer hangouts and outposts of cool.

Top Sights

California Academy of Sciences

MH de Young Memorial Museum

Worth a Trip

Top Sights

Alcatraz

The Haight (p146)
Flashbacks and fashion-forwardness, with free music, free-thinkers and pricey skateboards.

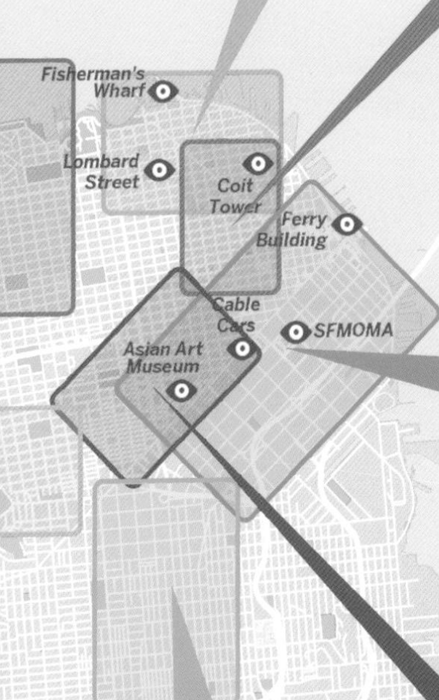

Fisherman's Wharf & the Piers (p34)
Sea-lion antics, creepy wooden fortune-tellers and underwater adventures.

Top Sights

Fisherman's Wharf

Lombard Street

North Beach & Chinatown (p52)
Hit poetry-paved Jack Kerouac Alley for tearooms and temples or pizza and jukebox opera, and get a parrot's-eye view of the city atop Coit Tower.

Top Sights

Coit Tower

Downtown & SoMa (p74)
Where high technology meets high art, cable cars lurch uphill, and everyone gets down and dirty on the dance floor.

Top Sights

SFMOMA

Ferry Building

Cable cars

Hayes Valley & Civic Center (p104)
Priceless masterpieces and great performances amid bargain gourmet finds, local designs in Victorian storefronts, and rum drinks fit for pirates.

Top Sights

Asian Art Museum

The Mission (p126)
In these mural-covered streets, join food revolutions, art movements and quasi-professional slacking already in progress.

Explore San Francisco

San Francisco, the Coit Tower and Alcatraz

Explore

Golden Gate Bridge & the Marina

The waterfront neighborhood near Golden Gate Bridge boasts chic boutiques, scientific wonders and veggie cuisine in a former Army depot, but 120 years ago, it reeked with dirty laundry and drunken cows. Swanky Union St was once Cow Hollow, where laundry was done and cows munched mash from waterfront whiskey stills. Today's spiffy Mex-Deco Marina was mostly built in the 1930s, using debris from the 1906 quake.

The Sights in a Day

Troll Union St boutiques for local designs, stylish bargains and pedigreed Pacific Heights vintage; try **ATYS** (p32), **Mingle** (p32) and **Marmalade SF** (p33). Then head over to **Fort Mason** (p28; pictured left) for organic Greens chili takeout by the docks, where you might discover an art or craft fair in progress.

Stroll the waterfront from the Marina to the picturesque **Palace of Fine Arts** (p29), and explore weird science at the **Exploratorium** (p28). Cross **Crissy Field** (p28) for sweeping Golden Gate Bridge views, and pop into the **Warming Hut** (p30) for coffee, pastries and nature-book browsing. Head onward to **Fort Point** (p25) for a Hitchcock-worthy view of the bridge, and if you've got another couple miles in you before sunset, walk across the **Golden Gate Bridge** (p24).

Take the bus back toward Union St to hit happy hour at **California Wine Merchant** (p31) before your reservations at **A16** (p29). Enjoy a performance at **Magic Theatre** (p31), or take the stage yourself at **BATS** (p31).

Top Sight

Golden Gate Bridge (p24)

Best of San Francisco

Outdoors

Crissy Field (p28)

Baker Beach (p28)

Architecture

Golden Gate Bridge (p24)

Shopping

Mingle (p32)

Past Perfect (p32)

Bargain Gourmet

Off the Grid (p31)

Entertainment

Fort Mason (p28)

For Kids

Exploratorium (p28)

Getting There

Bus 47 and 49 connect Marina to downtown; 41, 30 and 45 run to North Beach; 43 connects to the Haight; 22 runs to the Mission.

Car There's parking at Fort Mason and Crissy Field, and free parking in the adjoining Presidio.

Top Sight
Golden Gate Bridge

Strange but true: San Francisco's iconic suspension bridge was almost nixed by the navy in favor of yellow-striped concrete pylons. Joseph B Strauss is the engineering mastermind behind the 1937 marvel, but architects Gertrude and Irving Murrow get credit for the soaring deco design and custom 'International Orange' color. Before the War Department could insist on an eyesore, laborers braved treacherous riptides and got to work, constructing the nearly two-mile span and 746ft suspension towers in just four years.

Map p26, A1

goldengatebridge.org/visitors

Off Lincoln Blvd

Muni bus 28 runs near the Toll Plaza; all Golden Gate Transit buses cross the bridge ($3.65 one-way), including 70 and 80

Golden Gate Bridge viewed from Vista Point

Don't Miss

Vista Points

San Franciscans have passionate perspectives on every subject, but especially their signature landmark. Fog aficionados prefer the north-end lookout at Marin's Vista Point to watch clouds tumble like Olympic gymnasts over bridge cables. Crissy Field (p28) is a key spot to appreciate the span in its entirety, with windsurfers and kite-fliers adding action to your snapshots. From clothing-optional Baker Beach (p28), you can appreciate the bridge in all its naked glory.

Bridge Crossings

To see both sides of the Golden Gate, hike or bike the span. From the parking area and bus stop, a pedestrian pathway leads past the toll plaza to the **eastern sidewalk** (5am-6pm daily). Near the toll plaza is a cross-section of suspension cable, with the tensile strength to support thousands of cars and buses daily. If you'd rather not walk back, Golden Gate Transit buses head back to SF from Marin. Bikes share the eastern sidewalk, but must yield to pedestrians.

Fort Point

Completed in 1861 with 126 cannons, **Fort Point** (www.nps.gov/fopo; Marine Dr; admission free; 10am-5pm Fri-Sun; Lincoln Blvd) stood guard against certain invasion by Confederate soldiers during the Civil War...or not. Despite its guns, this fort saw no action – at least until Alfred Hitchcock shot scenes from *Vertigo* here, with stunning views of the Golden Gate Bridge from below. Stop by for panoramic viewing decks and Civil War displays.

Top Tips

Southbound toll is $6, northbound is free.

Carpools (three or more) are free 5am–9am and 4pm–6pm.

Dress warmly before crossing the bridge on foot or bike, with a water-resistant outer layer to break the wind and fog.

Skating and pets (except guide animals) are not allowed on bridge sidewalks. Wheelchairs are permitted on the east sidewalk.

Glimpse the underbelly of the bridge from the Municipal Pier in front of the Warming Hut. By reservation Saturday mornings March–October, Fort Point staff demonstrate how to catch crabs here.

Take a Break

Stop by the certified-green **Warming Hut** (p30) for fair-trade coffee and pastries.

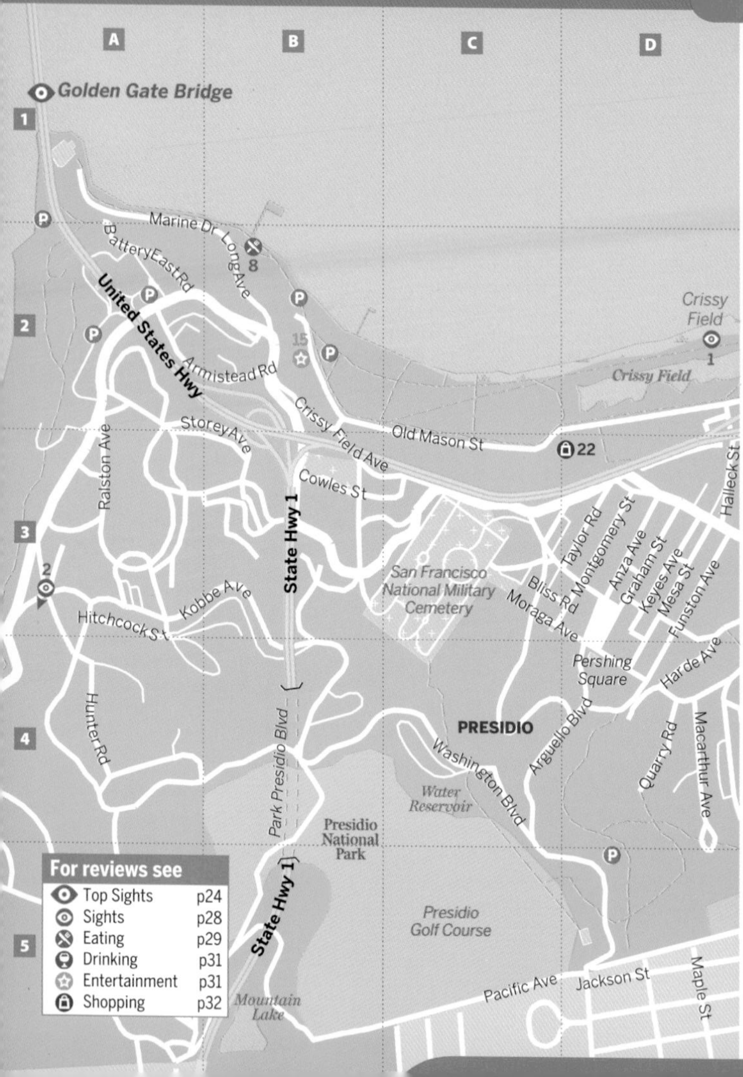

A B C D
1 2 3 4 5

Golden Gate Bridge
Marine Dr
Battery East Rd
Long Ave
8
United States Hwy
Armistead Rd
15
Crissy Field Ave
Storey Ave
Old Mason St
22
Crissy Field
1
Crissy Field
Halleck St
Ralston Ave
Cowles St
State Hwy 1
2
Kobbe Ave
Hitchcock St
San Francisco National Military Cemetery
Taylor Rd
Montgomery St
Anza Ave
Graham St
Keyes Ave
Mesa St
Funston Ave
Bliss Rd
Moraga Ave
Pershing Square
Hardie Ave
Hunter Rd
Park Presidio Blvd
PRESIDIO
Arguello Blvd
Washington Blvd
Quarry Rd
Macarthur Ave
Water Reservoir
Presidio National Park
State Hwy 1
Presidio Golf Course
Mountain Lake
Pacific Ave
Jackson St
Maple St

For reviews see

Top Sights	p24
Sights	p28
Eating	p29
Drinking	p31
Entertainment	p31
Shopping	p32

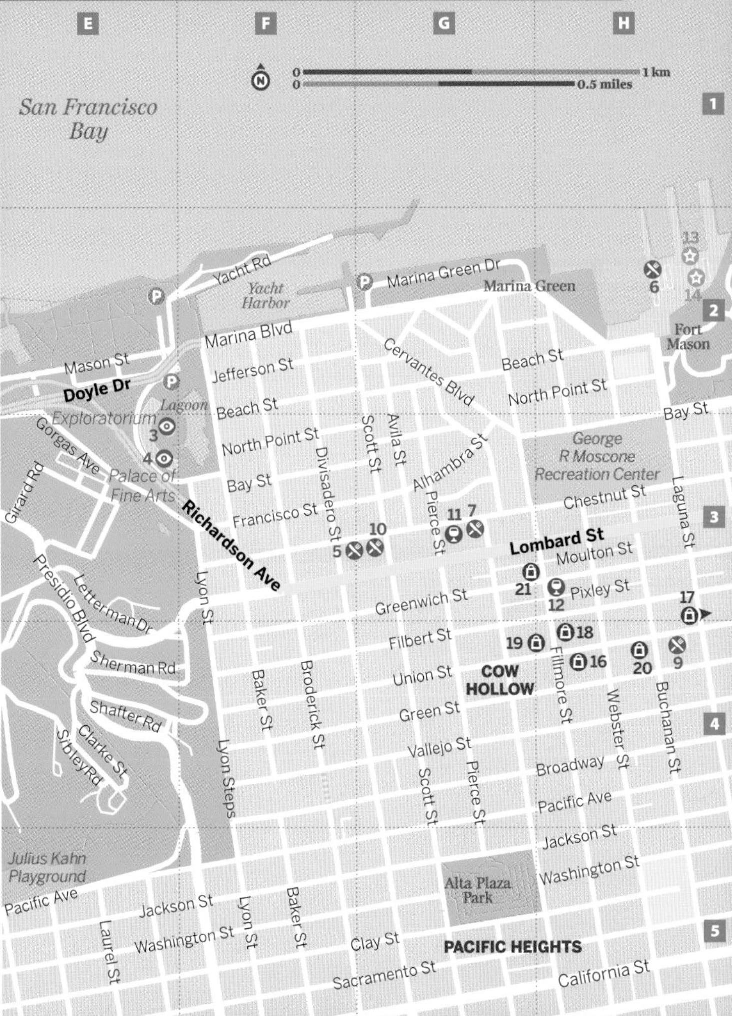

E
F
G
H
0
1 km
0
0.5 miles
1
2
3
4
5
San Francisco Bay
Yacht Rd
Yacht Harbor
Marina Green Dr
Marina Green
Fort Mason
Marina Blvd
Mason St
Doyle Dr
Jefferson St
Cervantes Blvd
Beach St
North Point St
Lagoon
Exploratorium
Gorgas Ave
Palace of Fine Arts
Beach St
North Point St
Bay St
Bay St
Francisco St
Divisadero St
Scott St
Avila St
Alhambra St
Pierce St
George R Moscone Recreation Center
Chestnut St
Laguna St
Girard Rd
Richardson Ave
Lombard St
Moulton St
Pixley St
Greenwich St
Presidio Blvd
Letterman Dr
Lyon St
Filbert St
Union St
COW HOLLOW
Fillmore St
Webster St
Buchanan St
Sherman Rd
Shafter Rd
Clarke St
Sibley Rd
Baker St
Broderick St
Green St
Vallejo St
Broadway
Lyon Steps
Scott St
Pierce St
Pacific Ave
Jackson St
Washington St
Julius Kahn Playground
Pacific Ave
Jackson St
Laurel St
Washington St
Lyon St
Baker St
Alta Plaza Park
Clay St
PACIFIC HEIGHTS
Sacramento St
California St

Sights

Crissy Field

PARK

1 Map p26, D2

War is for the birds in this military airstrip turned nature preserve, featuring sprawling Golden Gate Bridge panoramas. Birdwatchers huddle in reclaimed tidal-marsh rushes once paved with oil-stained asphalt, and the landing strip is now vigilantly patrolled by preschool kite-flyers and lolling puppies. On blustery days, bird-watch from the comfort of **Crissy Field Center** (9am-5pm), at the binocular-equipped cafe counter. (www.crissyfield.org; Btwn Mason St & Golden Gate Promenade; sunrise-sunset; Mason St)

Local Life

Fort Mason

San Francisco takes subversive glee in turning military installations into venues for nature, fine dining and experimental art – including **Fort Mason** (Map p26, H2; www.fortmason.org; cnr Bay & Franklin Sts; Marina Blvd), a former shipyard that was the embarkation point for WWII Pacific troops. The military mess halls have been replaced by vegan-friendly Greens (p30) and Off the Grid food trucks (see p31), and dockside Herbst Pavilion includes art fairs and wine-tasting in its arsenal (check the website for events). Warehouses now host cutting-edge theater at Magic Theatre and BATS (see p31) and the **Long Now Foundation** (http://longnow.org; bldg A, Fort Mason; 10:30am-5pm Mon-Fri, 11am-6pm Sat-Sun; Marina Blvd), a non-profit sponsoring four-dimensional (time-based) art and technology projects.

Baker Beach

BEACH

The city's best beach is a mile-long stretch of sand beneath windswept pines, offering fishing from waterfront rocks and a whole lot of exposed goose bumps on the breezy, clothing-optional north end. Yes, you're still in the city, with spectacular views of Golden Gate Bridge and the Lincoln Golf Course to prove it. Crowds come on weekends; mind the currents and the c-c-cold water. (Presidio; sunrise-sunset; Lincoln Blvd)

Exploratorium

MUSEUM

Budding Nobel Prize winners swarm this hands-on discovery museum, which answers the questions everyone always wanted to ask in science class: does gravity apply to skateboarding, do robots have feelings and do toilets ever flush counterclockwise? One especially far-out exhibit is the Tactile Dome, a pitch-black space that you can crawl, climb and slide through (reservations required). The Exploratorium is moving to Fisherman's Wharf (p36) in 2013. (415-561-0360; www.exploratorium.edu; 3601 Lyon St; adult/

Palace of Fine Arts

child $15/10, incl Tactile Dome $20; ⏲10am-5pm Tue-Sun; 🚌Lyon St)

Palace of Fine Arts

NOTABLE BUILDING

4 Map p26, E3

When San Francisco's 1915 Panama-Pacific exposition was over, the city simply couldn't bear to part with this Greco-Roman plaster palace. California Arts and Crafts architect Bernard Maybeck's artificial ruin was recast in concrete, so that future generations could gaze up at the rotunda relief to glimpse Art under attack by Materialists, with Idealists leaping to her rescue. (www.lovethepalace.org; 3301 Lyon St; 🚌Lyon St)

Eating

A16

PIZZERIA $$

5 Map p26, F3

SF's James Beard Award–winning Neapolitan pizzeria requires reservations, then haughtily makes you wait in the foyer like a high-maintenance date. The house-made mozzarella *burrata* and chewy-but-not-too-thick-crust pizza topped with kicky calamari makes it worth your while. Skip the spotty desserts and concentrate on adventurous appetizers, including house-cured salumi platters and delectable marinated tuna. (☎415-771-2216; www.a16sf.com; 2355 Chestnut St; pizza $12-18, mains $18-26; ⏲lunch Wed-Fri, dinner nightly; 🚌Chestnut St)

Greens Restaurant & Greens to Go
CALIFORNIAN, VEGETARIAN **$$**

6 Map p26, H2

Career carnivores won't realize there's no meat in the hearty black-bean chili with crème fraîche and pickled jalapeños, or that roasted eggplant *panino* (sandwich), packed with flavor from organic ingredients mostly grown on a Zen farm in Marin. On sunny days, get yours to go so you can enjoy it on a wharf-side bench – but if you're planning a sit-down weekend dinner or Sunday brunch you'll need reservations. (415-771-6222; www.greensrestaurant.com; Fort Mason Center, bldg A; lunch & dinner mains $7-24; noon-2:30pm Tue-Sat, 5:30-9pm Mon-Sat, 9am-4pm Sun; Marina Blvd)

Blue Barn Gourmet
SANDWICHES **$**

7 Map p26, G3

Forget ordinary salads and think organic produce, heaped with fixings such as artisan cheeses, caramelized onions, heirloom tomatoes, candied pecans, pomegranate seeds, even Meyer grilled sirloin. For something hot, try the toasted panini oozing with Manchego cheese, fig jam and salami. (www.bluebarngourmet.com; 2105 Chestnut St; salads & sandwiches $8-10; 11am-8:30pm Sun-Thu, to 7pm Fri & Sat; Chestnut St)

Warming Hut
SANDWICHES **$**

8 Map p26, B2

When the fog rolls over the Golden Gate Bridge, warm up with a steaming cup of Fair Trade coffee, organic pastries and organic hot dogs inside this eco-shack insulated with recycled denim. Browse an excellent selection of field guides and sample honey made by Presidio honeybees while you wait – all purchases support Crissy Field's ongoing conversion from Army airstrip to wildlife preserve. (www.parksconservancy.org; 983 Marine Dr; dishes $4-6; 9am-5pm; Mason St)

La Boulange
FRENCH, BAKERY **$**

9 Map p26, H4

Refuel with caffeine and freshly baked treats in the middle of the Union St shopping strip. La Combo is a $7.25 lunchtime deal to justify your next boutique purchase: half a *tartine* (open-faced sandwich) with soup or salad, plus all the Nutella and pickled *cornichons* (gherkins) you desire from the condiment bar. (http://laboulangebakery.com; 1909 Union St; 7am-6pm; Fillmore St)

Mamacita
MEXICAN **$$**

10 Map p26, G3

Made-completely-from-scratch tortillas, tamales, and two-dozen fresh-daily sauces are among the secrets to this crowd-pleasing yet adventurous Mexican menu, which features dishes ranging from spit-roasted goat to duck *carnitas*. The knock-out cocktail menu lists 60 tequilas, which explains the room's constant roar. Make reservations. (415-346-8494; www.mamacitasf.com; 2317 Chestnut St; dishes $10-18; dinner; M28, 30, 43)

Drinking

California Wine Merchant

WINE BAR

11 Map p26, G3

Pair your pick of 35 to 50 local wines by the glass with mild flirting in this wine cave, and be surprised by the unexpected nuances of Central Coast Pinots and Marina playboys earnestly trying to improve their game. Arrive early to score a table, and have a nice flight. (www.californiawinemerchant.com; 2113 Chestnut St; 10am-midnight Mon-Wed, 10am-1:30am Thu-Sat, 11am-11pm Sun; Fillmore St)

MatrixFillmore

COCKTAIL LOUNGE

12 Map p26, H3

The one bar in town where the presumption is that you're straight and interested. The smoky glass, fireplace and dangerous cocktails set a '70s key-party vibe, bringing out the inner freak in the stockbroker/sales rep crowd. The overall effect is modern and sleek, if not especially subtle – and the same can be said of the crowd. (www.matrixfillmore.com; 3138 Fillmore St; M22, 28, 30, 43)

Entertainment

Magic Theatre

THEATER

13 Map p26, H2

SF's upstart theatre company earns its risk-taking rep with provocative plays by Terrence McNally, Edna O'Brien, David Mamet and Sam Shepard (longtime playwright-in-residence), performed by talents like Ed Harris, Sean Penn and Woody Harrelson. Watch the next generation break through in professionally staged works written by teenagers from the Young California Writers Project. (415-441-8822; www.magictheatre.org; 3rd fl, bldg D, Fort Mason Center; Fort Mason)

BATS Improv

COMEDY, THEATER

14 Map p26, H2

Crash an office party, sabotage a fast-food drive-thru, meet your long-lost twin in jail: Bay Area Theatersports throws ordinary people into awkward scenarios and lets hilarity

Local Life

Off the Grid

Food trucks circle like pioneer wagons every Friday night at **Off the Grid** (Map p26, H2; http://offthegridsf.com; Fort Mason parking lot; dishes under $10; 5-10pm Fri; Marina Blvd), SF's largest mobile-gourmet hootenanny of up to 30 trucks (other nights/locations attract less than a dozen trucks; check the website). Arrive before 6:30pm or expect 20-minute waits for Chairman Bao's clamshell buns stuffed with duck and mango, Roli Roti's free-range herbed roast chicken, and dessert from The Créme Brûlée Man. Cash only; take dinner to nearby docks for Golden Gate Bridge sunsets.

ensue. Watch what happens next at completely improvised weekend shows, or take center stage yourself at an improv comedy workshop. Think fast: classes fill quickly. Shows are usually $15, but admission depends on the class/event. (Bay Area Theatersports; ☎415-474-8935; www.improv.org; 3rd fl, bldg B, Fort Mason Center; ⌚weekend shows 8pm; 🚌Fort Mason)

House of Air TRAMPOLINE PARK

 Map p26, B2

Bounce off the walls – quite literally – on 42 attached-together trampolines that cover an area roughly the size of a basketball court, located in a converted Army airplane hangar on Crissy Field. Little kids have dedicated play areas. Reservations strongly recommended, especially on weekends. (☎415-345-9675; www.houseofairsf.com; 926 Old Mason St, Crissy Field; adult/child $14/10; ⌚10am-10pm Mon-Thu, 10am-11pm Fri, 9am-9pm Sun; 👪)

Shopping

ATYS HOMEWARES, GIFTS

 Map p26, H4

Tucked away in a courtyard, this design showcase offers version 2.0 of essential household items: a zero-emissions solar-powered toy airplane, a radio carved from sustainably harvested wood, and a birchwood spyglass fit for a modern pirate. (www.atysdesign.com; 2149b Union St; ⌚11am-6:30pm Mon-Sat, noon-6pm Sun; 🚌Fillmore St)

Mingle CLOTHING, LOCAL DESIGNER

17 Map p26, H3

When you're tired of seeing the same clothes in your closet and the world over, it's time to get out there and Mingle with local designers. Cultivate a signature SF style with swingy smocked dresses, slouchy butter-leather bags and handmade gemstone necklaces, all for less than you'd pay for mall brands. Men emerge date-ready and dandy in dark denim and wind-turbine ties. (www.mingleshop.com; 1815 Union St; ⌚11am-7pm; 🚌Union St)

My Roommate's Closet WOMEN'S CLOTHING

18 Map p26, H4

All the half-off designer bargains and none of the clawing dangers of a normal sample sale. You'll find cloudlike Catherine Malandrino chiffon party dresses, executive-office Diane Von Furstenburg wrap dresses, and cult denim at prices approaching reality. (www.myroommatescloset.com; 3044 Fillmore St; ⌚11am-6pm, noon-5pm Sun; 🚌Fillmore St)

Past Perfect ANTIQUES

19 Map p26, H4

If you wonder how Pacific Heights eccentrics fill up those mansions, here's your answer: mercury glass apothecary jars, Big Sur driftwood sculpture and wall-to-wall mid-century teak credenzas. The store is a collective, so prices are all over the place – some sellers apparently believe their belongings owe them back-rent, while others are happy to be rid of wedding presents from first marriages. (2224 Union St; ⌚11am-7pm; 🚌Fillmore St)

Marmalade SF

CLOTHING, LOCAL DESIGNER

20 Map p26, H4

Girly-girl clothes by local and indie designers, and personalized service hell bent on helping you find your own personal style – hard to believe nothing at Marmalade costs over $100. Sizes run small, but bags and shoes are crowd-pleasers. (www.marmaladesf.com; 2059 Union St; 🚌Union St)

PlumpJack Wines

WINE

21 Map p26, G3

Before SF Mayor Newsom took office, he plied the electorate with 900 fine Italian, French and of course Californian wines as the co-owner/founder of PlumpJack and the local PlumpJack winery. A more knowledgeable staff is hard to find anywhere in SF, and they'll set you up with the right bottles under $30 to cross party lines. (www.plumpjack.com; 3201 Fillmore St; ⌚11am-8pm Mon-Sat, to 6pm Sun; 🚌Fillmore St)

GREG BALFOUR EVANS / ALAMY

Shopfronts and stalls along Union St

Sports Basement

SPORTS

22 Map p26, D3

This 80,000-sq-ft sports-and-camping equipment emporium was once a US Army PX, which is why you'll find hiking boots near the Fresh Produce sign. Get closeout prices on cross-training shoes to hit Crissy Field's paths, find rental snowboards for Tahoe slopes, and score yoga gear to strike warrior poses at free yoga classes here on Sundays. (www.sportsbasement.com; 610 Old Mason St; ⌚9am-9pm Mon-Fri, 8am-8pm Sat & Sun; 🚌Old Mason St)

Explore

Fisherman's Wharf & the Piers

The waterfront that today welcomes families fresh off the boat from Alcatraz tours was a dodgy dock area during California's Gold Rush. After the 1906 earthquake and fire, a retaining wall was built, and Sunday strollers gradually replaced drifters and grifters along Embarcadero boardwalks. But Wild West manners remain on Pier 39, where sea lions snore and belch like drunken sailors on the dockside.

The Sights in a Day

Escapees from Alcatraz end up on the piers but families might become captives at Pier 39's kid-friendly attractions, especially the **Aquarium of the Bay** (p37) and **San Francisco Carousel** (p38). Otherwise, say hi to the resident **sea lions** (p37) dockside, and race boardwalk crowds to an early lunch at **Boudin's** (p47) or **Salty's Famous Fishwich** (p47).

Recover from the inevitable starch stupor over vintage arcade games at **Musée Mecanique** (p37), then make your getaway from the crowds below decks on an actual WWII submarine: the **USS Pampanito** (p37). Back on dry land, explore 1930s murals inside the ship-shape **Aquatic Park Bathhouse** (p43) and wine-taste at the **Winery Collective** (p49). Hop off the Hyde St cable car at wiggly **Lombard Street** (p40) to hit highlights worth writing home about: the poetry-inspiring Golden Gate vistas at **Sterling Park** (p41), **Jack Kerouac's back-alley love shack** (p43), and Armistead Maupin's novel-worthy stairway walks to **Ina Coolbrith Park** (p44).

Head to Larkin St for pizza and ice cream or **Gary Danko** (p44) for California cuisine.

Top Sights

Fisherman's Wharf (p36)

Lombard Street (p40)

Best of San Francisco

Freebies

Sea Lions at Pier 39 (p37)

Aquatic Park Bathhouse (p43)

San Francisco Art Institute (p43)

Kids

Musée Mecanique (p37)

Aquarium of the Bay (p37)

San Francisco Carousel (p38)

Outdoors

Sterling Park (p41)

San Francisco Maritime National Historic Park (p38; pictured left)

Getting There

Streetcar Historic F Market streetcars

Cable Car Powell-Hyde and Powell-Mason lines

Bus Wharf-downtown buses include 30, 47 and 49

Car Public garages at Pier 39 and Ghiradelli Square

Top Sights
Fisherman's Wharf

Where fishermen once snared sea life, San Francisco now traps tourists in a commercial sprawl between the cable car terminus and Alcatraz Cruises port. But where you'd least expect it, Fisherman's Wharf offers surprise and delight. Here you can sunbathe with sea lions, ride carousel unicorns, experience stealth mode inside a WWII submarine, consult vintage mechanical fortune-tellers, and watch sharks circle from the safety of glass tubes built right into the bay.

Map p42, B1

www.fishermanswharf.org

Embarcadero & Jefferson St waterfront

Admission free

M 19, 37, 47, 49, F

Powell-Mason, Powell-Hyde

Sea lions at Pier 39

Don't Miss

Sea Lions at Pier 39

Pop stars wish they could live like San Francisco's sea lions, who've taken over an entire yacht marina with their harems since 1990. Since California law requires boats to make way for marine mammals, up to 1300 sea-lion squatters oblige yacht owners to relinquish valuable slips from January through July – making them heroes to beach bums everywhere.

Musée Mecanique

Laughing Sal has freaked out visitors with her coin-operated cackle for 100 years, but don't let this manic mannequin deter you from the best arcade west of Coney Island. A few quarters at the **Musée Mecanique** (www.museemecanique.org; Pier 45, Shed A; admission free; 10am-7pm Mon-Fri, to 8pm Sat-Sun;) let you start bar brawls in mechanical Wild West saloons, save the world from Space Invaders and get your fortune told by an eerily lifelike wooden swami.

USS Pampanito

Dive, dive, dive! Head into the belly of a restored **WWII US Navy submarine** (www.maritime.org; Pier 45; adult/child $10/4; 9am-5pm) that sunk six Japanese ships (including two carrying British and Australian POWs). Submariners' stories of tense moments in underwater stealth mode will have you holding your breath – caution, claustrophobes – and all those brass knobs and hydraulic valves make 21st-century technology seem overrated.

Aquarium of the Bay

Take a long walk off a short pier right into the bay, and stay perfectly safe and dry as sharks circle, manta rays flutter and schools of fish flit overhead. The **aquarium** (www.aquariumofthebay.com;

Top Tips

- Afternoon fog blows in around 4pm, sometimes earlier in summer. Carry a jacket and don't wear shorts, except in a rare heat wave.
- Most people cover the waterfront attractions on foot or bike – wear comfortable shoes and sunscreen.
- Fisherman's Wharf is most popular with families, who pack the waterfront by early afternoon. To dodge the crowds, hit Pier 43½ for an early lunch and visit the USS *Pampanito* and Aquatic Park Bathhouse in the afternoon.

Take a Break

Snack shacks line the Pier 39 boardwalk and flank picnic benches at Pier 43½, including Salty's Famous Fishwich (p47). The best sweet treats are at Ghirardelli Square, including Kara's Cupcakes (p46) and Crown & Crumpet (p45).

Pier 39; adult/child $17/8; ⏲9am-8pm summer, 10am-6pm winter; 🚸) is built right into the bay, and a conveyor belt transports you through underwater glass tubes for an up-close-and-personal look at local aquaculture.

San Francisco Carousel

Chariots await to whisk you and the kiddies past the Golden Gate Bridge, Alcatraz and other SF landmarks hand-painted onto this Italian **carousel** (www.pier39.com; Pier 39; admission $3; ⏲11am-7pm; 🚸) twinkling with 1800 lights. The old-timey organ carnival music inspires goofy sing-a-longs on the four-minute ride, and it's loud enough to drown out the tiny tot clinging for dear life to a high-stepping horsey.

San Francisco Maritime National Historic Park

'Aye, she's a beauty,' you'll growl like a salty dog once you've visited the **historic boats** (www.nps.gov/safr; Pier 45; adult/child $5/free; ⏲9:30am-5pm Oct-May, to 7pm Jun-Sep) open as museums along Hyde St Pier – especially elegant are 1891 schooner *Alma* and c 1890 steamboat *Eureka*. Floating alongside like giant bath toys are steam-powered paddlewheel tugboat *Eppleton Hall* and triple-masted, iron-hulled 1886 *British Balclutha*, which hauled coal to San Francisco via the dreaded Cape Horn.

Adventure Cat

Centuries of sailors are right: there's no better view of San Francisco than from its silvery bay, especially on a sunset sail. After seeing the historic ships of the San Francisco Maritime National Historic Park, hulking modern cruise boats may seem to lack that easy grace and sense of adventure – but you can still sail off into the sunset with **Adventure Cat** (☎415-777-1630; www.adventurecat.com; Pier 39; adult/child $35/15, sunset cruise $50;

Understand

The Left Coast

San Francisco's port thrived in 1934, but local longshoremen pulling long hours unloading heavy cargo for scant pay didn't see the upside of the shipping boom. When they protested dangerous working conditions, shipping tycoons sought dockworkers elsewhere – only to discover San Francisco's longshoremen had coordinated their strike with 35,000 workers along the West Coast. After 83 days, police and the National Guard broke the strike, killing 34 strikers and wounding 40 sympathizers. Public sympathy forced concessions from shipping magnates, and 1930s murals by Diego Rivera and Works Project Administration (WPA) artists reflect the pro-worker sentiment that swept the city known henceforth as America's 'Left Coast.'

Fisherman's Wharf;). The catamaran cruises offer sweeping views, trampolines between hulls for bouncy kids and windless cabins in case of fog (dress warmly). Three daily cruises depart March to October; weekends only November to February.

Red & White Fleet

No need to fear the fog on bay cruises with this crew – one-hour tours are available, and alcohol served on board takes the edge off chilly days on the bay. The **Red & White Fleet** (415-673-2900; www.redandwhite.com; Pier 43 1/2; adult/child $24/16;) audio tours provides narrative in multiple languages from the comfort of indoor decks, but for unbeatable views of the Golden Gate Bridge from water level, brave the wind and sit on the outdoor upper deck. Raise a toast underneath the Golden Gate Bridge and it's bound to come true…especially if it's to getting another drink.

LEE FOSTER/LONELY PLANET IMAGES ©

San Francisco Carousel at Pier 39

Top Sights
Lombard Street

Giddiness comes with the territory atop Lombard St, peering down at eight switchbacks down the 27% grade of Russian Hill. Lombard's title as 'world's crookedest street' may be grammatically and factually incorrect, but the thrills are real: Hitchcock used this steep block to induce *Vertigo*, and skate legend Tony Hawk included its thrills in his *Pro Skater* video game.

Map p42, B3

900 block of Lombard St

Admission free

24 hr

Columbus;
Powell-Hyde

Switchbacks on Lombard St

Don't Miss

Switchbacks

After one too many drivers went careening into front gardens after visits to speakeasies in the Roaring '20s, local property owners added eight turns punctuated by flowerpots to transform this block from a lethal shortcut into a scenic route. The result is what you see today: a red-brick street with lovingly tended flower beds at every turn, flanked by 250 steps.

Sterling Park

Drivers rushing toward Lombard St's tricky turns miss glorious Golden Gate Bridge vistas along the zigzagging paths of hilltop **Sterling Park** (www.rhn.org/pointofinterestparks.html; Lombard & Hyde Sts;). Sunsets framed by windswept Monterey pines are pure poetry, as befits the park's namesake, bohemian poet George Sterling. He embraced nature, free love and opium, and was frequently broke. But San Francisco's high society indulged his eccentricities and had this park named after him.

Powell-Hyde Cable Car

Never mind all those movie car-chase scenes and car commercials shot in San Francisco, the best way to hit Lombard isn't by car, but by cable car. Powell-Hyde summits Nob Hill before clanging up Russian Hill, passing multimillion-dollar mansions and secret stairway gardens. Leap off at Lombard for unbeatable hilltop views.

Top Tips

- To avoid traffic jams heading down Lombard, come early morning; for sunlit photo-ops, swing by mid-afternoon, when the fog clears.
- No need to hold up traffic, angling for the best shot – the best photos of Lombard are from the bottom of the street and atop Coit Tower, one hill over.
- Don't try anything funny. The recent clampdown on renegade skaters means that the challenges featured in skater video games will remain strictly virtual – at least until the cops get slack.

Take a Break

Before you get your kicks heading down Lombard, detour to Larkin St for crowd-pleasing ice cream at Swensen's (p47) or pizza by the slice at Za (p45).

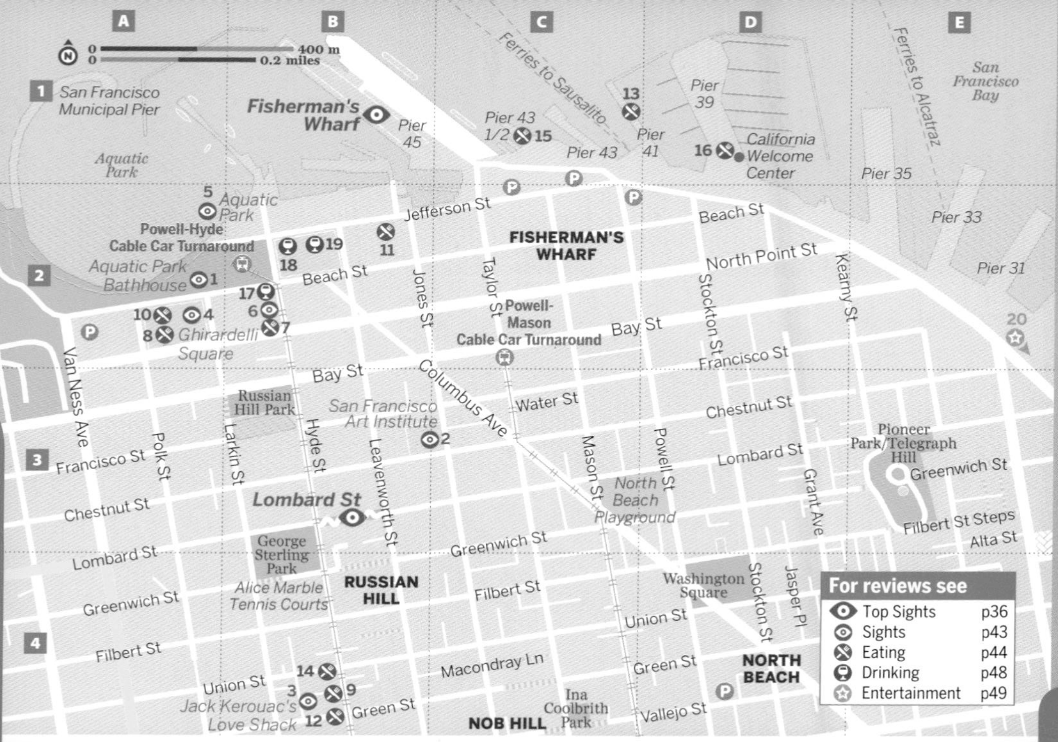
For reviews see
Top Sights p36
Sights p43
Eating p44
Drinking p48
Entertainment p49
San Francisco Bay
Ferries to Alcatraz
Ferries to Sausalito
Pier 31
Pier 33
Pier 35
Pier 39
Pier 41
Pier 43
Pier 43 1/2
Pier 45
California Welcome Center
Fisherman's Wharf
FISHERMAN'S WHARF
San Francisco Municipal Pier
Aquatic Park
Powell-Hyde Cable Car Turnaround
Powell-Mason Cable Car Turnaround
Aquatic Park Bathhouse
Ghirardelli Square
Russian Hill Park
San Francisco Art Institute
Lombard St
George Sterling Park
Alice Marble Tennis Courts
RUSSIAN HILL
Jack Kerouac's Love Shack
NOB HILL
Ina Coolbrith Park
North Beach Playground
Washington Square
NORTH BEACH
Pioneer Park/Telegraph Hill
Filbert St Steps
Alta St
Kearny St
Grant Ave
Jasper Pl
Stockton St
Powell St
Mason St
Taylor St
Jones St
Leavenworth St
Hyde St
Larkin St
Polk St
Van Ness Ave
Jefferson St
Beach St
North Point St
Bay St
Francisco St
Chestnut St
Lombard St
Greenwich St
Filbert St
Union St
Green St
Vallejo St
Water St
Columbus Ave
Macondray Ln
400 m
0.2 miles

Sights

Aquatic Park Bathhouse

HISTORIC BUILDING

1 Map p42, A2

A monumental hint to sailors in need of a scrub, this recently restored 1939 streamline moderne landmark is decked out with Works Project Administration (WPA) art treasures, including a playful seal sculpture by Beniamino Bufano, Hilaire Hiler's surreal underwater murals and acclaimed African American artist Sargent Johnson's carved green-slate doorway. Johnson left his veranda aquatic mosaics unfinished in protest at plans to include a private restaurant in this public facility. (www.nps.gov/safr/historyculture/bathhousebuilding.htm; 499 Jefferson at Hyde; admission free; 10am-4pm)

San Francisco Art Institute

ART GALLERY

2 Map p42, B3

Founded during the 1870s, SFAI was the vanguard for 1960s Bay Area Abstraction, 1970s conceptual art, and 1990s new media art – glimpse what's next in **Walter and McBean Gallery** (11am-6pm Mon-Sat). Diego Rivera's 1931 *The Making of a Fresco Showing a Building of a City* sprawls across **Diego Rivera Gallery**, showing the artist pausing to admire the constant work-in-progress that is San Francisco. (www.sfai.edu; 800 Chestnut St; admission free; 9am-5pm; Powell-Mason)

Take a Break The terrace cafe offers eye-opening espresso with panoramic bay views.

Jack Kerouac's Love Shack

HISTORIC SITE

3 Map p42, B4

This modest house on a quiet alley witnessed major drama in 1951 and 1952, when Jack Kerouac shacked up with Neal and Carolyn Cassady to pound out his 120ft-long scroll draft of *On the Road*. Jack and Carolyn became lovers at Neal's suggestion, but Carolyn frequently kicked them both out – though Neal moved back for the birth of John Allen Cassady (named for Jack and Allen Ginsberg). (29 Russell St; Powell-Hyde)

Ghirardelli Square

HISTORIC SITE

4 Map p42, A2

Willy Wonka would tip his hat to Domingo Ghirardelli (*gear*-ar-deli), who founded the West's largest chocolate factory c 1893. After the company moved to the East Bay, developers reinvented the factory as a mall in 1964. Today, the square has entered its third incarnation as a gourmet timeshare complex with wine-tasting rooms, dessert parlors and boutiques. (www.ghirardellisq.com; 900 North Point St; 10am-9pm; North Point St; Powell-Hyde;)

Take a Break Try the Cable Car Sundae at **Ghirardelli Ice Creams** (10am-11pm): marshmallow and hot fudge atop rocky road ice cream.

Local Life

Ina Coolbrith Park

On the San Francisco literary scene, all roads eventually lead to Ina Coolbrith, California's first poet laureate. She was a colleague of Mark Twain and Ansel Adams; mentor of Jack London, Isadora Duncan, George Sterling and Charlotte Perkins Gilman; and a lapsed Mormon (she kept secret from her bohemian posse that her uncle was Mormon prophet Joseph Smith). Hidden hilltop **Ina Coolbrith Park** (Map p42, C4; Vallejo St; Powell-Mason) is a fitting honor, with flowery passages leading to exclamation-inspiring vistas. Climb past gardens, decks and flower-framed apartment buildings and, as the fog blows in, listen for the whooshing wind in the treetops. On the way down, take the stairway past **Macondray Lane** (Map p42, C4; btwn Taylor & Leavenworth Sts; Powell-Mason), lined with gravity-defying wooden cottages. This enchanted byway looks like something out of a novel, and so it is: Armistead Maupin used it as the model for Barbary Lane in his *Tales of the City* series.

Aquatic Park — CULTURAL BUILDING

5 Map p42, A2

Eccentricity along Fisherman's Wharf is mostly staged, but at this beach-front park, it's the real deal: extreme swimmers dive into the bone-chilling bay waters in winter, weirdos mumble conspiracy theories on the grassy knoll of Victoria Park, and wistful tycoons stare off into the distance and contemplate sailing far away from Silicon Valley. (Hyde & Jefferson Sts; Van Ness Ave; Powell-Hyde;)

Blazing Saddles — BICYCLE RENTAL

6 Map p42, B2

To gear up for a Gary Danko feast after a round of Kara's Cupcakes, cover the waterfront from Pier 39 to the Golden Gate Bridge by bike. Bicycle rentals are readily available at Blazing Saddles, with a main shop on Hyde St and five rental stands around Fisherman's Wharf (good weather permitting). Reserve online for a 10% discount; rentals includes all extras (helmets, bungee cords, packs etc). (415-202-8888; www.blazingsaddles.com; 2715 Hyde St; bikes per hour $8-15, per day $32-88; 8am-7:30pm; 19, 30, 47, F; Powell-Hyde;)

Eating

Gary Danko — CALIFORNIAN $$$

7 Map p42, B2

The true test of romance is who you'll grant a taste of your trio of crème brûlées here. Gary Danko racks up James Beard Awards for impeccable dining experiences – perhaps try the oysters with caviar and lettuce cream, then duck breast with rhubarb compote, and tiny chocolate cakes as parting gifts? Choose three or five courses, but don't skip the cheese cart.

Reservations essential. (415-749-2060; www.garydanko.com; 800 North Point St; 3-/5-course menus $68/102; dinner; North Point; Powell-Hyde)

Crown & Crumpet

DESSERT, SANDWICHES **$$**

8 Map p42, A2

Designer style and rosy cheer usher teatime into the 21st century here, as dads and daughters clink teacups with crooked pinkies, pinafore-clad Lolita Goth teens nibble cucumber sandwiches and girlfriends dish the dirt on dates over scones and champagne. Reservations recommended on weekends. (415-771-4252; www.crownandcrumpet.com; 207 Ghirardelli Sq; dishes $8-12; 10am-9pm Mon-Fri, 9am-9pm Sat, 9am-6pm Sun; North Point; Powell-Hyde;)

Za

PIZZA **$**

9 Map p42, B4

Pizza lovers brave the uphill climb for cornmeal-dusted, thin-crust pizza by the slice, piled with fresh ingredients, accompanied by a pint of Anchor Steam and a cozy bar setting with highly flirtatious pizza-slingers – all for under 10 bucks and a smile. (www.zapizzasf.com; 1919 Hyde St; noon-10pm Sun-Wed, to 11pm Thu-Sat; Powell-Hyde)

Cycling the pier toward Transamerica Pyramid

Ghirardelli Sq (p43)

Kara's Cupcakes

DESSERTS $

10 Map p42, A2

Proustian nostalgia washes over adults as they bite into cupcakes that recall childhood birthday parties. Varieties range from campfire-worthy chocolate marshmallow to classic carrot cake with cream-cheese frosting, all meticulously calculated for maximum glee, and some available gluten-free. (www.karascupcakes.com; 3249 Scott St; cupcakes $3.25; 10am-8pm Mon-Sat, to 6pm Sun; North Point; Powell-Hyde)

In-N-Out Burger

BURGERS $

11 Map p42, B2

Gourmet burgers have taken SF by storm, but In-N-Out has had a good thing going for 60 years: prime chuck beef they process themselves, plus fries and shakes made with ingredients you can pronounce, all served by employees paid a living wage. Ask for yours off the menu 'wild style,' cooked in mustard with grilled onions. (www.in-n-out.com; 333 Jefferson St; 10:30am-1am Sun-Thu, 10:30am-1:30am Fri & Sat; Jefferson St; Powell-Hyde;)

Frascati

CALIFORNIAN, ITALIAN $$$

12  Map p42, B4

'Clang clang clang went the trolley/zing zing zing went my heartstrings...' That classic Judy Garland tune makes a whole lot more sense after a romantic evening at this hilltop neighborhood charmer, with storefront windows looking out to passing cable cars. The Mediterranean menu features flavor-drenched dishes like duck confit, pork chops with ratatouille, and roast chicken with lemon-oregano jus. Make reservations. (415-928-1406; www.frascatisf.com; 1901 Hyde St; mains $20-30; 5:30pm-9:45pm Mon-Sat, 5:30pm-9pm Sun; Powell-Hyde)

Forbes Island GRILL $$$

13 Map p42, C1

No man is an island – well, except for an eccentric millionaire named Forbes Thor Kiddoo that is. His moored houseboat is now a restaurant that is strong on grilled meats and island atmosphere, including a miniature lighthouse, thatched hut, a waterfall, sandy beach and swaying palms. Reserve ahead and catch boat shuttles from Pier 39; landlubbers dining below deck should bring motion-sickness medication. (415-951-4900; www.forbesisland.com; Pier 41; mains $28-40; 5-10pm Wed-Sun; North Point St;)

Swensen's ICE CREAM $

14 Map p42, B4

Bite into your ice-cream cone, and get instant brain-freeze and a hit of nostalgia. Oooh-ouch, that peppermint stick really takes you back, doesn't it? The 16-ounce root beer floats are the 1950s version of Prozac, but the classic 'chocolate ring-a-ding' hot fudge sundae is pure serotonin with sprinkles on top. (www.swensensicecream.com; 1999 Hyde St; noon-10pm Tue-Thu, to 11pm Fri-Sun; Powell-Hyde)

Salty's Famous Fishwich SANDWICHES $

15  Map p42, C1

Despite the name, Fisherman's Wharf drives a hard bargain for seafood – good luck finding a satisfying meal under $10. The exception is Salty's Famous Fishwich, a crispy slab of fried Pacific cod smothered in tangy, cilantro-spiked coleslaw overflowing the bun. The $5 'halfwich' makes

Local Life

Sourdough Bread

San Francisco's climate isn't great for bikinis, but it's perfect for lactobacillus sanfranciscensis, the lactic-acid bacteria that gives sourdough bread its distinctive tang and helps activate yeast. Any self-respecting San Francisco bakery serves sourdough, but the most famous is **Boudin Bakery** (Map p42, C2; www.boudinbakery.com; 160 Jefferson St; 8am-9:30pm Sun-Thu, to 10pm Fri-Sat; Fisherman's Wharf; Powell-Hyde;), a San Francisco institution since 1849. Brave the crowds at Boudin's Bakers Hall on the wharf for sourdough sandwiches (especially local Fra' Mani ham and brie) and peeks at bakers cramming human-sized lumps of dough into Jacuzzi-size mixers. But fair warning: gloppy clam chowder in a sourdough-bread bowl is a marathon of starch that tests even the toughest stomachs.

vacating the boardwalk picnic bench difficult, and $4 garlic fries could keep munchies and vampires away for days. (Pier 43 1/2; sandwiches $5-8; 11am-6:30pm; Fisherman's Wharf; Powell-Hyde;)

Eagle Cafe

AMERICAN $$

16 Map p42, D1

The best breakfast/lunch spot on Pier 39, the Eagle's food is simple and straightforward – pancakes, omelets and crab-salad sandwiches are reliable bets. The views are good, the prices decent for the prime location, and they even accept reservations, which you should definitely make on weekends to save yourself a long wait. (415-433-3689; www.eaglecafe.com; Pier 39, 2nd floor, Ste 103; mains $10-20; 7:30am-9pm; Fisherman's Wharf; Powell-Mason;)

Drinking

Buena Vista Café

BAR

17 Map p42, B2

Warm fog-chilled toes with a frothy goblet of creamy, bittersweet Irish coffee, introduced to the US at this destination bar with the nerve to serve such dainty drinks to sailors and cannery hands. The creaky Victorian floor still takes a pounding nightly from carousers and families, served

Pouring Irish coffees at Buena Vista Café

community-style at round tables looking out over the Wharf. (www.thebuenavista.com; 2765 Hyde St; ⌚9am-2am Mon-Fri, 8am-2am Sat & Sun; Powell-Hyde)

Winery Collective WINE TASTING ROOM

18 Map p42, B2

Ditch supermarket standards and discover new favorite indie wines with tastings at this California small-producer showcase. Featured wines vary, but popular flights include sublimely spicy Copain Anderson Valley pinot noir with a cult following; single-vineyard syrah and pinot blanc custom-blended by crafty sommeliers at Boulevard (p92) to delight foodies; and lightweight, biodynamic Evolve Sonoma sauvignon blanc, from reality-TV winemaker Benjamin Flajnik (of *The Bachelor* fame/notoriety). (www.winerycollective.com; 485 Jefferson St; ⌚noon-9pm; Powell-Hyde)

Jack's Cannery Bar BAR

19 Map p42, B2

Escaping Alcatraz and Pier 39 crowds definitely calls for a beer or two – and with 60 to 85 options on tap, Jack's got your back. Some locals balk at $6.50 and up for a pint of their usual Anchor Steam, Anderson Valley and Sierra Nevada brews. With outdoor seating and flatscreen TVs indoors, however, this is a neighborhood hangout on sunny days and big-game nights. Family-friendly; cash only. (2801 Leavenworth St ⌚11am-2am; Powell-Hyde)

Entertainment

Pier 23 LIVE MUSIC

20 Map p42, E2

It looks like a surf shack, but this waterfront bar-restaurant on Pier 23 regularly features live R&B, reggae, Latin bands, mellow rock and the occasional jazz pianist. Wander out to the bayside patio to soak in views – especially if you're visiting during early-October Fleet Week or the 2013 **Americas Cup** (www.americascup.com). The dinner menu features seaworthy options like batter-fried oysters and whole roasted crab. (www.pier23cafe.com; Pier 23; admission free-$10; ⌚shows 5-7pm Tue, 6-8pm Wed, 7-10pm Thu, 10pm-midnight Fri & Sat, 4-8pm Sun; Embarcadero)

Top Sight
Alcatraz

Getting There

Alcatraz is 1.25 miles across San Francisco Bay from Fisherman's Wharf.

Ferry Departures from Pier 33 every half-hour 9am to 3:55pm, plus 6:10pm and 6:45pm

Step into the cell, shut the iron door, and listen carefully: beyond these bars and across the bay, you can hear the murmur of everyday life. Now you appreciate how Alcatraz became America's most notorious prison, and why inmates risked rip tides to escape. Day visits include captivating audio tours with prisoners and guards recalling cell-house life, while popular, creepy twilight tours are led by park rangers. On the boat back to San Francisco, freedom never felt so good.

Cells inside Alcatraz

Don't Miss

The Cell Block

In 1934, America's first military prison became a maximum-security cell block housing the most-wanted criminals, from Chicago crime boss Al Capone to convicted Soviet spy Morton Sobell. Though Alcatraz was considered escape-proof, in 1962 the Anglin brothers and Frank Morris floated away on a makeshift raft and were never seen again. Their escape plot is showcased on the fascinating cell-block tour, which also covers riots, censorship, and solitary confinement.

Native American Landmarks

After the prison was closed in 1963, the state rejected a petition to turn Alcatraz into a Native American study center. Native American leaders occupied the island in 1969 in protest, and their 19-month standoff with the FBI is commemorated in a dockside museum and 'This is Indian Land' water-tower graffiti. Public support for the protesters pressured president Richard Nixon to restore Native territory and strengthen self-rule for Native nations.

Nature Trails

After the government regained control of Alcatraz from Native American protesters, it became a national park. By 1973, it had already become a major draw for visitors and the namesake birds of Isla de Alcatraces (Isle of the Pelicans). Wear sturdy shoes to explore unpaved trails to the prison laundry area that has become a prime bird-watching zone, and glimpse native plants thriving in the ruins of prison-guard homes.

☎ 415-981-7625

tickets: www.alcatrazcruises.com

park info: www.nps.gov/alcatraz

adult/child day $26/16, night $33/19.50

Top Tips

- Book at least two weeks ahead for self-guided daytime visits, longer for ranger-led night tours. Try to book the first or last boat of the day, when there are fewer people.
- Be prepared to hike. A steep path ascends from the ferry landing to the cell block.
- Most people spend two to three hours on the island. You only need to reserve the ferry to Alcatraz; several ferries return in the afternoon.
- Weather changes fast and it's often windy. Wear layers, long pants and sun block.

Take a Break

There is no food available on the island, only bottled water.

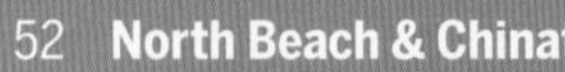

Explore

North Beach & Chinatown

Coffee or tea? East or west? You'll never have to decide in San Francisco, where historic Chinese and Italian neighborhoods are linked by poetry-lined Jack Kerouac Alley. Wander backstreets dotted with pagoda-topped temples and saloons where the Gold Rush, Chinese revolution and the Beat movement started. Rising above it all is Coit Tower, ringed by murals and jealously guarded by parrots.

The Sights in a Day

Enter **Dragon Gate** (p61) onto Grant Ave, lined with pagoda-topped buildings purpose-built in the 1920s by Chinatown merchants to attract curiosity seekers and souvenir shoppers – clearly their plan worked like a charm. It's hard to believe that this cheerful vintage-neon-signed street was once a notorious red-light district – at least until you see the fascinating displays at the **Chinese Historical Society** (p59). Wander temple-lined **Waverly Place** (p58) to glimpse a neighborhood that's survived against daunting odds, and detour for dim sum at **City View** (p61).

Cross into North Beach via **Jack Kerouac Alley** (p58) and **City Lights** (p68), San Francisco's free-speech landmark. Espresso at **Caffe Trieste** (p65) frees your inner Beatnik for the **North Beach Beat** walking tour (p184), and hikes up giddy, garden-lined Filbert Steps to **Coit Tower** (p54).

Kick off a Barbary Coast happy-hour crawl from **15 Romolo** (p66) to **Tosca** (p65) and **Comstock Saloon** (p65). San Franciscans will only excuse you from another round for one of three reasons: dinner reservations at **Coi** (p61), tickets to **Beach Blanket Babylon** (p67), or shows at **Bimbo's 365 Club** (p68).

Top Sight

Coit Tower & Filbert St Steps (p54)

Best of San Francisco

Eating

Coi (p61)

Cotogna (p61)

City View (p61)

Caffe Trieste (p65)

Drinking

Comstock Saloon (p65)

Specs (p65)

Tosca (p65)

Entertainment

Beach Blanket Babylon (p67)

Cobb's Comedy Club (p68)

Bimbo's 365 Club (p68)

Getting There

Cable car From downtown or the wharf, take Powell-Mason line through Chinatown and North Beach. The California cable car passes through Chinatown.

Bus Key routes are 30, 41 and 45.

Top Sight
Coit Tower

The exclamation point on San Francisco's skyline is the white Deco Coit Tower that eccentric heiress Ms Lillie Hancock Coit left a fortune to build as a monument to San Francisco's firefighters. This concrete projectile has been a lightning rod for controversy for its colorful, provocative 1930s Works Project Administration murals – but there's no debating the quality of the 360-degree panoramas from the viewing platform. The climb here along Filbert Steps is an adventure, with wild parrots squawking encouragement.

Map p56, D2

http://sfrecpark.org/CoitTower.aspx

Telegraph Hill Blvd

adult/child $7/2

10am-5:30pm summer, 9am-4:30pm winter

39

Coit Tower on Telegraph Hill, with a statue of Columbus in foreground

Don't Miss

WPA Murals

Coit Tower's lobby murals show San Franciscans during the Great Depression, gathered at soup kitchens and dock-workers' unions, partying despite Prohibition, and poring over library books – including *The Communist Manifesto*. These federally funded artworks proved controversial in 1934, and authorities denounced their 26 artists as communist – but San Franciscans embraced Coit Tower's bright, bold murals as beloved city landmarks.

Viewing Platform

After the 20-minute walk uphill to Coit Tower, the wait and admission fee to take the elevator to the top of the tower is well worth it. From the panoramic open-air platform 210 feet above San Francisco, you can spot two bridges, cable cars and skyline-defining landmarks.

Filbert St Steps

In the 19th century, a ruthless entrepreneur began quarrying Telegraph Hill and blasting away roads – much to the distress of his neighbors. City Hall eventually stopped the quarrying of Telegraph Hill, but the views of the bay from garden-lined, cliffside Filbert St Steps is still (wait for it) dynamite.

Napier Lane

Along the steep climb from Sansome St up Filbert St Steps toward Coit Tower, stop for a breather along Napier Lane, a wooden boardwalk lined with cottages and gardens where wild parrots have flocked for decades.

Top Tips

- To see more murals hidden inside Coit Tower's stairwell, take the free docent-led tours at 11am on Saturdays.
- Curious about why parrots flock to Telegraph Hill? Don't miss the award-winning 2005 documentary *The Wild Parrots of Telegraph Hill*, featuring flock caretaker and local character Mark Bittner.
- Bus 39 heads to Coit Tower from Fisherman's Wharf – but scenic walks climb Filbert St or Greenwich St Steps. Shorter, steeper Filbert St climbs lead from Washington Square.

Take a Break

Pick up a freshly baked snack off Washington Square at **Liguria Bakery** (p62) to savor with sparkling Bay views – a worthy reward for the climb up Telegraph Hill to Coit Tower.

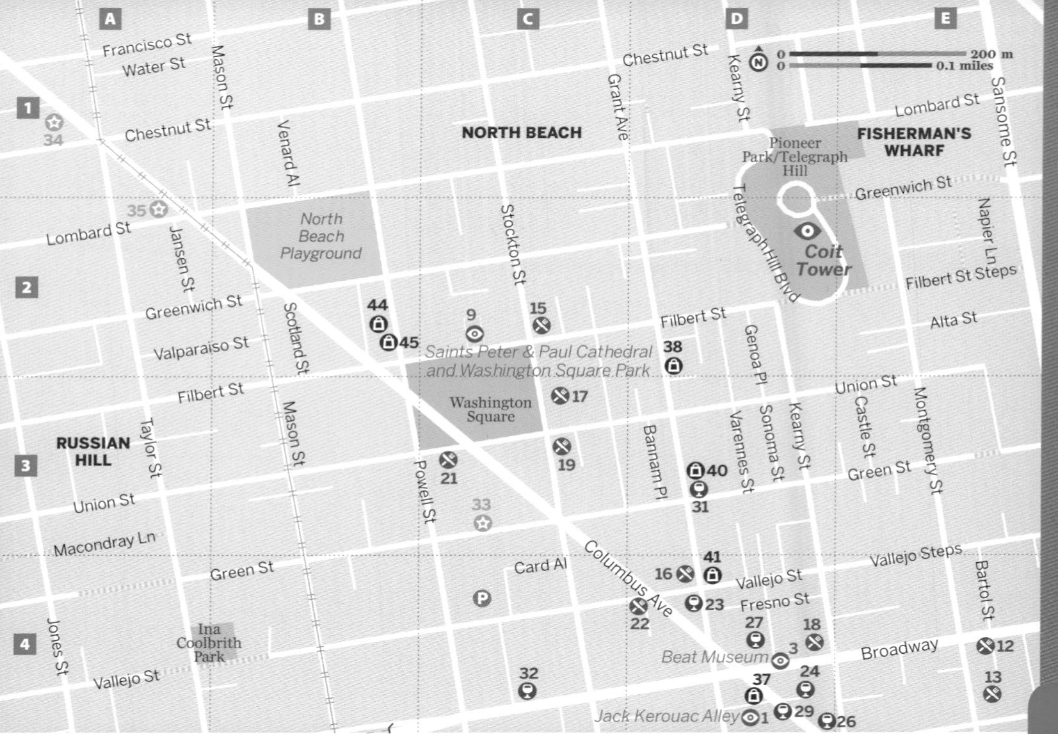

A
B
C
D
E
1
2
3
4
0
200 m
0.1 miles
N
Francisco St
Water St
Mason St
Chestnut St
Venard Al
NORTH BEACH
Grant Ave
Chestnut St
Kearny St
Lombard St
Sansome St
Pioneer Park/Telegraph Hill
FISHERMAN'S WHARF
Greenwich St
Napier Ln
Telegraph Hill Blvd
Coit Tower
Filbert St Steps
Alta St
Lombard St
Jansen St
North Beach Playground
Stockton St
Greenwich St
Scotland St
Valparaiso St
Filbert St
Genoa Pl
Saints Peter & Paul Cathedral and Washington Square Park
Filbert St
Union St
Washington Square
Mason St
RUSSIAN HILL
Taylor St
Powell St
Bannam Pl
Varennes St
Sonoma St
Kearny St
Castle St
Montgomery St
Green St
Union St
Macondray Ln
Card Al
Columbus Ave
Vallejo Steps
Green St
Vallejo St
Fresno St
Bartol St
Jones St
Ina Coolbrith Park
Vallejo St
Beat Museum
Broadway
Jack Kerouac Alley
34
35
44
45
9
15
38
17
19
21
40
31
33
41
16
23
22
27
18
3
12
32
37
24
13
1
29
26

Broadway
Broadway Tunnel
Pacific Ave
Bernard St
Taylor St
Auburn St
Pacific Ave
John St
Grant Ave
Beckett St
Columbus
Tower
Jackson St
Montgomery St
Jackson St
Cable Car
Museum
Stone St
Chinese
Telephone Exchange
Chinese
Culture
Center
Mark Twain St
Jones St
Washington St
Wetmore St
Chinese
Historical
Society
Waverly
Place
Clay St
Waverly Pl
Kearny St
Commercial St
NOB HILL
CHINATOWN
Sacramento St
Reed St
Priest St
Clay St
Sproule La
Old St Mary's Church &
St Mary's Square
Spring St
Pleasant St
Joice St
Sacramento St
Mason St
Powell St
Stockton St
FINANCIAL
DISTRICT
Huntington
Park
Cushman St
California St
Grant Ave
Quincy St
St Mary's
Square
Pine St
Belden St
For reviews see
Top Sights p54
Sights p58
Eating p61
Drinking p65
Entertainment p67
Shopping p68
Taylor St
Dragon
Gate
Bush St
UNION SQUARE
Harlan Pl
Claude La

Sights

Jack Kerouac Alley STREET

1 Map p56, D4

'The air was soft, the stars so fine, and the promise of every cobbled alley so great...' The *On the Road* author's ode is fittingly inscribed in the pavement of his signature shortcut between Chinatown and City Lights bookstore (p68). Spiffy with murals yet fragrant as ever, this alleyway is where Kerouac was tossed after one epic binge at Vesuvio (p67).

Waverly Place STREET

2 Map p56, D6

Off Sacramento St are the flag-festooned balconies of Chinatown's historic temples, where services have been held since 1852 – even in 1906, while altars were still smoldering after San Francisco's earthquake and fire. Due to 19th century race-based restrictions, family associations and temples were built right on top of barber shops, laundries and restaurants lining Waverly Place. (Stockton St; California, Powell-Mason)

Beat Museum MUSEUM

3 Map p56, D4

This is the closest you can get to the complete Beat experience without breaking a law. The 1950 to 1969 ephemera collection ranges from magnificent (the banned edition of

Understand

Chinatown Alleyways

Forty-one historic alleyways packed into Chinatown's 22 blocks have seen it all since 1849: Gold Rushes and revolution, incense and opium, fire and icy receptions. Though Chinese miners were among the first to arrive in San Francisco's gold rush, 1870s anti-Asian state and local laws restricted Chinese immigration, employment and housing. Anyone of Chinese origin was denied property ownership and union jobs, and many resorted to dangerous work blasting trans-continental railway tunnels through the mountains – or worse. Chinatown's white landlords profited handsomely from basement opium dens along Duncombe Alley, and brothels lining Ross Alley.

When the 1906 earthquake and fire devastated Chinatown, developers convinced the city to oust Chinese residents altogether. But with the support of China's consulate and gun-toting merchants, Chinatown refugees defied the expulsion order and returned to rebuild their community from the ground up. Family associations ousted opium and flesh trades, and 1920s merchants gave the neighborhood a tourist-friendly 'Chinatown Deco' makeover. Today you can hear the clatter of mahjong tiles at 36 Spofford Alley, where Sun Yat-sen once plotted revolution.

Allen Ginsberg's *Howl*) to tawdry (a 1961 Jack Kerouac liquor store check). Downstairs, watch fascinating Beat-era films; upstairs, pay respects at shrines to individual Beats. Entry to the adjoining bookstore and frequent poetry readings are free. (☎1-800-537-6822 (1-800-KER-OUAC); www.thebeatmuseum.org; 540 Broadway; admission $5; ⏰10am-7pm Tue-Sun; 🚌Columbus Ave)

Chinese Historical Society

MUSEUM

4 Map p56, C6

Picture what it was like to be Chinese in America during the Gold Rush, transcontinental railroad construction or the Beat heyday in this 1932 landmark, built as Chinatown's YWCA by Julia Morgan (of Hearst Castle fame). Century-old photos, gold-mining tools and mesmerizing miniatures of Chinatown landmarks bring local history to life, alongside vintage advertisements and toys conveying Chinese stereotypes. (☎415-391-1188; www.chsa.org; 965 Clay St; adult/child $5/2, 1st Thu of month free; ⏰noon-5pm Tue-Fri, 11am-4pm Sat; 🚌Stockton St, California St; 👪)

Chinese Culture Center

ART GALLERY

5 Map p56, E6

You can see all the way to China inside this cultural center, which hosts exhibits of traditional Chinese arts, cutting-edge contemporary art installations and a new Art at Night series showcasing Chinese-inspired art, jazz,

SABRINA DALBESIO/LONELY PLANET IMAGES ©

Silk shirts in Chinatown

and food. Check the center's schedule for upcoming concerts, hands-on arts workshops, arts festivals and walking tours (see p60). (☎415-986-1822; www.c-c-c.org; 3rd fl, Hilton Hotel, 750 Kearny St; gallery free (donation requested); ⏰10am-4pm Tue-Sat; 🚌Kearny St)

Chinese Telephone Exchange

HISTORIC BUILDING

6 Map p56, D6

This triple-decker pagoda pioneered telecoms c 1894, when operators fluent in English plus five Chinese dialects began connecting calls to 1500 Chinatown residents. Throughout the Chinese Exclusion era (1882 to 1943), this switchboard was San Franciscans'

Top Tip

Chinatown Walks

Local-led, kid-friendly Chinatown Heritage Walking Tours guide visitors through the living history and mythology of Chinatown in two hours, winding through backstreets to key historic sights: Chinese Telephone Exchange, Golden Gate Fortune Cookie Factory, Waverly Place and Portsmouth Square. All proceeds support Chinatown community programming at the **Chinese Cultural Center** (415-986-1822; adult/child $30/25; 10am Sat, groups of 4 or more with 2-day advance booking at 10am, noon and 2pm Tue-Sat), and bookings can be made online or by phone.

primary contact with family and business partners in China. Managers lived onsite, ensuring no call was missed. The landmark was restored by Bank of Canton in 1960. (743 Washington St; Stockton St; California)

Columbus Tower HISTORIC BUILDING

7 Map p56, E5

Shady political boss Abe Ruef finished this copper-topped tower just before the 1906 earthquake, then restored it right before his 1907 bribery conviction. Folk band the Kingston Trio bought Columbus Tower in the 1960s, recording the Grateful Dead in the basement. Since 1970, the building has belonged to Francis Ford Coppola, who leases offices to fellow filmmakers Sean Penn and Wayne Wang. (916 Kearny St; Kearny St)

Take a Break Sip Coppola's Director's Cut wine at ground-level **Cafe Zoetrope** (11am-10pm Tue-Sat, noon-9pm Sun).

Old St Mary's Church & St Mary's Square CHURCH & PLAZA

8 Map p56, D7

Built by an Irish entrepreneur determined to give wayward San Francisco religion in 1854, St Mary's offered confessionals alongside the city's most notorious brothels. The 1906 earthquake destroyed a bordello directly across from the church, making room for **St Mary's Square**. Today, skateboarders stealthily ride park handrails while Beniamino Bufano's 1929 statue of Chinese revolutionary Sun Yat-sen keeps a lookout. (www.oldsaintmarys.org; 660 California St; 11am-6pm Mon-Tue, 11am-7pm Wed-Fri, 9am-6:30pm Sat, 9am-4:30pm Sun; Stockton St; California;)

Saints Peter & Paul Cathedral and Washington Square Park CHURCH & PARK

9 Map p56, C2

Wedding-cake cravings are inspired by this frosted-white, triple-layer 1924 cathedral (666 Filbert St) where Joe DiMaggio and Marilyn Monroe posed for wedding photos (as divorcees, they were denied a church wedding here). The cathedral faces Washington Sq, where grandmothers practice tai chi by the 1897 statue of Ben Franklin, donated by an eccentric dentist who made fortunes in gold teeth. (Columbus Ave & Union St; Columbus Ave; Powell-Mason)

Take a Break Even wild parrots descend from park treetops for oven-fresh focaccia from **Liguria Bakery** (p62).

Dragon Gate

MONUMENT

10 Map p56, D8

Enter this dragon archway donated by Taiwan in 1970, and you'll find yourself on the once-notorious street known as Dupont in its red-light heyday. The pagoda-topped 'Chinatown Deco' architecture beyond this gate was innovated by forward-thinking Chinatown businessmen led by Look Tin Ely in the 1920s, transforming the street from a playground for alcoholics into a stomping ground for shopaholics. (Intersection of Bush St & Grant Ave; Stockton St; California;)

Cable Car Museum

MUSEUM

11 Map p56, B6

Grips, engines, braking mechanisms...if these words warm your heart, you'll be completely besotted with the Cable Car Museum, housed in SF's still-functioning cable-car barn. See three original 1870s cable cars and watch as cables glide over huge bull wheels – as awesome a feat of physics now as when the mechanism was invented by Andrew Hallidie in 1873. (www.cablecarmuseum.org; 1201 Mason St; admission free; 10am-6pm Apr-Sep, to 5pm Oct-Mar; Powell-Mason, Powell-Hyde;)

Eating

Coi

CALIFORNIAN **$$$**

12 Map p56, E4

Chef Daniel Patterson's wild, 11-course tasting menu featuring foraged morels, wildflowers and Pacific seafood is like licking the California coastline: purple ice-plant petals may appear atop Sonoma duck's tongue, wild-caught abalone and organic arugula. Decor rivals '70s Big Sur nudist colonies with shaggy cushions, grasscloth walls and terrariums – but only-in-California flavors and wine pairings ($95; generous enough for two) inspire California dreaming. (415-393-9000; http://coirestaurant.com; 373 Broadway; set menu per person $145/; 6-10pm Tue-Fri, 5:30-10pm Fri-Sat; Columbus Ave;)

Cotogna

ITALIAN **$$**

13 Map p56, E4

No wonder chef-owner Michael Tusk won the 2011 James Beard Award – his rustic Italian pastas and toothsome pizzas magically balance a few pristine, local flavors. Book ahead; the $24 prix-fixe is among SF's best dining deals. (415-775-8508; www.cotognasf.com; 470 Pacific Av; mains $14-24; noon-3pm & 7-10pm Mon-Sat; Kearny St;)

City View

DIM SUM **$**

14 Map p56, E6

Take your seat in a sunny dining room and your pick from carts loaded with delicate shrimp and leek dumplings, tangy spare ribs, garlicky Chinese broccoli and other tantalizing dim sum. Time your arrival before or after the lunch rush, so you can nab seats in the sunny upstairs room and avoid having to flag down speeding carts. (662 Commercial St; ⏲11am-2:30pm Mon-Fri, 10am-2:30pm Sat & Sun; Kearny St; California)

Liguria Bakery
BAKERY $

15 Map p56, C2

Bleary-eyed art students and Italian grandmothers are in line by 8am for the cinnamon-raisin focaccia, leaving 9am dawdlers a choice of tomato or classic rosemary, and noon stragglers out of luck. Take what you can get, and don't kid yourself that you're going to save it for lunch. (1700 Stockton St; ⏲8am-1pm Mon-Fri, 7am-1pm Sat, 7am-noon Sun; Columbus Ave; Powell-Mason).

Ideale
ITALIAN $$

16 Map p56, D4

Other North Beach restaurants put on Italian accents, but Ideale is the one

Understand

Portsmouth Square Landmarks

The action begins early and runs late in Portsmouth Sq at 733 Kearny St, where tai chi practitioners greet the dawn, and summertime and Chinese New Year bring a lively night market (July to October). Chinatown's unofficial living room is named after John B Montgomery's sloop, which pulled up near here in 1846 to stake the US claim on San Francisco and has been making history ever since. Look for the following monuments around the square:

- A plaque near the children's playground where California's first public school was founded, c 1848.
- The hillside where tabloid publisher and real-estate speculator Sam Brannan kicked off California's Gold Rush, waving a vial of gold dust and shouting: 'Gold! Gold from the American River!'
- A plaque commemorating San Francisco's first bookshop and Brannan's newspaper office, abruptly abandoned during the Gold Rush.
- The bawdy Jenny Lind Theater, which, over the protests of its patrons, became San Francisco's first City Hall in 1852.
- A ship with golden sails dedicated to adventure author Robert Louis Stevenson, who found inspiration here c 1879.
- A bronze replica of the Goddess of Democracy statue made by the 1989 Tiananmen Square protesters.

restaurant where you'll find actual Italians in the kitchen, on the floor and at the table. Roman chef Maurizio Bruschi whips up gorgeous ricotta gnocchi and truffled zucchini, but try any pasta involving house-cured pancetta and ask Tuscan staff to recommend wine, and everyone goes home happy. (www.idealerestaurant.com; 1315 Grant Ave; ⏲5:30-10:30pm Mon-Sat, 5-10pm Sun; 🚌 Columbus Ave)

Park Tavern CALIFORNIAN-ITALIAN $$$

17 Map p56, C3

An instant Washington Square institution, this Kiwi-founded newcomer is a genuine North Beach character. Instead of Tuscan bona fides, the PT presents totally twisted Italian standards with California produce: sea urchin crudo atop velvety avocado, yellow watermelon wrapped in prosciutto, wood-fired oven-roasted chicken lounging on a bed of crispy spinach. Never mind the noise; have a Negroni and join the happy din. (☎415-989-7300; www.parktavernsf.com; 1652 Stockton St; ⏲5:30-11pm Tue-Thu, until 12:30am Fri-Sat; 🚌Columbus Ave)

Naked Lunch SANDWICHES $

18 Map p56, D4

Unpredictable, utterly decadent cravings worthy of a William S Burroughs novel are satisfied by the ever-changing menu at this lunch stall near the Beat Museum. Foie gras, duck prosciutto and black truffle salt are liable to sprawl across a sandwich,

Tosca (p65)

keeping company with salty-sweet, artisan-made *chicharrones* (fried pork rinds) and sweet-talking Southern cinnamon iced tea. (www.nakedlunchsf.com; 504 Broadway; ⏲11:30am-2pm Tue-Sat; 🚌Columbus Ave, Powell-Mason)

Tony's Coal-fired Pizza & Slice House PIZZA $

19 Map p56, C3

Fuggedaboudit... This may be San Francisco, but you can still grab a cheesy, thin-crust slice to go in a New York minute from nine-time world champ pizza-slinger Tony Gemignani. Difference here is, you can take that slice to sunny Washington Square Park, and watch tai chi practice and

Nob Hill

Once the California cable car made blustery Nob Hill accessible c 1873, gold-mining moguls jockeyed for hilltop views. But fire engines couldn't reach these hilltop mansions during the 1906 earthquake and fire, and almost all were destroyed. Swanky hotels sprung up, offering million-dollar sunsets over martinis at **Top of the Mark** (Map p56, C7; www.topofthemark.com; 999 California St; cover $5-15; 5pm-midnight Sun-Thu, 4pm-1am Fri & Sat; California). Locals recover from workdays and foggy nights over Scorpion Bowls at **Tonga Room** (Map p56, C7; www.fairmont.com; Fairmont Hotel, 950 Mason St; cover $5-8; 5-11:30pm Sun, Wed & Thu, 5:30pm-12:30am Fri & Sat; M1, 27; California), SF's classic tiki bar where thundershowers erupt over the indoor pool and cover bands play popular music after 8pm. Episcopal **Grace Cathedral** (Map p56, B7; www.gracecathedral.org; 1100 California St; 7am-6pm Sun-Fri, 8am-6pm Sat; California), rebuilt thrice since the gold rush, has an AIDS Memorial Chapel altarpiece by Keith Haring, stained-glass windows featuring Albert Einstein and a labyrinth for private meditation.

wild parrots in the trees year-round. Sorry, Manhattan – whaddayagonnado? (www.tonyspizzanapoletana.com; 1556 Stockton St; noon-11pm Wed-Sun; Columbus Ave; Powell St)

House of Nanking — ASIAN $$

20  Map p56, E5

Like older sisters, staff here are bossy because they know what's best for you. Meekly suggest an interest in seafood, nothing deep-fried, perhaps some greens – and in minutes, you'll be devouring pan-seared scallops, garlicky noodles and spicy braised long beans. Come prepared to wait, and bearing cash. (919 Kearny St; 11am-10pm Mon-Fri, noon-10pm Sat, noon-9pm Sun; Kearny St)

Cinecittá Pizzeria — PIZZA $

21 Map p56, C3

Squeeze in at the counter for your thin-crust pie and Anchor Steam on draft with a side order of sass from Roman owner Romina. Vegetarians swear by the Funghi Selvatici (wild mushroom with grilled zucchini and sundried tomato), but that saliva-prompting aroma that elicits untranslatable exclamations from Italian regulars is O Sole Mio, with capers, olives, mozzarella and anchovies. (663 Union St; noon-10pm Sun-Thu, to 11pm Fri & Sat; Columbus Ave; Mason St;)

Molinari — ITALIAN DELI $

22  Map p56, D4

Grab a number and a crusty roll, and when your number rolls around the guys in paper hats behind the counter will stuff it with translucent sheets of prosciutto di Parma, milky buffalo mozzarella, tender marinated artichokes or slabs of the legendary house-cured salami (the city's best).

(373 Columbus Ave; 9am-5:30pm Mon-Fri, 7:30am-5:30pm Sat; M Columbus Ave).

Drinking

Caffe Trieste CAFE

23 Map p56, D4

Poetry on bathroom walls, opera on the jukebox, live Italian accordion jams weekly, and sightings of Beat poet laureate Lawrence Ferlinghetti: this is North Beach at its best, since the 1950s. Linger over a legendary espresso and scribble your screenplay under the Sicilian mural just as young Francis Ford Coppola did. Perhaps you've heard of the movie *The Godfather*? (601 Vallejo St; 6:30am-11pm Sun-Thu, to midnight Fri & Sat; Columbus Ave;)

Specs Museum Café DIVE BAR

24 Map p56, D4

Ever wondered what to do with a drunken sailor? Here's your answer. The walls are plastered with mementos from the Merchant Marine, and you'll be plastered too if you try to keep pace with the salty old-timers holding court out back. Surrounded by nautical memorabilia, your order is obvious: pint of Anchor Steam, coming right up. (12 William Saroyan Pl; 5pm-2am; Columbus Ave)

Comstock Saloon BAR

25 Map p56, D5

Cocktails remain period-perfect in this vintage Victorian saloon; the Pisco Punch is made with real pineapple gum, and the Hop Toad with Jamaican rum, bitters and apricot brandy would make sea captains abandon ship. The adjacent restaurant serves dainty, decadent 'pig in a blanket' (sausage in a fluffy biscuit) and maple-bourbon cake. (155 Columbus Ave; 11:30am-2am Mon-Fri, 2pm-2am Sat; Columbus Ave)

Tosca COCKTAIL LOUNGE

26 Map p56, D4

Sean Penn, Bobby De Niro and Sofia Coppola might lurk in the VIP room, but they could base their next character study on regulars sipping *caffe corretto* (espresso 'corrected' with liquor) in these retro red-vinyl booths. Opera on Tosca's jukebox (with genuine

Local Life

Parking Luck

You'd be lucky to find parking anywhere near Chinatown or North Beach, but a free space in the **Good Luck Parking Garage** (Map p56, C4; 735 Vallejo St; Stockton St; California, Powell-Mason; P) brings double happiness. Each parking spot offers fortune-cookie wisdom stenciled onto the asphalt: 'You have already found your true love. Stop looking.' These car-locating omens are brought to you by West Coast artists Harrell Fletcher and Jon Rubin, who also gathered the photographs of local residents' Chinese and Italian ancestors that grace the entry in heraldic emblems.

45rpm platters) sometimes has to compete with the thump-thump of Larry Flynt's Hustler Club next door, but Tosca wins for high-drama romance. (http://toscacafesf.com; 242 Columbus Ave; 5pm-2am Tue-Sun; Columbus Ave)

15 Romolo

BAR

27 Map p56, D4

Strap on your spurs – finding this Western saloon in an alleyway between burlesque joints is an adventure. Arrivals are rewarded with stiff Victorian-inspired cocktails – the Pim's Cup strikes a rigorous gin/cucumber/bitters ratio. Happy hour runs 5pm to 7:30pm daily; stick around for pub grub like smoked pulled-pork sliders and fries with curry ketchup (15 Romolo Pl; 5pm-2am; M Columbus Ave)

Barrique

BAR

28 Map p56, E5

For hot dates on foggy nights, roll out the barrel at Barrique. Choose your varietal and vintage, and barkeeps pour your wine selection straight from the cask – or let them custom-blend you a glass. Many wines come from small California artisan winemakers you've never heard of before, but who could be your new best friends before the night and your charcuterie plate are through. (www.barriquesf.com; 461 Pacific Ave; 3pm-10pm Tue-Sat; M 10, 12, 30, 41, 45)

EMILY RIDDELL/LONELY PLANET IMAGES ©

Li Po Cocktails bar in Chinatown

Vesuvio

MICROBREWERY

29 Map p56, D4

Guy walks into a bar, roars, and leaves. Without missing a beat, the bartender says to the next customer, 'Welcome to Vesuvio, honey – what can I get you?' Kerouac blew off Henry Miller to go on a bender here, and after joining neighborhood characters for microbrews or Kerouac's namesake drink (a bucket of rum, tequila, and OJ), you'll understand why. (www.vesuvio.com; 255 Columbus Ave, btwn Grant & Columbus Aves; 6am-2am; Columbus Ave)

Li Po Cocktails

DIVE BAR

30 Map p56, D5

Beat a hasty retreat from Grant Ave souvenir shops to the bar where Allen Ginsberg and Jack Kerouac debated the meaning of life by the golden Buddha. Enter the faux-grotto doorway, and dodge the red lanterns to place your order for whiskey, Tsing Tao beer, or the Chinese mai tai made with *bai ju* (Chinese rice liquor). (916 Grant Ave; 2pm-2am; Stockton St)

Church Key

BAR

31 Map p56, D3

Warm North Beach nights call for your favorite beer – whether Brazilian or Kiwi, bacon-flavored or pomegranate-scented. Look for the discreet white key sign over the door, and head on back to the copper-topped bar for your selection of 55 international craft brews. With potent 10% to 12% beer, you won't miss cocktails. Cash only. (1402 Grant Ave; 5pm-midnight; Columbus Ave)

Rosewood

BAR

32 Map p56, C4

San Franciscans still like their bars the way Chinatown's Prohibition bootleggers preferred their bills: small and unmarked. There's no sign outside, but mood lighting illuminates sleek rosewood-paneled walls and low-slung black-leather sofas. Basil gimlets and crafty DJs add intrigue to the bamboo-enclosed smokers' patio. Arrive before 10 if you're here for casual conversation. (732 Broadway; 5:30pm-2am Wed-Fri, 7pm-2am Sat; Stockton St)

Entertainment

Beach Blanket Babylon

CABARET

33 Map p56, C3

Killer drag, razor-sharp satires of current events and oddly touching musical odes to San Francisco are highlights of the city's longest-running comedy cabaret. Big onstage personalities in giant hats deliver huge belly laughs – spectators must be 21-plus for the occasionally racy humor, except at cleverly sanitized matinees. Reservations essential; arrive one hour early for best seats (415-421-4222; www.beachblanketbabylon.com; 678 Green St; admission $25-100; shows 8pm Wed, Thu & Fri, 6:30pm & 9:30pm Sat, 2pm & 5pm Sun; Stockton St, Powell-Mason).

Bimbo's 365 Club
LIVE MUSIC

34 Map p56, A1

Cibo Matto, Ben Harper and Coldplay have recently played this vintage-1931 speakeasy, where stiff drinks get the crowd on the polished parquet dance floor. Cash only, and bring something extra to tip the ladies' powder room attendant – this is a classy joint. (www.bimbos365club.com; 1025 Columbus Ave; tickets from $20; check calendar; Columbus; Powell-Mason)

Cobb's Comedy Club
COMEDY

35 Map p56, A2

Bumper-to-bumper shared tables make for an intimate (and vulnerable) audience for stand-up acts. Come to see rising talents before they nab their own sitcoms, and watch big-name acts from HBO's Dave Chapelle to NBC's Tracy Morgan try out risky new material. Check the website for shows. (www.cobbscomedyclub.com; 915 Columbus Ave; admission $18-33 plus 2-drink minimum; shows 8pm & 10:15pm; Columbus Ave)

Purple Onion
COMEDY

36  Map p56, E5

Legendary comics including Woody Allen, Robin Williams and Phyllis Diller clawed their way up from underground at this grotto nightclub. Recently, comics have been taking back the stage from lackluster lounge acts – Zach Galifianakis shot an excruciatingly funny comedy special here. Bookings are sporadic; see online event calendar. (415-956-1653; www.caffemacaroni.com; 140 Columbus Ave; admission $10-15; check calendar; M Columbus Ave)

Shopping

City Lights
BOOKS

37 Map p56, D4

Poetic justice has been served here since 1957, when City Lights founder and Beat poet Lawrence Ferlinghetti won a landmark free speech ruling over publishing Allen Ginsberg's incendiary, magnificent *Howl and Other Poems*. Celebrate your freedom to read freely in the designated Poet's Chair upstairs, load up on zines on the mezzanine, or entertain big ideas in the nonfiction cellar. (www.citylights.com; 261 Columbus Ave; 10am-midnight; Columbus Ave).

Aria
ANTIQUES

38 Map p56, D2

An art installation that doubles as an antiques boutique, with anatomy diagrams of the human heart propped on medicine chests, rusty castle keys scattered across worn pews, and bundles of 19th-century French love letters tied with ribbon. Hours are erratic whenever owner/chief scavenger Bill Haskell is out treasure-hunting. (1522 Grant Ave; 11am-6pm Mon-Sat, noon-5pm Sun; Columbus Ave)

Golden Gate Fortune Cookie Company
FORTUNE COOKIES

39 Map p56, D5

You too can make a fortune in San Francisco at this bakery, where fortune cookies are stamped out on antique presses. Make your own customized cookies (50¢ each), or pick up a bag of the risqué/adult fortune cookies – no need to add 'in bed' at the end to make these interesting. Cash only; 50¢ tip requested for photos. (56 Ross Alley; admission free; 8am-7pm; Stockton St; Powell-Mason)

101 Music

MUSIC & INSTRUMENTS

40 Map p56, D3

You'll have to bend over those bins to let DJs and hardcore collectors pass (and, hey, wasn't that Tom Waits?!), but among the \$3–\$10 discs are obscure releases *(Songs for Greek Lovers)* and albums by Nina Simone, Janis Joplin, and SF anthem-rockers Journey. At the sister shop – 513 Green St – don't bonk your head on the vintage Les Pauls. (1414 Grant Ave; 10am-8pm Tue-Sat, noon-8pm Sun; Columbus Ave)

Al's Attire

CLOTHING & ACCESSORIES, LOCAL DESIGNER

41 Map p56, D4

Hepcats and slick chicks get their duds at Al's, where vintage styles are reinvented in noir-novel twill, dandy high-sheen cotton, and midcentury flecked tweeds. Prices aren't exactly bohemian, but turquoise wing-tips are custom-made to fit your feet, and svelte hand-stitched jackets have silver-screen star quality. (www.alsattire.com; 1314 Grant Ave; 11am-7pm Mon-Sat, noon-5pm Sun; Columbus Ave)

Understand

The Barbary Coast

By 1854, San Francisco's harbor near Portsmouth Sq was filling with rotting ships abandoned by crews with gold-rush fever. Here on the ragged piers of the 'Barbary Coast,' a buck might procure whiskey, opium or a woman's company at 500 saloons, 20 theaters and numerous brothels – but buyer beware. Saloon owners like Shanghai Kelly and notorious madam Miss Piggot would ply new arrivals with booze, knock them out with drugs or billy-clubs, and deliver them to sea captains in need of crews. At the gaming tables, luck literally was a lady: women card dealers dealt winning hands to those who engaged their back-room services.

Prohibition and California's Red Light Abatement Act drove the Barbary Coast's illicit action underground, but it never really went away. US obscenity laws were defied post-WWII in anything-goes North Beach clubs near Broadway and Columbus, where burlesque dancer Carol Doda went topless and comedian Lenny Bruce dropped F-bombs. Today San Francisco is undergoing a Barbary Coast saloon revival, with potent 19th-century-style cocktails served by apparently harmless bartenders – just don't forget to tip.

Red Blossom Tea Company TEA

42 Map p56, D6

Venture beyond mass-market tea bags to discover 100-plus specialty white teas, herbal infusions and namesake blossoms – tightly wound balls of tea-leaves that unfurl into flowers in hot water. Score a free sample with purchase, or enroll in a tea-tasting class – half-hour tea classes with freshly brewed tastings from a daily menu, including an immersion course on preparing tea for maximum flavor ($30 for up to four participants). Drop in weekdays or call ahead on weekends; seating is limited. (415-395-0868; www.redblossomtea.com; 831 Grant Ave; 10am-6:30pm Mon-Sat, 10am-6pm Sun; M Stockton St, Powell St)

Clarion Music Center MUSICAL INSTRUMENTS

43 Map p56, D6

With this impressive range of *erhus* (Chinese fiddles), African congas, Central American marimbas and gongs galore, you could become your own multiculti one-person band. Check the website for concerts, workshops and demonstrations by master musicians. (www.clarionmusic.com; 816 Sacramento St; 11am-6pm Mon-Fri, 9am-5pm Sat; California St)

SF Rock Posters & Collectibles ANTIQUES & COLLECTIBLES

44 Map p56, B2

Anyone who hazily remembers the '60s may recall long-lost bands (and

Understand

The Beat Generation

US armed services personnel dismissed in WWII for disobeying orders, homosexuality and other 'subversive' behavior were discharged in San Francisco, as though that would teach them a lesson. Instead, they found themselves at home in nonconformist North Beach. So during McCarthyism, rebels and romantics headed for San Francisco – including Jack Kerouac. By the time *On the Road* was published in 1957, the fellow writers, artists and dreamers Kerouac affectionately called 'the mad ones' and the press derisively dubbed 'beatniks' were San Francisco regulars.

Police fined 'beatnik chicks' for wearing sandals, and were taunted in verse by African American street-corner prophet Bob Kaufman (there's now a North Beach alley in his name). Poet Lawrence Ferlinghetti and manager Shigeyoshi Murao of City Lights Bookstore (p68) fought the law and won, after their arrest for 'willfully and lewdly' publishing Allen Ginsberg's *Howl*. The kindred Beat spirits *Howl* describes as 'angel-headed hipsters burning for the ancient heavenly connection' made more waves, art and love than money, upending 1950s social-climbing conventions and making way for the 1960s.

brain cells) in this trippy temple to the rock gods. Nostalgia isn't cheap – first-run psychedelic Fillmore concert posters featuring Jimi Hendrix or the Grateful Dead run $250 and up – but you can score deals on handbills for 1970s local acts like Santana or the Dead Kennedys. (www.rockposters.com; 1851 Powell St; ⏲10am-6pm Tue-Sat; 🚋Columbus Ave; Powell-Mason)

Double Punch TOYS, ART

45 Map p56, B2

Doubly dangerous for collectors with kids: original artworks by emerging local artists line the upstairs gallery, while downstairs shelves feature coveted limited-edition toys by KAWS and other major graffiti artists. *Star Wars* action figures from local Lucasfilm are usually in stock, and the $5 bargain bin offers kid-friendly finds. (http://doublepunch.com; 1821 Powell St; ⏲11am-7pm Mon-Sat, to 6pm Sun; 🚋Columbus Ave; Powell-Mason; 👪)

Chinatown Kite Shop GIFTS

46 Map p56, D6

Be the star of Crissy Field (p28) and wow any kids in your life with a fierce 6ft-long flying shark, a surreal set of flying legs or a flying panda bear that looks understandably stunned. Pick up a papier-mâché two-person lion-dance costume, and invite a date to bust ferocious moves with you next lunar new year. (www.chinatownkite.com; 717 Grant Ave; ⏲10am-8.30pm; 🚋 Kearny St; Powell-Mason)

SABRINA DALBESIO/LONELY PLANET IMAGES ©

101 Music store (p69)

Local Life
Upper Polk Bars & Boutiques

Sailors on shore leave set the tone for Polk St, a historic nightlife hub that was San Francisco's original gay neighborhood. Today most gay bars have relocated to SoMa and the Castro, but dive bars with live music and literary credentials still make the scene. By day, Marina party girls and slumming Nob Hill socialites shop funky Polk St boutiques.

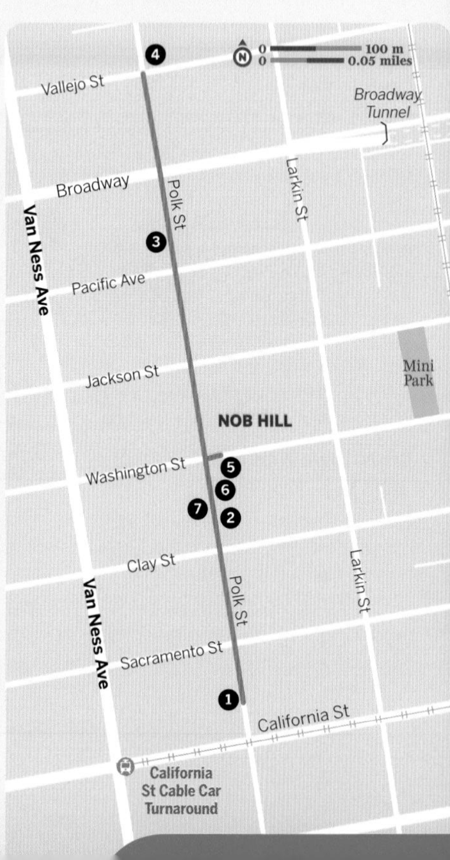

Getting There

Upper Polk St is 0.5 miles south of Aquatic Park

Bus No 19 runs up Polk St to the wharf.

Cable Car Powell-Hyde climbs Russian Hill, the California line connects Polk St to downtown.

❶ Seafood Lunch

Decadent lunches at decent prices are the specialty of **Swan Oyster Depot** (1517 Polk St; dishes $10-20; ⏰8am-5:30pm Mon-Sat). Join the line for a spot at the counter to savor crab salad with a glass of bubbly along with the obligatory oysters, shucked in front of you and drizzled with mignonette (wine and shallot sauce).

❷ Handmade SF at Studio

Spiff up your pad with locally made arts and crafts at bargain prices at **Studio** (www.studiogallerysf.com; 1815 Polk St; ⏰11am-8pm Wed-Fri, to 6pm Sat & Sun). Bring San Francisco home in Katie Gilman's pulp-fiction-inspired prints of SF haunts, architectural etchings by Alice Gibbons, and Heather Logsdon's repurposed San Francisco map-wallets.

❸ Statement Jewelry

Craftsmanship meets high concept at **Velvet da Vinci** (www.velvetdavinci.com; 2015 Polk St; ⏰11am-6pm Tue-Sat, to 4pm Sun), where one-of-a-kind handmade jewels have been celebrated and exhibited for 20 years. Look for Amy Tavern's industrial recreations of her grandmother's jewelry, and Niki Ulelha's marionette-inspired jointed ebony necklaces.

❹ Sustainable Chic

Idealism meets streetwise fashion at **Eco Citizen** (www.ecocitizenonline.com; 2255 Polk St), a boutique of eco-friendly, fair-traded fabulousness. Gear up for San Francisco hills in easygoing, thoughtful style from head to foot, from hand-printed organic cotton sunhats to hand-stitched, California-made black oxfords. Prices are fair for the quality, and sale racks a total steal.

❺ Wine at Amélie

No Polk St boutique trawl is complete without a toast to shopping scores at **Amélie** (www.ameliesf.com; 1754 Polk St), where wine-bottle sconces on wine-stained walls hint at the house specialty. Happy hour flights run $10, but daily specials may include a bottle with cheese plate for under $35.

❻ Kitsch Cocktails at Bigfoot

After one sobriety stomping Sasquatch cocktail (Wild Turkey, brandy, and a droplet of ginger ale) at log cabin–themed **Bigfoot Lodge** (www.bigfootlodge.com; 1750 Polk St), you'll swear you've seen Bigfoot – the hairy monster lurks in the corner. Stick around after the 3pm–7pm happy hour, and the night turns urban-legendary: bartenders light the bar on fire around midnight.

❼ Gay Old Times at Cinch

Finding a fun gay dive bar on Polk St isn't as easy as it once was, but here it's a **Cinch** (www.thecinch.com; 1723 Polk St; ⏰9am-2am Mon-Fri, 6am-2am Sat & Sun). Come out and play in an old-timey saloon with pool, pinball, free popcorn, a big smokers patio, year-round holiday decorations and occasional amateur drag nights.

Explore

Downtown & SoMa

Get to know SF from the inside out, from art galleries to farmers markets. Discover fine dining that's unfussy yet fabulous, and find out why some cocktails are worth double digits – just don't plan to sleep. Social media pioneers and MacWorld conferences might co-exist alongside historic clubs and drag venues *So*uth of *Ma*rket St (SoMa), but everyone gets down and dirty on the dance floor here after 10pm.

The Sights in a Day

Brace yourself with a fortifying bayside brunch at **Boulette's Larder** (p93) before your SoMa art binge: the **Cartoon Art Museum** (p88) for superheroes and indie comics; **Catharine Clark Gallery** (p88) for art revolutions in the making; and **SFMOMA** (p76) for photography and mind-bending new media art.

Swing by the **Contemporary Jewish Museum** (p88; pictured left) and **Museum of Craft & Folk Art** (p90) on your way to **Blue Bottle** (p97), for a cup of coffee that cost $20,000 to make. Hop the **Powell-Hyde cable car** (p81) for one wild ride, with giddy views and poetry inducing sunsets.

Return downtown for the happy hour of your choice: oysters and bubbly at **Hog Island** (p79), Prohibition-pedigreed cocktails at **Bar Agricole** (p94), beer flights at **City Beer** (p95) or dangerously tasty tequila drinks at **Cantina** (p95). Plan the rest of your night around tickets at **ACT** (p97), reservations at **Benu** (p91), dance performances at **Yerba Buena Center for the Arts** (p97), or drag dinner theatre at **AsiaSF** (p98).

For a local's night in SoMa, see p84.

Top Sights

SFMOMA (p76)

Ferry Building (p78)

Cable cars (p80)

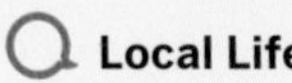

Local Life

SoMa Nightlife (p84)

Best of San Francisco

Museums & Galleries

SFMOMA (p76)

Cartoon Art Museum (p88)

Contemporary Jewish Museum (p88)

Catharine Clark Gallery (p88)

Gallery Paule Anglim (p88)

49 Geary (p89)

77 Geary (p90)

Getting There

M S Along Market St

Bus East–west buses include 14 Mission and 47 Harrison (to Fisherman's Wharf); north–south include 27 Bryant (Mission to Russian Hill) and 19 Polk

Car Garage at Mission & 5th St

Top Sights

San Francisco Museum of Modern Art

When SFMOMA outgrew its Civic Center galleries and moved to architect Mario Botta's light-filled box in 1995, it became clear just how far this museum was prepared to push the art world. It showed its brick backside to New York, taking risks on then-unknown SF artist Matthew Barney's poetic videos involving industrial quantities of Vaseline, and mounting art-history-altering photography retrospectives by Japanese postwar photographers Daido Moriyama and Shomei Tomatsu.

Map p86, E3

www.sfmoma.org

151 3rd St

adult/student/child $18/11/free

11am-6pm Fri-Tue, to 9pm Thu

M S Montgomery St

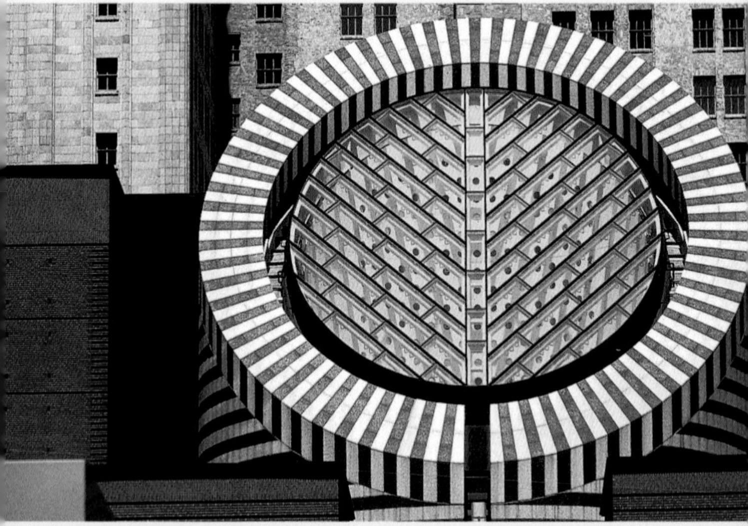

Architectural detail of the San Francisco Museum of Modern Art

Don't Miss

Photography

Since photography has flourished in Northern California since early Gold Rush days, SFMOMA got a head-start on other museum collections with a groundbreaking photography collection. Works range from 19th-century daguerreotypes and early innovators – including local pioneers Eadweard Muybridge, Ansel Adams, Pirkle Jones, Imogen Cunningham, Edward Weston and Dorothea Lange – to such boundary-breaking photographers as William Eggleston and Diane Arbus.

New Media

New media art took off with SFMOMA's 1995 relaunch, just as new technology was launching around the Bay (the original iPhone mock-up is in the Design collection). SFMOMA hosted groundbreaking shows of video art by Bill Viola and Olafur Eliasson's outer-space light installations, and collectors took note: donations have doubled SFMOMA's holdings since 1995, including video art, wall-drawing installations and relational art.

Modern Masters

From its start in 1935, SFMOMA has shown what's on our modern minds, from Paul Klee's manic dreamscapes to Diego Rivera's poignant paintings of laborers. A $480 million expansion is currently underway with Norway-based Snøhetta architects to accommodate 1100 more key modern works recently donated by the Fisher family (founders of SF-based clothiers The Gap/Old Navy/Banana Republic).

Top Tips

- Admission is half-price on Thursday after 6pm, the first Tuesday of the month is free.
- There are regular, free gallery tours, but exploring on your own gives you the thrill of discovery – which is what SFMOMA is all about.
- Begin self-guided tours in the 3rd-floor photography galleries, heading up through 4th- and 5th-floor contemporary exhibits to the rooftop sculpture garden.
- Descend via the dramatic stairwell for vertiginous perspectives over atrium installations.
- SF's most artful flirting happens Thursday nights at SFMOMA, when late hours and cocktail events loosen up shy artists.

Take a Break

The rooftop sculpture garden offers extraordinary city perspectives, best appreciated with Blue Bottle cappuccino and Mondrian cake at the cafe.

Top Sights
Ferry Building

Slackers have the right idea at this transport hub turned gourmet emporium, where no one's in a hurry to leave. Boat has traffic tapered off since the grand hall was built in 1898, so in 2003 the city converted the Ferry Building into a monumental tribute to the Bay Area's local specialty foods, garnished with California's most famous farmers market. Further reasons to miss that ferry await indoors: James Beard Award–winning restaurants, wine tasting, and foodie boutiques to bring inspiration home.

Map p86, H2

www.ferrybuildingmarketplace.com

Market St & Embarcadero

10am-6pm Mon-Fri, 9am-6pm Sat, 11am-5pm Sun

M S Embarcadero

Don't Miss

Ferry Plaza Farmers Market

SF's professional chefs and semiprofessional eaters trawl **farmers market stalls** (www.cuesa.org; ⌚10am-2pm Tue & Thu, 8am-2pm Sat) for samples of NorCal produce, goat cheese and wild boar jerky, plus gourmet street food such as Korean tacos and organic tamales. Prices may be higher, but you'll find unique local specialty foods – though you may have to elbow *Top Chef* contestants out of your way.

Hog Island Oyster Company

Decadence with a conscience: sustainably farmed, local Tomales Bay oysters are served raw or cooked with Sonoma bubbly at **Hog Island** (www.hogislandoysters.com; samplers $15-30; ⌚11:30am-8pm Mon-Fri, 11am-6pm Sat & Sun). Choose yours au naturel, with caper *beurre blanc* or spiked with bacon and paprika. Oysters are half-price and pints $4 Monday and Thursday 5pm to 7pm.

Mijita

Sustainable fish tacos reign supreme and *agua fresca* (fruit punch) is made with fresh juice at James Beard Award–winning chef/owner Traci des Jardins' casual Cal-Mex family joint **Mijita** (www.mijitasf.com; small plates $2-9; ⌚10am-7pm Mon-Wed, to 8pm Thu-Sat, to 4pm Sun;), paying tribute to her Mexican grandmother's cooking.

Slanted Door

Unsurprisingly it's hard to get a table without reservations at **Slanted Door** (☎415-861-8032; www.slanteddoor.com; mains $13-36; ⌚lunch & dinner). James Beard Award–winning chef/owner Charles Phan reinvents Vietnamese classics, from fragrant five-spice duck with figs to garlicky Niman Ranch 'shaking beef' atop watercress. Reserve tables with bay-views or picnic on takeout from the Open Door stall.

Top Tips

- Among the locavore gourmet stalls lining the grand arrivals hall are three standout local purveyors: Heath Ceramics (p99), Recchiuti Chocolates (p100), and Ferry Plaza Wine Merchant (p102).
- For bayside picnics, find benches flanking the bronze statue of Gandhi by the ferry docks, or walk to the end of pedestrian Pier 14 for perches with unobstructed bay views.
- Across the Embarcadero from the Ferry Building in Justin Hermann Plaza, lunchtime picnickers join a classic SF scene, where wild parrots, protestors, skaters and craftspeople mingle.

Take a Break

Before you choose a restaurant from our listings, don't miss the gourmet food trucks and stalls flanking the Ferry Building's southwest corner.

Top Sights
Cable Cars

A creaking handbrake seems to be the only thing between you and cruel fate as your 15,000lb cable car picks up speed downhill, careening toward oncoming traffic. But Andrew Hallidie's 1873 contraptions have held up miraculously well on San Francisco's giddy slopes, and groaning brakes and clanging brass bells only add to the carnival-ride thrills. Powell-Mason cars are quickest to reach Fisherman's Wharf; Powell-Hyde cars are more scenic; and the original east–west California line is the most historic.

Map p86, D2

schedules: transit.511.org
maps: www.sfmuni.com

$6 per ride; all-day unlimited $14

about 6am–1am daily

California, Powell-Mason, Powell-Hyde

Cable car with Transamerica Pyramid in the background

Don't Miss

Powell-Hyde Cable Car

The journey is the destination on this hilly line, with the Golden Gate Bridge popping in and out of view. Hop off the cable car atop zig-zagging Lombard St (p40) to see Russian Hill's priceless pine-framed panorama, naming rights to which belong not to resident billionaire and Oracle CEO Larry Ellison, but penniless poet George Sterling, to whose memory Sterling Park (p41) was dedicated.

Powell-Mason Cable Car

Powell-Mason's ascent up Nob Hill feels like the world's longest roller-coaster climb. Stop for a hilltop martini (p64), or continue on to Chinatown's Chinese Historical Society (p59). The route crosses North Beach at Washington Sq Park (p60), ringed with pizza-purchasing possibilities, and offers a glimpse of Diego Rivera murals at the nearby San Francisco Art Institute (p43). Near the terminus are two riveting attractions: USS *Pampanito* (p37) and Musée Mecanique (p37).

California St Cable Car

History buffs and crowd-shy visitors will probably prefer the California St cable car. In operation since 1878, this divine ride heads west through Chinatown, past Old St Mary's (p60) and climbs Nob Hill to Grace Cathedral (p64). Alight at Polk St for boutique-browsing and cocktails with Sasquatch at Bigfoot Lodge (p73). The Van Ness terminus is a few blocks northeast of Japantown (p124).

☑ Top Tips

- Cable cars stop almost every block on California and Powell-Mason lines, and stop every block on north–south stretches of the Powell-Hyde line.
- To board on hills, act fast: leap onto the baseboard and grab the closest leather hand-strap.
- Powell St and Fisherman's Wharf cable car turnarounds usually have lines, but they move fast. To skip the queue, head further up the line and jump on when the cable car approaches.
- This Victorian transport is not childproof – you won't find car seats or seat belts. Kids love open-air seating in front, but holding them inside the car is safer.
- Cable cars are not wheelchair-accessible.

Take a Break

Hop off for scenic invented-in-SF martinis at Top of the Mark (p64) or sundaes from Swensen's (p47).

Understand

The Cable Car's Timeless Technology

Legend has it that the idea for cable cars occurred to Andrew Hallidie in 1869, as he watched a horse carriage struggle up Jackson St – until one horse slipped on wet cobblestones, and the carriage went crashing downhill. Such accidents were considered inevitable on steep San Francisco hills, but Hallidie knew better. His father was the Scottish inventor of wire cable, which Hallidie had used hauling ore out of Gold Rush mines. If hemp-and-metal cable could carry rock through High Sierras snowstorms, surely it could transport San Franciscans through fog.

'Wire rope railway' was a name that didn't inspire confidence, and skeptical city planners granted the inventor just three months to make his contraption operational by August 1, 1873. Hallidie had missed his city deadline by four hours when his cable car was poised on Jones St for the descent. The operator was terrified, and Hallidie himself is said to have grabbed the brake and steered the car downhill.

By the 1890s, 53 miles of track crisscrossed the city. Hallidie became a rich man, and even ran for mayor; defamed as an opportunistic Englishman despite his civic contributions and US citizenship, he lost. He remained a lifelong inventor, earning 300 patents and becoming a prominent member of the California Academy of Sciences (p162).

Today the cable car seems more like a steampunk carnival ride than modern transport. Cable cars still can't move in reverse, and require burly gripmen and one buff gripwoman to lean hard on hand-operated brakes to keep from careening downhill. The city receives many applicants for this job, but 80% fail the strenuous tests of upper-body strength and hand-eye coordination, and rarely try again.

Although cables groan piteously with uphill effort, they seldom fray and have rarely broken in more than a century of near-continuous operation. The key to the cable car's amazing safety record is the cable gripwheel: clips click into place and release gradually to prevent cables from slipping. There are newer, faster ways to get around town, but this Victorian technology remains the killer app to conquer San Francisco's highest hills.

Powell Street Cable Car Turnaround

At Powell and Market Sts, you'll spot cable-car operators gripping trolleys and slooowly turning them around by hand on a revolving wooden platform. Cable cars can't go in reverse, and this 'turnaround' is where the Powell-Mason and Powell-Hyde lines end and begin. Tourists line up here to secure a seat, with street performers and doomsday preachers for entertainment. Locals hop on further uphill.

Friedel Klussmann Cable Car Turnaround

The Powell-Hyde turnaround at Fisherman's Wharf is named after the gardener who rallied her ladies' garden club in 1947 against the mayor's scheme to replace Powell cable car lines with buses – the mayor lost to the 'Cable Car Lady' by a landslide. In 1952, Klussmann campaigned to rescue the insolvent California line. Upon her death in 1986, cable cars citywide were draped in black.

Local Life
SoMa Nightlife

In San Francisco's work hard, play harder district, warehouse clubs and leather bars are conveniently located near business-class hotels. Once the sun sets and timid commuters clear out, the scene turns spicy and a little seedy – clubhoppers should take cabs or drive. Call clubs ahead to get on the list for reduced/free admission, and dress like you mean it.

❶ Brazen Hussy Behavior at Harlot

Vampire bordello is the vibe at **Harlot** (☎415-777-1077; www.harlotsf.com; 46 Minna St; admission free 5-9pm Wed-Fri, otherwise $10-20; ⏰5pm-2am Wed-Fri, 9pm-2am Sat; M S Montgomery St), with intense red lighting, velvet curtains over-exposed brick walls and cocktail tables featuring illustrated pinups wearing nothing but boa constrictors. Before 9pm it's a lounge, but after that the

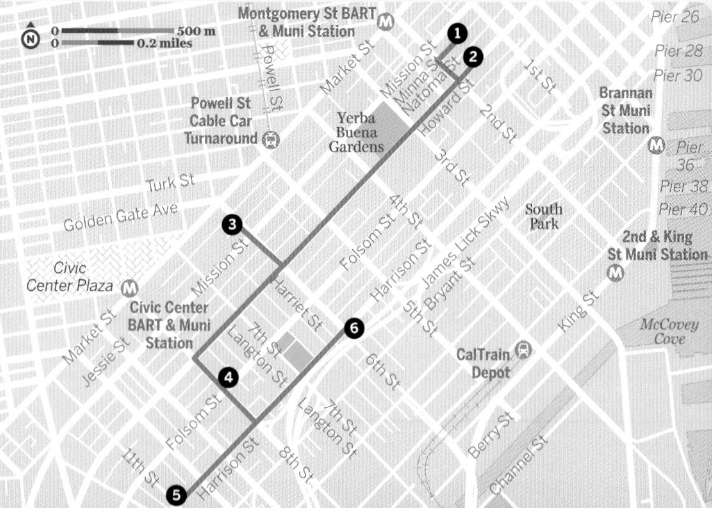

killer sound system pumps. Expect house on Thursdays, indie-rock Wednesdays, and monthly women-only Fem Bar parties. Dress funky to get past bouncers.

❷ Generate Electricity at Temple

The city's greenest club is an *izakaya* (bar snack) and sustainably sourced sushi bar before 10pm, when it turns into a glowing LED-lit **Temple** (415-978-8853; www.templesf.com; 540 Howard St; admission $20, often $5 before 11pm; 10pm-4am Thu-Sun; M S Montgomery St) of house music, with libations in biodegradable cups. Buddha presides over the all-white upstairs room; downstairs, two smaller dance floors harness the energy of stomping feet to generate electricity.

❸ Groove Underground at Club Six

Smack on Skid Row, but don't be daunted: **Club Six** (415-863-1221, 415-531-6593; www.clubsix1.com; 60 6th St; admission $5-15; 7pm-midnight Mon, 9pm-2am Tue-Thu, to 4am Fri & Sat; M Market St, S Powell St) defines casual cool with lumpy sofas, worn hardwood floors and easy beats. Hang in the street-level lounge when there's live music, or dive into the thick of it on the basement dance floor.

❹ Go Retro at Cat Club

Jump to 90s power pop at Saturday's Club Vogue and shuffle winsomely at Friday and Sunday goth/new wave nights at **Cat Club** (415-703-8965; www.catclubsf.com; 1190 Folsom St; admission after 10pm $5; 9pm-3am Tue-Sun; M S Civic Center) – but plan your week around Thursday night's 1984, when the euphoric bi/straight/gay/indefinable crowd belts out Aha's *Take on Me*, like a scene from a lost John Hughes movie.

❺ Rock Your Alter Ego at DNA Lounge

Cops keep trying and failing to shut down rowdy **DNA Lounge** (415-626-1409; www.dnalounge.com; 375 11th St; admission $3-25; 9:30pm-3am Fri-Sat, other nights vary; M Market St), where big-name DJs disturb the peace at twice-monthly Saturday Bootie, the original mashup party. Dress the part for events ranging from major drag king competitions to Death Guild, the Monday all-ages goth dance party with free tea service.

❻ End Up at EndUp

Straight club-kids do surface at **EndUp** (415-646-0999; www.theendup.com; 401 6th St; admission $5-20; 10pm-4am Mon-Thu, 11pm Fri-11am Sat, 10pm Sat-4am Mon; M Bryant St), SF's only 24-hour club – but epic gay Sunday tea dances have been held here since 1973, beginning with Ghettodisco Saturdays and ending Monday, watching the sunrise over the freeway ramp.

A
B
C
D
1
2
3
4
5
Elm St
Post St
Larkin St
Polk St
Hyde St
Leavenworth St
Geary St
Shannon St
McAllister St
Van Ness Ave
Grove St
Dr Carlton B Goodlett Pl
Eddy St
Jones St
Taylor St
Mason St
Hayes St
Fell St
Civic Center Plaza
United Nations Plaza
Turk St
Golden Gate Ave
San Francisco Visitors Information Center
Powell St Cable Car Turnaround
Cable Cars
Market St
Civic Center BART & Muni Station
Powell St BART & Muni Station
Stevenson St
Jessie St
Laskie St
Electric Works
Mission St
Minna St
Natoma St
Grace St
8th St
6th St
Mary St
5th St
Howard St
10th St
Dore Al
Tehama St
Langton St
7th St
Moss St
Russ St
Harriet St
Clementina St
Folsom St
Juniper St
Victoria Manalo Draves Park
Shipley St
Clara St
4th St
Harrison St
SOUTH OF MARKET (SOMA)
11th St
9th St
James Lick Skwy
Morris St
Bryant St
Gilbert St
Brannan St
Bluxome St
Townsend St
5
14
19
23
24
26
28
33
35
36
37
38
45
46
47
52
For reviews see
Top Sights p76
Sights p88
Eating p91
Drinking p94
Entertainment p97
Shopping p99

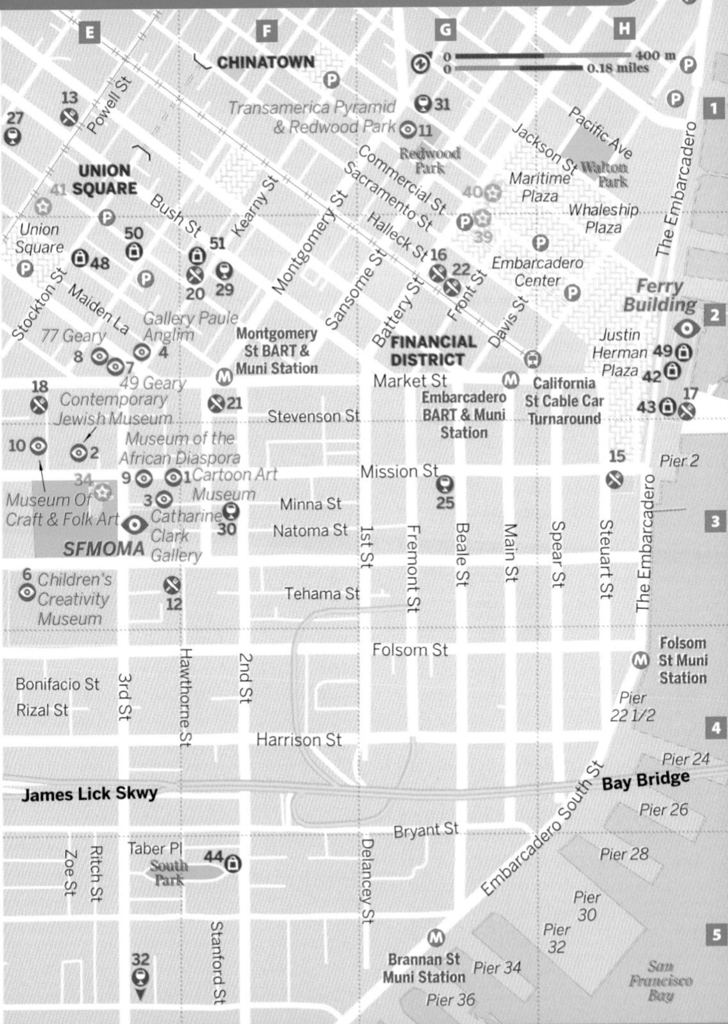

E
F
G
H
1
2
3
4
5
CHINATOWN
400 m
0.18 miles
Transamerica Pyramid & Redwood Park
Redwood Park
UNION SQUARE
Union Square
Powell St
Bush St
Kearny St
Montgomery St
Sansome St
Battery St
Front St
Davis St
Commercial St
Sacramento St
Halleck St
Jackson St
Pacific Ave
Walton Park
Maritime Plaza
Whaleship Plaza
Embarcadero Center
The Embarcadero
Ferry Building
Justin Herman Plaza
Stockton St
Maiden La
77 Geary
Gallery Paule Anglim
49 Geary
Montgomery St BART & Muni Station
FINANCIAL DISTRICT
Market St
Embarcadero BART & Muni Station
California St Cable Car Turnaround
Contemporary Jewish Museum
Stevenson St
Museum of the African Diaspora
Cartoon Art Museum
Museum Of Craft & Folk Art
SFMOMA
Catharine Clark Gallery
Mission St
Minna St
Natoma St
Pier 2
Children's Creativity Museum
Tehama St
1st St
Fremont St
Beale St
Main St
Spear St
Steuart St
Folsom St
Folsom St Muni Station
Bonifacio St
Rizal St
3rd St
Hawthorne St
2nd St
Pier 22 1/2
Harrison St
Pier 24
Bay Bridge
James Lick Skwy
Pier 26
Bryant St
Embarcadero South St
Pier 28
Taber Pl
South Park
Zoe St
Ritch St
Delancey St
Pier 30
Pier 32
Stanford St
Brannan St Muni Station
Pier 34
Pier 36
San Francisco Bay

Sights

Cartoon Art Museum — MUSEUM

1 Map p86, E3

Comics fans need no introduction to this museum founded on a grant from Bay Area cartoon legend Charles M Schultz *(Peanuts)*, featuring movie-marquee superheroes plus cult classics by local comics heroes R Crumb *(Mr Natural)*, Daniel Clowes *(Ghostworld)*, Gene Yang *(American Born Chinese)* and Adrian Tomine *(Optic Nerve)*. Don't miss openings, political cartoon retrospectives and animation workshops with Pixar Studio heads. First Tuesday of the month is 'pay what you wish' day. (CAM; www.cartoonart.org; 655 Mission St; adult/student $7/5; 11am-5pm Tue-Sun; M S Montgomery St)

Contemporary Jewish Museum — MUSEUM

2 Map p86, E3

Daniel Liebskind's 2008 blue steel-and-brick building incorporates the facade of the 1881 Jesse Street Power Substation to form the shape of the Hebrew word *l'chaim* ('to life') – a fine idea in theory, though best appreciated from a helicopter. But inside, these galleries are most illuminating, with fascinating recent shows on Warhol, Houdini, and the Bay Area's own Gertrude Stein. (www.thecjm.org; 736 Mission St; adult/child $10/free, after 5pm Thu $5; 11am-5pm Fri-Tue, 1-8pm Thu; M S Montgomery St)

Catharine Clark Gallery — ART GALLERY

3 Map p86, E3

Art revolutions are instigated at Catharine Clark, a showcase for such gorgeous provocations as Al Farrow's miniature religious monuments made from ammunition, and Masami Teraoka's paintings of geishas and goddesses banding together like superheroines to fend off wayward priests. Don't miss the video/new media room, featuring works such as Anthony Discenza's mesmerizing digital remix of suburban dream homes. (www.cclarkgallery.com; 150 Minna St; admission free; 11am-6pm Tue-Sat; M S Montgomery St)

Gallery Paule Anglim — ART GALLERY

4 Map p86, E2

Big names make bold gestures here, from Tony Oursler's video projections of rolling eyes to Louise Bougeois' expressionistic watercolors of afterbirth. Think pieces in new media are standouts here, from Lynn Hirschman's toxin-sensing broom to Ann Hamilton's circular book, re-bound into an infinite, loosely tied narrative. (www.gallerypauleanglim.com; 14 Geary St; admission free; 10am-5:30pm Tue-Fri, 10:30am-5pm Sat; S Montgomery)

Electric Works — ART GALLERY

5 Map p86, B3

Light-bulb moments abound at Electric Works, where David Byrne's diagrams reveal the overlap between

RICK GERHARTER/LONELY PLANET IMAGES ©

Catharine Clark Gallery

hairstyles and long division, Talia Greene's portraits show dandies rocking beards of swarming bees, and Sandow Birk's take on Dante's *Inferno* stars traffic-jammed LA as hell and San Francisco as foggy purgatory. The small, select gallery store is what museum stores ought to be, with limited-edition gifts and print editions benefiting nonprofits. (www.sfelectricworks.com; 130 8th St; admission free; ⌚11am-6pm Tue-Fri, to 5pm Sat; M S Civic Center)

Children's Creativity Museum

MUSEUM

6 Map p86, E3

No velvet ropes or hands-off signs here: kids have the run of the place, with high-tech displays double-daring them to make their own music videos, claymation movies and soundtracks. Jump right into a live-action video game, sign up for workshops with Bay Area robot-builders or hop a ride on the restored 1806 Looff Carousel out front ($3 for two rides). (www.zeum.org; 221 4th St; admission $10; ⌚11am-5pm Tue-Sun, carousel to 6pm; M S Powell St; 👪)

49 Geary

ART GALLERY

7 Map p86, E2

Pity collectors politely nibbling endive in austere Chelsea galleries – at 49 Geary, openings bring provocative art, outspoken crowds and animal crackers. Four floors of galleries feature standout international and local works including classic photography at **Fraenkel Gallery** (www.fraenkelgallery.com), social commentary at **Steven Wolf Fine Art** (www.stevenwolffinearts.com), spirited minimalism at **Gregory Lind** (www.gregorylindgallery.com) and sublime environmental art at **Haines Gallery** (www.hainesgallery.com). Come weekdays for quieter contemplation. (www.sfada.com; 49 Geary St; admission free; 10:30am-5:30pm Tue-Fri, 11am-5pm Sat; M S Powell St)

77 Geary
ART GALLERY

8 Map p86, E2

Step out of the elevator and your usual frame of reference on the 2nd floor, where you'll discover the Bay Area's next art star among the painter-provocateurs at **Marx & Zavattero** (www.marxzav.com), raise an eyebrow at think-pieces at **Rena Bransten Gallery** (www.renabranstengallery.com) and debate political art at **Togonon Gallery** (www.togonongallery.com). Stop on the mezzanine at **Patricia Sweetow Gallery** (www.patriciasweetowgallery.com) for seductive minimalism. (77 Geary St; admission free; 10:30am-5:30pm Tue-Fri, 11am-5pm Sat; M S Montgomery St)

Local Life

Rincon Annex Post Office

Only in San Francisco could a post office be controversial. Art deco **Rincon Annex** (Map p86, H3; 101 Spear St; admission free; M S Embarcadero) is lined with Works Project Administration murals of San Francisco history. Russian-born painter Anton Refregier began in 1941, only to be interrupted by WWII and political squabbles over differing versions of history. After 92 changes, his mural cycle was completed in 1948 with *War and Peace*, pointedly contrasting Nazi book-burning and postwar promises for 'Freedom from fear/want/of worship/speech.' Initially denounced as communist by McCarthyists, Refregier's masterpiece is now a National Landmark.

Museum of the African Diaspora
MUSEUM

9 Map p86, E3

MoAD has assembled an international cast of characters to tell the epic story of the African diaspora: a regal couple by Nigerian British sensation Chris Ofili, Harlem jazz portraits by Romare Bearden, and Siddi family quilts by Indians descended from African slaves. Don't miss the moving video of slave narratives narrated by Maya Angelou. (MoAD; www.moadsf.org; 685 Mission St; adult/student $10/5; 11am-6pm Wed-Sat, noon-5pm Sun; M S Montgomery St)

Museum of Craft & Folk Art
MUSEUM

10 Map p86, E3

Vicarious hand cramps are to be expected from a trip to this small but utterly absorbing museum, where remarkable handiwork comes with fascinating backstories. Recent exhibits showcased Korean *bojagi* (hand-pieced textiles), playful modern takes on iconic Mexican handicrafts, and internationally acclaimed SF artist Clare Rojas' urban folklore mural installations. Check the website for DIY crafts workshops, trunk shows and kids' events. (www.mocfa.org; 51 Yerba Buena Lane; adult/child $5/free; 11am-6pm Wed-Sat; M S Montgomery St)

Transamerica Pyramid & Redwood Park PARK

11 Map p86, G1

The defining quirk of San Francisco's skyline is the Transamerica Pyramid, built atop a whaling ship abandoned in the 1849 Gold Rush. The building is closed to visitors, but you can picnic under redwood trees beneath the pyramid, on a half-acre where Mark Twain's favorite saloon once stood. These transplanted redwoods have shallow roots, but the network of intertwined roots they form with neighboring trees allows them to reach dizzying heights. Mark Twain himself couldn't have scripted a more perfect metaphor for San Francisco. (http://thepyramidcenter.com; 600 Montgomery St; park 9am-6pm Mon-Fri; Kearny St, S Montgomery St)

Eating

Benu CALIFORNIAN FUSION $$$

Map p86, E3

SF has refined Cal-Asian fusion over 150 years, but no one rocks it like chef Corey Lee (formerly of Napa's French Laundry), who remixes local, sustainable fine-dining staples and Pacific rim flavors with a SoMa DJ's finesse. His Dungeness crab and black truffle custard bring such outsize flavor to faux-shark's-fin soup, you'll swear Jaws is in there – especially paired with 1968 Madeira by star-sommelier Yoon Ha. (415-685-4860; www.benusf.com; 22 Hawthorne St; mains $25-40; 5:30-10pm Tue-Sat; M S Montgomery)

Sons & Daughters CALIFORNIAN $$$

13  Map p86, E1

Urban farm-to-table cuisine, made with ingredients grown by the staff gardener in the restaurant's one-acre garden combind with the quick wits and sharp knives of co-chef/owners Matt McNamara and Teague Moriarty Instead of meat and potatoes, they'll serve you wild boar cooked in hay and heirloom potato-skin consommé. Book ahead. (415-391-8311; www.sonsanddaughterssf.com; 708 Bush St; 4-course menu $58; dinner; Geary St, Powell-Hyde & Powell-Mason, S Powell St)

Zero Zero PIZZA $$

The name is a throw-down of Neapolitan pizza credentials – 00 flour is used exclusively for Naples' famous puffy-edged crust – and these pies deliver on that promise, with inspired SF-themes toppings. The Geary is a crossover hit with Manila clams, bacon and chilies, but the real crowd-pleaser is the Castro, turbo-loaded with house-made sausage. (www.zerozerosf.com; 826 Folsom

St; pizza $10-15; noon-2:30pm & 5:30-10pm Sun-Thu, to 11pm Fri & Sat; M P Powell St)

Boulevard

CALIFORNIAN **$$**

15 Map p86, H3

Belle époque decor adds grace notes to this 1889 building that once housed the Coast Seamen's Union, but chef Nancy Oakes has kept the menu honest and reliable with juicy pork chops, enough Dungeness crab on salads to satisfy a sailor and crowd-pleasing desserts like chocolate ganache cake with housemade bourbon ice cream. (www.boulevardrestaurant.com; 1 Mission St; lunch $17-25, dinner $29-39; 11:30am-2pm Mon-Fri, 5:30-10pm Sun-Thu, 5:30-10:30pm Fri & Sat; M S Embarcadero)

Michael Mina

CALIFORNIAN **$$$**

16  Map p86, G2

The multiple James Beard Award winner has reinvented his posh namesake restaurant as a lighthearted Californian take on French-Japanese cooking – there's still caviar and lobster, but you will also discover foie gras PB&J and a deconstructed lobster pot pie on the menu. Reservations essential, or grab bar bites and cocktails at the bar. (415-397-9222; www.michaelmina.net; 252 California St; lunch menus $49-59, dinner mains $35-42; 11:30-2pm Mon-Fri, 5:30-10pm nightly; M S Montgomery St; California)

Understand

South Park Schemes

'Dot-com' entered the global vernacular during the mid-'90s, when venture capitalists and techies first plotted website launches in cafes ringing South Park (enclosed by 2nd, 3rd, Bryant & Brannan Sts). But when online ice-cream delivery services failed to deliver profits, South Park became a dot-com ghost town, adding another bust to its checkered history.

Speculation is nothing new to South Park, originally planned by a 1850s real-estate developer as a gated community. A party celebrating a Crimean War victory was thrown here in 1855 to attract gold-rush millionaires – but it degenerated into a cake-throwing food fight, and the development flopped. Yet the neighborhood remained fertile ground for wild ideas: 601 3rd St was the birthplace of Jack London, best-selling author of *The Call of the Wild*, *White Fang* and other adventure stories.

After WWII, Filipino American war veterans formed a quiet community in South Park – at least until dot-com HQs moved in and out of the neighborhood. South Park offices weren't vacant for long before Web 2.0 moved in, including a scrappy startup with the outlandish notion of communicating in online haiku. Twitter has since moved its operations and 200 million users downtown.

Boulette's Larder INTERNATIONAL $$

17  Map p86, H2

Dinner theater doesn't get better than communal-table brunches at Boulette's, strategically placed inside a working kitchen amid a swirl of chefs preparing for dinner service. Inspired by their truffled eggs and beignets? Get spices and mixes at the counter. (www.bouletteslarder.com; 1 Ferry Bldg, mains $7.50-22; breakfast Mon-Fri, lunch Mon-Sat, brunch Sun)

Amber India INDIAN $$

18 Map p86, E2

Tandoori in the Tenderloin is fine for kicks, but for vindaloo-hot dates and cool cucumber martinis with venture capitalists, upgrade to complex spices and organic meats at Amber India. The lighting is warm and so is the lunch buffet featuring butter chicken, a velvety tomato-based concoction engineered to impress both Indian-food novices and Silicon Valley execs just back from Hyderabad. (www.amber-india.com; 25 Yerba Buena Lane; dishes $10-20, lunch buffet $14; noon-2:30pm & 5-10pm daily; M S Powell St)

Citizen's Band CALIFORNIAN, NEW AMERICAN $

19 Map p86, B4

The name refers to CB radio, and the menu is retro American diner with a California difference: mac-n-cheese with Sonoma jack cheese and optional truffle, wedge-lettuce salads with local Point Reyes blue cheese, and local Snake River kobe beef burgers (the best in town). Don't miss small-production local wines, and after-lunch treats from the pop-up cupcake shop on the premises. (http://citizensbandsf.com; 1198 Folsom St; meals $13-23; 11:30am-2pm & 5:30-11pm Tue-Fri, 10am-2pm & 5:30-11pm Sat, 10am-2pm & 5:30-9:30pm Sun; M Folsom St, S Civic Center)

Gitane BASQUE, MEDITERRANEAN $$

20  Map p86, F2

Slip out of the Financial District and into something more comfortable at this boudoir-styled bistro, where co-workers flirt shamelessly over craft cocktails and friends dish over sharable plates of Basque- and Moroccan-inspired stuffed squash blossoms, silky pan-seared scallops and herb-spiked lamb tartare. (www.gitanerestaurant.com; 6 Claude Lane; mains $15-25; 5:30pm-midnight Tue-Sat, bar to 1am; M S Montgomery;)

Sentinel SANDWICHES $

21 Map p86, F2

Rebel SF chef Dennis Leary revolutionizes lunchtime take-out, taking on the classics with top-notch seasonal ingredients. Tuna salad gets radical with chipotle mayo and the snap of crisp summer vegetables, and corned beef crosses borders with Swiss cheese and housemade Russian dressing. Menus change daily; come prepared for about a 10-minute wait, since every sandwich is made to order. (www.thesentinelsf.com; 37 New Montgomery St; sandwiches $8.50-9; 7:30am-2:30pm Mon-Fri; M S Montgomery St)

Barbacco

ITALIAN $$

22 Map p86, G2

Grab a stool facing the open kitchen or schmoozy communal tables along exposed-brick walls, and prepare to share decadent plates of housemade *'nduja* (spicy salami paste), Brussels sprouts fried in duck fat, and chicken thighs braised with olives, escarole, and almonds. The iPad wine list is gimmicky, but helps you build wine flights with 3oz pours at fair prices. (www.barbaccosf.com; 220 California St; lunch mains $10-13, dinner $11-17; 11:30am-10pm Mon-Fri, 5:30-10pm Sat; M S Embarcadero, California)

Drinking

Bar Agricole

BAR

23 Map p86, A4

Drink your way to a history degree with well-researched cocktails: Bellamy Scotch Sour with egg whites passes the test, but Tequila Fix with lime, pineapple gum, and hellfire bitters earns honors. This overachiever won a James Beard Award for restaurant design – don't miss the sleek deck – and serves sophisticated bar bites like pork pate with aspic and farm egg with pork belly. (www.baragricole.com; 355 11th St; 6-10pm Sun-Wed, to late Thu-Sat, brunch 11am-2pm Sun; Folsom St, M Van Ness)

Bloodhound

BAR

24 Map p86, B4

The murder of crows painted on the ceiling is definitely an omen: nights at Bloodhound assume mythic proportions with top-shelf booze served in Mason jars and pool marathons under a Viking deer-antler chandelier. SF's best food trucks often park out front; ask the barkeep to suggest a pairing. (www.bloodhoundsf.com; 1145 Folsom St; 4pm-2am; Folsom St, M Van Ness)

RN74

WINE BAR

25 Map p86, G3

Wine collectors and encyclopedia authors must envy the Rajat Parr–designed wine menu at RN74, a definitive volume that covers obscure Italian and Austrian entries, long-lost French vintages, and California's most thorough account of cult wines. Settle into a couch for the duration of your self-guided wine adventure, and don't skip bar menu food pairings created by star chef/owner Michael Mina. (http://michaelmina.net; 301 Mission St; 11:30am-1am Mon-Fri, 5pm-1am Sat, 5pm-11pm Sun; M S Embarcadero)

The Stud

GAY CLUB

26 Map p86, A4

Rocking the gay scene since 1966, The Stud branches out beyond the obvious leather daddies and preppy twinks to create new genres of gay good times. Check the schedule for rocker-grrrl Mondays, anything-goes Meow Mix Tuesday drag variety, raunchy comedy

Bar Agricole

and karaoke Wednesdays, art/drag dance parties on Fridays, and drag-disco cabaret whenever hostess/DJ Anna Conda gets the notion. (www.studsf.com; 399 9th St; admission $5-8; 5pm-3am; 10th St, M S Civic Center)

Cantina BAR

27 Map p86, E1

All the Latin-inspired cocktails (think tequila, Cachaça and Pisco) are made with fresh juice – there's not even a soda gun behind the bar – at this mixologist's dream bar that's mellow enough on weeknights for quiet conversation. The all-local crowd includes many off-duty bartenders – always a good sign. DJs spin weekends. (www.cantinasf.com; 580 Sutter St; Mon-Sat; Geary St, Powell-Mason)

City Beer Store & Tasting Room BAR

28 Map p86, B4

Taste exceptional local and Belgian micro-brewed beer from the 300-brew menu (6oz to 22oz, depending how thirsty you are) with killer cheese and salami pairings, served in a spiffy brick bar that'll win over lounge-lizard friends. Assemble your own six-pack to go, and check the website for bottle release parties and tapping events. (www.citybeerstore.com; 1168 Folsom St; noon-10pm Tue-Sat, to 6pm Sun; Folsom St, M Van Ness)

Children's Creativity Museum (p89)

Rickhouse

BAR

29 Map p86, F2

Like a shotgun shack plunked downtown, Rickhouse is lined with repurposed whisky casks imported from Kentucky, and back-bar shelving from an Ozark Mountains nunnery that once secretly brewed hooch. The emphasis is on rare bourbon, but authentic Pisco Punch is served in garage-sale punchbowls. (www.rickhousebar.com; 246 Kearny St; Mon-Sat; M S Montgomery)

111 Minna

BAR, CLUB

30 Map p86, F3

The night is young and so is the crowd of MFA students, minor YouTube sensations and Google engineers trying to score with emerging fashion designers. A street-wise art gallery by day, 111 Minna serves a techie crowd around happy hour and busts club moves after 9pm, when '90s and '80s dance parties take the back room by storm. (www.111minnagallery.com; 111 Minna St; admission free-$15; noon-5pm Wed-Sat, evening hours vary; M S Montgomery St)

Taverna Aventine

BAR

31 Map p86, G1

In the days of the Barbary Coast, the 150-year-old building that houses the Aventine fronted on the bay, and you can still observe the saltwater marks on the brick walls in the parlor downstairs. But the main action happens between 3pm and 7pm weeknights in the brick-walled upstairs bar, where bartenders whip up happy hour bourbon cocktails in the old-new fashion.

(www.aventinesf.com; 582 Washington St; 11:30am-midnight Mon-Fri, 8:30pm-2am Sat; Kearny St)

Blue Bottle Coffee Company

CAFE

32 Map p86, E5

Don't mock SF's coffee geekishness until you try a superior fair-trade organic drip that spurts through the mad-scientist glass tubes of Blue Bottle's $20,000 coffee siphon. This coffee micro-roaster gets crafty with ferns drawn on cappuccino foam and bittersweet mocha with mysterious mood-curative powers. Expect a wait and $4 for your fix. (www.bluebottlecoffee.net; 66 Mint St; 7am-7pm Mon-Fri, 8am-6pm Sat, 8am-4pm Sun; M S Powell St, Powell-Mason, Powell-Hyde)

Entertainment

American Conservatory Theater

THEATER

33 Map p86, D1

Breakthrough shows destined for Broadway and London's West End must first pass muster at the turn-of-the-century Geary Theater, which hosts landmark ACT productions like Tony Kushner's *Angels in America* and Robert Wilson's *Black Rider*, with a libretto by William S Burroughs and music by the Bay Area's own Tom Waits. (415-749-2228; www.act-sf.org; 415 Geary St; Geary St, Powell-Mason, Powell-Hyde)

Yerba Buena Center for the Arts

LIVE MUSIC, DANCE, ART

34  Map p86, E3

Oh how rock stars must envy art-stars at YBCA openings. These events attract overflowing crowds of art groupies, coat-checking their skateboards to consume live hip-hop, spontaneous light shows set to the music of unrehearsed bands, and Vik Muniz

Local Life

SF Dance Scene

Ballet follows the strictly classical Balanchine method at San Francisco Ballet (p119) – but San Francisco's dance scene makes big, bold, modern moves at ODC (p139) and Yerba Buena Center for the Arts. The main stage here hosts the annual **Ethnic Dance Festival** (www.sfethnicdancefestival.org) and the regular season of notable SF modern dance companies: **Liss Fain Dance** (www.lissfaindance.org), champions of muscular modern movement; **Alonzo King's Lines Ballet** (www.linesballet.org), recently showcasing martial-arts-inspired angular shapes; **Smuin Ballet** (www.smuinballet.org), with relatable dance befitting their tagline, 'Ballet, but Entertaining'; and **Joe Goode Performance Group** (www.joegoode.org), an early adaptor of performance art and spoken word into dance.

Local Life

San Francisco Giants

Hometown crowds go wild April–October for the **San Francisco Giants** (Map p86, F5; http://sanfrancisco.giants.mlb.com; AT&T Park; tickets $5-135; M Townsend;). The city's National League baseball team has won the World Series with superstitious practices that might seem eccentric elsewhere, but endear them to SF: on winning streaks, players sport bushy beards and pitchers have worn women's underwear. Behind-the-scenes **tours** (415-972-2400; tickets $12.50; nongame days 10:30am & 2:30pm) cover the clubhouse, dugout, field and solar-powered scoreboard. Inside a hideous giant Coca-Cola bottle 'sculpture' there's a kids' play structure. When games sell out, you might score tickets through the Double Play Ticket Window (see website), eBay.com or craigslist.org – or join fans jostling for free views of right field along the Waterfront Promenade.

documentaries on subjects such as making art from trash. Touring dance companies perform at YBCA's theater across the sidewalk, see p97. (415-978-2787; www.ybca.org; 700 Howard St; gallery adult/senior & student $7/5, tickets free-$35; gallery noon-5pm Tue, Wed & Fri-Sun, noon-8pm Thu, park sunrise-10pm; M S Montgomery St)

Slim's

LIVE MUSIC

35 Map p86, A4

Guaranteed good times by Gogol Bordello, Tenacious D and AC/DShe (a hard-rocking female tribute band) fit the bill at this midsized club, where Prince and Elvis Costello have shown up to play sets unannounced. Shows are all-ages, though shorties may have a hard time seeing once the floor starts bouncing. Come early to score burgers with balcony seating. (www.slims-sf.com; 333 11th St; tickets $11-28; 5pm-2am; Folsom St, M Van Ness)

Mezzanine

LIVE MUSIC, CLUB

36 Map p86, C3

Big nights come with bragging rights at the Mezzanine, where the best sound system in SF bounces off the brick walls at breakthrough hip-hop shows by Quest Love, Method Man, Nas and Snoop Dogg, plus throwback alt-classics like the Dandy Warhols and Psychedelic Furs. (www.mezzaninesf.com; 444 Jessie St; admission $10-40; varies; M Market St, S Powell St)

AsiaSF

NIGHTCLUB, THEATER

37  Map p86, A3

Cocktails and Asian-inspired dishes are served with a tall order of sass and a secret: your servers are drag stars. Hostesses rock the bar/runway hourly, but once inspiration and drinks kick in, everyone mixes it up on the downstairs dance floor. The three-course 'Menage á Trois Menu' runs

$39, cocktails around $10, and honey, those tips are well-earned. (☎415-255-2742; www.asiasf.com; 201 9th St; minimum per person $35; ⏲7-11pm Wed-Thu, 7pm-2am Fri, 5pm-2am Sat, 7-10pm Sun, reservation line 1-8pm daily; M S Civic Center)

Hotel Utah Saloon

LIVE MUSIC

38 ☆ Map p86, D5

The ground-floor bar of this Victorian hotel has hosted SF's underground scene since the '70s, when upstarts Whoopi Goldberg and Robin Williams took the stage. The thrill of finding SF's hidden talents draws crowds to singer-songwriter Open Mic Mondays, featuring indie-label debuts and local favorites like Riot Earp, Saucy Monkey and The Dazzling Strangers. (www.hotelutah.com; 500 4th St; bar admission free, shows $5-10; ⏲11:30am-2am Mon-Fri, 2pm-2am Sat & Sun; M 4th St)

Embarcadero Center Cinema

CINEMA

39 ☆ Map p86, G2

Forget blockbusters – here locals queue up for the latest Almodóvar film, whatever won best foreign film at the Oscars, late-night showings of *Rocky Horror* and *The Big Lebowski*. The snack bar caters to discerning tastes with locally roasted coffee, fair-trade chocolate and popcorn with real butter. (www.landmarktheatres.com; top fl, 1 Embarcadero Center; adult/senior & child $10.50/8.25; M S Embarcadero)

Punch Line

COMEDY

40  Map p86, G1

Known for launching big talents (perhaps you've heard of Robin Williams, Chris Rock, Ellen DeGeneres and David Cross?) this historic stand-up venue is small enough that you can hear sighs of relief backstage when comics kill, and teeth grinding when jokes bomb. Strong drink loosens the crowd, but be warned: you might not be laughing tomorrow morning. (www.punchlinecomedyclub.com; 444 Battery St; admission $12-23, plus 2-drink minimum; ⏲shows 8pm Sun, Tue-Thu, 8pm & 10pm Fri & Sat; M S Embarcadero)

Starlight Room

LIVE MUSIC

41  Map p86, E1

Views are mesmerizing from the 21st floor of the Sir Francis Drake, where bands get tourists and locals mingling on the dance floor at weekends, and DJs breath life into downtown on weekdays. Sundays there's a kooky drag-show brunch (make reservations). (☎415-395-8595; www.harrydenton.com; 21st fl, 450 Powell St; cover varies, often free; ⏲8:30pm-2am Tue-Sat; M S Powell St, Powell-Mason, Powell-Hyde)

Shopping

Heath Ceramics

HOUSEWARES, HANDICRAFTS

42 Map p86, H2

No local, artisanal SF restaurant tablescape is complete without handmade modern Heath stoneware, thrown by local potters in Heath's Sausalito studio since 1948. Chef Alice Waters (p186) has served her definitive California fare on Heath dishware for decades – hence the popular Chez Panisse ceramics in earthy, food-friendly shades. Pieces are priced for fine dining except studio seconds, sold here on weekends. (www.heathceramics.com; 1 Ferry Bldg; ⌚10am-7pm Mon-Fri, 8am-6pm Sat, 11am-5pm Sun; M S Embarcadero)

Recchiuti Chocolates

FOOD & DRINK

43 Map p86, H2

San Francisco invented the chocolate bar as a convenience food for gold miners, but Recchiuti is reviving a more luxuriant, indulgent approach to chocolate. Standouts include gold-leafed Kona coffee chocolates, dark-chocolate-dipped *fleur de sel* caramels, seasonal truffles with designs by SF artists, and for SF-style tailgate parties, beer-pairing chocolates. (www.recchiuticonfections.com; 1 Ferry Bldg; ⌚10am-7pm Mon-Fri, 8am-6pm Sat, 10am-5pm Sun; M S Embarcadero)

Local Life

Eden & Eden

Quirkiness is an SF style trademark that can be cultivated either through an MFA program or a quick stop at **Eden & Eden** (Map p86, G1; www.edenandeden.com; 560 Jackson St; M Kearny St). Everything you might dream up after diligent study of pop art is here: a necklace that looks like a giant zipper, shaggy-haired orange tea cozies, a cushion that says 'blahblahblah,' and hideous apartment buildings on elegant bone-china plates.

Jeremys

FASHION, CLOTHING

44 Map p86, F5

Score designer clothing at steep discounts direct from photo shoots, window displays and runways – which explains why Proenza Schouler dresses might only come in size 2-4 and glossy Zegna men's suits are occasionally smudged with makeup. Upstairs is a midrange sample sale, from J Crew to Rock & Republic. Returns are possible for store credit, but only within seven days. (www.jeremys.com; 2 South Park St; ⌚11am-6pm Mon-Wed & Fri, 11am-8:30pm Thu, noon-6pm Sun; M Townsend St)

Madame S & Mr S Leather

COSTUMES, FETISH WEAR

45 Map p86, B4

Only in San Francisco would an S&M superstore outsize Home Depot, with such musts as suspension stirrups, latex hoods and – for that really special someone – a chrome-plated codpiece. If you've been a very bad puppy, there's an entire doghouse department for you here, and gluttons for punishment will find home-decor inspiration in Dungeon Furniture. (www.madame-s.com; 385 8th St; ⌚11am-7pm; M S Civic Center)

Jeremys department store

Branch

HOUSEWARES

46 Map p86, A4

When you're looking for original home decor with a sustainable edge, it's time to Branch out. Whether you're in the market for a cork chaise lounge, beechwood-fiber bath towel, or a tiny bonsai in a reclaimed breath-mint tin, Branch has you covered – and yes, they ship. (www.branchhome.com; 345 9th St; 9:30am-5:30pm Mon-Fri; M 10th St)

Gama-Go

CLOTHING & ACCESSORIES

47 Map p86, B4

Every one of SF-designer Gama-Go's products seems calibrated for maximum glee: a hand-shaped cleaver called the Karate Chopper, T-shirts with a roaring powder-blue yeti, and a tape measure disguised as a cassette tape. Gama-Go is distributed nationally, but here in the showroom you'll find 70% off last season's lines and score 15% off all purchases noon-2pm daily. (www.gama-go.com; 335 8th St; noon-6pm Mon-Fri, to 5pm Sat & Sun; M S Civic Center)

Original Levi's Store

CLOTHING & ACCESSORIES

48 Map p86, E2

The flagship store in Levi Strauss' hometown sells classic jeans that fit without fail, plus limited-edition pairs made of tough Japanese selvage and organic cotton. Start with impressive discount racks (30% to 60% off), but don't hold out for sales – denim fanatics Tweet their finds, so rare lines like

1950s prison-model denim sell out fast. They'll hem your jeans for $10. (www.us.levi.com; 300 Post St; M S Powell St, Powell-Mason, Powell-Hyde)

Ferry Plaza Wine Merchant

WINES

49 Map p86, H2

Part tasting room, part wine bar, totally tasty (hic). Staff is knowledgeable and the wine list written to make non-snobs feel welcome. For $50–$75, you can take a class that promises to demystify sparkling wines and cult pinot noirs – or just hit the wine bar and ask the sommelier to surprise you, and enjoy 2oz blind tastings. (www.fpwm.com; 1 Ferry Bldg; 11am-8pm Mon, 10am-8pm Tue, 10am-9pm Wed-Fri, 8am-8pm Sat, 10am-7pm Sun; M S Embarcadero)

Le Sanctuaire

FOOD & DRINK

50 Map p86, E2

Mad scientists and professional chefs make appointments to browse this culinary curiosity shop selling salt for meat-curing, spherifiers to turn fruit into caviar, and the molecular gastronomy must-have: foaming agents. Check the website for classes on techniques like using liquid nitrogen to make powdered lard – too bad suspending disbelief with gellants isn't on the schedule. (415-986-4216; www.le-sanctuaire.com; 5th fl, 315 Sutter St; by appointment 10:30am-4:30pm Mon-Fri; Geary St; Powell-Mason, Powell-Hyde)

Margaret O'Leary

CLOTHING

51 Map p86, F2

Ignorance of the fog is no excuse in San Francisco – but should you confuse SF for LA (the horror!) and neglect to pack the obligatory sweater, Margaret O'Leary will sheathe you in knitwear, no questions asked. The Bay Area designer's specialties are whisper-light cardigans with an urban edge in ultrasoft wool, cashmere or organic cotton. (www.margaretoleary.com; 1 Claude Lane; 10am-5pm Tue-Sat; Kearny St, California)

Understand

SF Chain Stores

Young Levi Strauss brought fashion sense to the gold rush in 1850, making pants from tough French sailcloth from Nîmes (hence the name: 'de Nîmes' – denim) to hold heavy nuggets. The Gap/Old Navy/Banana Republic retail juggernaut also started out in San Francisco as a single Gap store selling wardrobe basics. Yet these and other mega-brands are largely confined downtown, around Union Square and inside nine-level Westfield San Francisco Centre, kept out of neighborhoods by city zoning resolutions and snarky vandalism. Read one recent addendum to a 'Peace. Love. Gap.' bus-shelter ad: 'It's Peace, Love & Understanding, you corporate tools.'

Ferry Plaza Wine Merchant

Westfield San Francisco Centre

DEPARTMENT STORE

52 Map p86, D2

The suburbs come to the city in this nine-level mall, with Bloomingdale's and Nordstrom, plus 400 other retailers and a movie theater. Highlights: post-holiday sales, H&M's Spanish cousin Mango, bathrooms (including lounges with baby-changing tables) and a respectable basement food court. (www.westfield.com/sanfrancisco; 865 Market St; 9:30am-9pm Mon-Sat, 10am-7pm Sun; M S Powell Street, Powell-Mason, Powell-Hyde;)

Explore

Hayes Valley & Civic Center

Don't be fooled by its grand formality – San Francisco's Civic Center is down to earth and cutting edge. City Hall helped launch gay rights and green politics internationally, and the arts institutions nearby ensure San Francisco is never lost for inspiration. West of City Hall lies Hayes Valley, where Victorian storefronts showcase breakthrough local designers and community gardens sprout from retired freeway ramps.

The Sights in a Day

Get a fresh start at **Farm:Table** (p113), then swing down Powell St to hop the historic F line streetcar to graze through twice-weekly **Heart of the City Farmers Market** (p115) to the **Asian Art Museum** (p106). Here you'll cover the Silk Rd in an hour and encounter cross-cultural sensations, from Persian-inspired Korean ceramics to mod Indian anime. Across the plaza at **City Hall** (p110; pictured left), you can see where sit-ins, gay marriage, universal healthcare and zero-waste mandates made US history.

Window-shop down Hayes Street to California-grown lunches at **Bar Jules** (p113) and stop by **Hayes Valley Farm** (p112) to smell the flowers and recharge your cell phone at the solar-power pump. Then head back into the fray of **Hayes Valley boutiques** (p120).

Haul your booty to pirate-themed speakeasy **Smuggler's Cove** (p115) – but don't let that Dead Reckoning cocktail delay your grand entrance at **San Francisco Opera** (p119), **Ballet** (p119) or **Symphony** (p117). End your night in a compromising position at **Rebel** (p115) or **Hemlock Tavern** (p115), and you've done SF proud.

Top Sight

Asian Art Museum (p106)

Best of San Francisco

Live Music

San Francisco Symphony (p117)

San Francisco Opera (p119)

Great American Music Hall (p119)

Warfield (p119)

Drinks

Smuggler's Cove (p115)

Bourbon & Branch (p116)

Two Sisters Bar & Books (p116)

Rye (p115)

Hemlock Tavern (p115)

Edinburgh Castle (p116)

Getting There

M Streetcar Historic F Market streetcars run along Market St; J, K, L, M and N metro lines run under Market St to Van Ness and Civic Center stations.

Bus 38 Geary heads from Union Square through the Tenderloin; lines 2, 5, 6, 14, 21, 30, 31, 38, 41, 45, 71 run down Market to downtown.

Car Garage under Civic Center Plaza.

Top Sight
Asian Art Museum

Take an escalator ride across oceans and centuries, from racy Rajasthani miniatures to Senju Hiroshi's modern, life-size silver waterfall – just don't go bumping into those priceless Ming vases. The Asian works are diplomatic wonders bringing Taiwan, China and Tibet together, uniting Pakistan and India, and reconciling Japan, Korea and China under one Italianate roof. The distinguished collection of 17,000 unique treasures also does the city proud, reflecting San Francisco's 150-year history as North America's gateway to Asia.

Map p108, E4

www.asianart.org

200 Larkin St

adult/child $12/free

10am-5pm Tue-Sun, to 9pm Thu Feb-Sep

5, 6, 21, 31, 71, F; M S Civic Center

Asian Art Museum

Don't Miss

Permanent Collection

Begin your artistic tour of Asia by taking a single-file escalator up to the top floor. The curatorial concept is to follow the geographical path of Buddhism through Asia from the top floor down, beginning with India and travelling to Japan. By the time you've cruised past rare Zoroastrian artifacts and splendid Balinese shadow puppets, all theological quibbles will yield to astonishment. Sticklers may complain that South Asia gets one gallery while the Chinese collection takes up two wings - but healthy cultural competition has encouraged donations of South Asian artifacts lately.

Ground Floor Galleries

After covering three floors and 6000 years of artifacts, return to the modern era by way of the Asian's rotating contemporary exhibits. Shows have ranged from nightclub advertisement lithographs from 1930s Shanghai to contemporary Cambodian sculptor Sopheap Pich's mesmerizing cell-structure forms woven from rattan. Flanking the galleries is a gauntlet of temptation better known as the museum shop.

Architecture

Italian architect Gae Aulenti's clever repurposing of the old San Francisco Main Library building left intact the much-beloved granite bas-relief on the building's face, the entryway's travertine arches and the polished stone staircase inside. She added two new indoor plazas for oversize installations, leaving plenty of room for debate and educational programs - check the schedule for artists' demonstrations and hands-on workshops for kids.

Top Tips

- First Sunday of the month admission is free
- On First Thursday MATCHA nights (every other month, 5–9pm), the Asian gets hip with *soju* cocktails, Asian dub DJs and special guests – lately, master henna artisans, martial art Olympians, and *Top Chef* Master Floyd Cardoz.
- Acclaimed contemporary artists and performers demonstrate their work at AsiaAlive events on the landing up the central grand staircase.
- Film festivals accompany most major exhibitions – anime for Japanese manga shows, Bollywood political musicals as a backdrop for maharajas' treasures etc. Screenings are free with museum admission.

Take a Break

Linger over a sustainable sushi bento box at Café Asia.

Wednesdays and Sundays, get fresh food at Heart of the City Farmers Market (p115).

For reviews see
Top Sights p106
Sights p110
Eating p112
Drinking p115
Entertainment p117
Shopping p120
A
B
C
D
1
2
3
4
5
PACIFIC HEIGHTS & JAPANTOWN
HAYES VALLEY
CIVIC CENTER
Jefferson Square
Hayward Playground
San Francisco Arts Commission Gallery
City Hall
Civic Center Plaza
Van Ness Muni Station
Larch St
Eddy St
McAllister St
Buchanan St
Ash St
Fulton St
Laguna St
Birch St
Grove St
Octavia Blvd
Ivy St
Turk St
Elm St
Gough St
Golden Gate Ave
Franklin St
Van Ness Ave
Redwood St
Linden St
Fell St
Hickory St
Oak St
Lily St
Hayes St
Dr Carlton B Goodlett Pl
Polk St
Haight St
Page St
Rose St
Market St
McCoppin St
Colton St
12th St
11th St
Jessie St
9th St
Mission St

E
F
G
H
1
2
3
4
5
0
400 m
0
0.2 miles
Daniel Burnham Ct
Fern St
Bush St
Pine St
Post St
Cedar St
Polk St
Hemlock St
Larkin St
18
Myrtle St
O'Farrell St
Olive St
Ellis St
Willow St
Eddy St
23
30
THE TENDERLOIN
Sutter St
Geary St
33
14
Jones St
Cosmo Pl
20
11
25
16
8
13
22
Polk St
Larkin St
Cohen Pl
Shannon St
Taylor St
Hyde St
Glide Memorial United Methodist Church
4
Mason St
Turk St
Golden Gate Ave
Asian Art Museum
3
San Francisco Main Library
32
McAllister St
Powell St Cable Car Turnaround
Grove St
United Nations Plaza
2
31
Market St
Luggage Store Gallery
Civic Center BART & Muni Station
Federal Building
Stevenson St
UNION SQUARE
7th St
6
Jessie St
8th St
6th St
5th St
Mission St

Sights

City Hall

HISTORIC BUILDING

1 Map p108, D4

Rising from the ashes of the 1906 earthquake, this beaux-arts building has witnessed historic firsts: America's first sit-in in 1960, protesting red-baiting McCarthy hearings; the 1977 election and 1978 assassination of America's first openly gay official, Supervisor Harvey Milk; and 4037 same-sex marriages performed onsite in 2004. Intriguing basement exhibits showcase local artists; weekly Board of Supervisors meetings are open to the public (2pm Tue). (415-554-4000, tour info 415-554-6023, art exhibit line 415-554-6080; www.ci.sf.ca.us/cityhall; 400 Van Ness Ave; 8am-8pm Mon-Fri, tours 10am, noon & 2pm; Van Ness, M S Civic Center;)

Top Tip

Street Smarts

Most first-time visitors are surprised to find that merely by crossing Powell St, they leave Union Sq department stores behind, and enter the down-and-out Tenderloin. Keep your street smarts about you in the area bounded by Powell, Geary to the north, Mission St to the south and Larkin St to the west. When possible, avoid these sketchy blocks, take public transit or cabs through the area, or walk briskly along Geary or Market Sts to reach specific destinations.

Luggage Store Gallery

ART GALLERY

2 Map p108, G5

A dandelion pushing through sidewalk cracks, this plucky nonprofit gallery has brought signs of life to one of the toughest blocks in the Tenderloin for two decades. By giving street artists a gallery platform, the Luggage Store helped launch graffiti art-star Barry McGee, urban folklorist Clare Rojas and muralist Rigo. Look for the graffitied door and rooftop mural of a firecracker-wielding kid by Brazilian duo Osgemeos. (www.luggagestoregallery.org; 1007 Market St; noon-5pm Wed-Sat; M S Civic Center)

San Francisco Main Library

LIBRARY

3 Map p108, E4

A grand lightwell illuminates favorite San Franciscan subjects. Downstairs excellent lectures cover everything from cooking to civil rights; upstairs you'll find graphic novels galore, James C Hormel Gay & Lesbian Center history exhibits and Skylight Gallery art shows. Check out the 2nd-floor wallpaper made from the old card catalog – artists Ann Chamberlain and Ann Hamilton plus 200 San Franciscans have added multilingual running commentary to 50,000 cards. (http://sfpl.org; 100 Larkin St; 10am-6pm Mon & Sat, 9am-8pm Tue-Thu, noon-6pm Fri, noon-5pm Sun; M S Civic Center;)

The Thomas Mayne–designed Federal Building

Glide Memorial United Methodist Church CHURCH

4 Map p108, H4

The Glide gospel choir takes to the stage beaming in rainbow robes and everyone squeezes in closer to make room along the pew for just one more person – the 1500-plus congregation at this hospitable Methodist is GLBT-friendly and warmly welcomes absolutely everyone. After Sunday celebrations, the progressive Methodist congregation keeps the inspiration coming, providing a million free meals a year and housing for 52 formerly homeless families. (www.glide.org; 330 Ellis St; celebrations 9am & 11am Sun; M S Powell St)

San Francisco Arts Commission Gallery ART GALLERY

5 Map p108, D3

Get in on the next art movement at the ground level in this lobby gallery featuring international perspectives and local talents. Besides hanging shows and hosting receptions in this gallery, the commission also curates City Hall exhibits and shop-window art installations at 155 Grove St. (www.sfacgallery.org; 401 Van Ness Ave; noon-5pm Wed-Sat; 5, 42, 47, 49, F; M Van Ness)

Federal Building NOTABLE BUILDING

6  Map p108, F5

The revolutionary green design of this new government office building by 2005 Pritzker Architecture Prize–winner

Local Life

Hayes Valley Farm

A freeway on-ramp is no place for a pumpkin...or is it? After the 1989 earthquake damaged the freeway on-ramp at Fell St, a 2-acre stretch of asphalt was left to crumble into urban blight – until renegade community gardeners transformed it into Hayes Valley Farm (Map p108; A3; www.hayesvalleyfarm.com; entry 450 Laguna St at Fell St; noon-5pm Sun, Wed & Thu; Hayes St). With neighbors' help and organic compost, the crops have hit the highway, from fava beans to pumpkins. During open hours, visitors can volunteer (arrive at noon) or recharge mobile devices at the solar-electricity-pumping station. Check the website for free yoga, kids' activities, and sliding-scale workshops.

Thomas Mayne conserves energy and eliminates office politicking over corner offices, with 90% of work stations enjoying direct sunlight, natural ventilation and window views (over the Tenderloin, but still). (Cnr Mission & 7th St; F, J, K, L, M, N, 5, 7, 14, 71; S Civic Center)

Eating

Jardinière — CALIFORNIAN $$$

7 Map p108, C3

Opera arias can't compare to the high notes hit by James Beard Award winner, Iron Chef and Top Chef Master Traci des Jardins, who lavishes braised oxtail ravioli with summer truffles and stuffs crispy pork belly with salami and Mission figs. Go Mondays, when $45 scores three market-inspired, decadent courses with wine pairings, or enjoy post-SF Opera meals in the bar downstairs. (415-861-5555; www.jardiniere.com; 300 Grove St; mains $18-38; 5-10:30 Tue-Sat, to 10pm Sun-Mon; M Van Ness).

Brenda's French Soul Food — CREOLE $

8 Map p108, E3

Chef and owner, Brenda Buenviaje, combines Creole cooking with French technique in a hangover-curing Hangtown fry (omelet with cured pork and corn-breaded oysters), shrimp-stuffed po' boys, and fried chicken with collard greens and hot-pepper jelly – all of which are well worth the inevitable wait on a sketchy stretch of sidewalk. (www.frenchsoulfood.com; 652 Polk St; mains $8-12; 8am-3pm Sun-Tue, 8am-10pm Wed-Sat; Polk St)

Nojo — JAPANESE $$

9 Map p108, C4

Everything you could possibly want skewered and roasted at happy hour, besides your boss. The house specialty is Japanese *izakaya* (bar snacks), especially grilled chicken *yakatori* (kebabs), panko-crusted anchovies and spicy beef heart slathered with earthy soy-based sauce. Save room for the house sundae: black sesame and white miso ice creams with rice crackers. Top-notch produce, wine and beer that's local and sustainable. (www.nojosf.com; 231 Franklin St; small plates $4-12 5-10pm Wed-Thu & Sun-Mon, to 11pm Sat-Sun; Hayes St Van Ness)

Bar Jules

CALIFORNIAN **$$**

10  Map p108, A3

Small, local and succulent is the credo at this corridor of a neighborhood bistro. The short daily menu thinks big with flavor-rich, sustainably minded fare: Sonoma duck breast with cherries, almonds and arugula, a local wine selection, and the dark, sinister 'chocolate nemesis' cake. Waits are a given – but so is simple, tasty food. (www.barjules.com; 609 Hayes St; mains $10-26; 6-10pm Tue, 11:30am-3pm & 6-10pm Wed-Sat, 11am-3pm Sun; Hayes St)

Lahore Karahi

PAKISTANI **$**

11  Map p108, G3

Only one thing can induce relatively sane San Franciscans to brave merciless fluorescent lighting and risky business propositions in the gritty Tenderloin: succulent, smoky tandoori chicken. Of all the linoleum-floored Pakistani tandoori joints this side of Geary, Lahore Karahi wins the loyalty of theater-goers and streetwalkers alike for its consistency, cleanliness and cheapness with a side of good cheer. (www.lahorekarahirestaurant.com; 612 O'Farrell St; 5-11pm Mon, 11am-11pm Tue-Sun; Geary St; Powell-Mason, Powell-Hyde)

Zuni Cafe

CALIFORNIAN, AMERICAN **$$$**

12 Map p108, B5

Zuni has been reinventing basic menu items as gourmet staples since 1979. Reservations and fat wallets are necessary, but see-and-be-seen seating is a kick and the cocktails and food beyond reproach: organic beef burgers on focaccia, Caesar salad with house-cured anchovies, wood-fired-oven-roasted chicken with horseradish mashed potatoes, and impeccable chocolate pudding. (415-552-2522; www.zunicafe.com; 1658 Market St; mains $14-29 11:30am-11pm Tue-Thu, 11:30am-midnight Fri & Sat, 11am-11pm Sun; Market St; Van Ness)

Saigon Sandwich Shop

VIETNAMESE **$**

13 Map p108, F3

Consider it frontier justice for the indecisive: order your $3.50 *banh mi* sandwich when the lunch ladies of the Saigon call you, or you'll get skipped. Act fast and be rewarded with a baguette piled high with your choice of roast pork, chicken, pâté, meatballs and/or tofu, plus pickled carrots, cilantro, jalapeño and thinly sliced onion. (560 Larkin St; sandwiches $3.50; 6:30am-5:30pm; Polk St; Civic Center)

Farm:Table

NEW AMERICAN **$**

14  Map p108, H2

A tiny storefront with one wooden communal table inside, two tables and

Farmers market fare

a stand-up counter outside, Farm:Table uses seasonal and regional organics in hearty California breakfasts and lunches, posting the daily menu on Twitter (@farmtable). Great coffee too; cash only. (www.farmtablesf.com; 754 Post St; dishes $6-9; 7:30am-6pm Mon-Fri, 8am-6pm Sat, 9am-3pm Sun; Geary St)

Suppenküche

GERMAN **$$**

15 Map p108, A3

Doesn't matter if you're caught in fog without a jacket or a Mahler symphony with a hangover, Suppenküche's German comfort food will put things right. Buck small-plate trends with inch-thick pancakes studded with brandied raisins, feast on housemade Bratwurst sausages and *spaetzle*, and toast your new friends at the unvarnished communal table with a 2L glass boot of draft beer. (www.suppenkuche.com; 525 Laguna St; mains $10.50-20; 5-10pm daily, brunch 10am-2:30pm Sun; Hayes St)

Millennium

SUSTAINABLE VEGAN & VEGETARIAN **$$**

16 Map p108, H3

Three words you're not likely to hear together outside these doors describe the menu: opulent vegan dining. GMO-free and proud of it, with wild mushrooms and organic fruit featuring in sumptuous seasonal concoctions. Reserve ahead for monthly themed feasts, especially aphrodisiac dinners and vegetarian Thanksgiving. (415-345-3900; www.millenniumrestaurant.com; 580 Geary St; menus $39-72; dinner; Geary St, M S Powell St;)

Drinking

Smuggler's Cove

BAR

17 Map p108, C3

Yo-ho-ho and a bottle of rum... or wait, make that a Dead Reckoning cocktail with tawny port, Nicaraguan rum, bitters and vanilla liqueur, unless someone wants to share the flaming Scorpion Bowl? Pirates are bedeviled by choice at this shipwreck tiki bar, hidden behind a tinted door. With 200 specialty rums and 70 well-researched cocktails, you won't be dry-docked for long. (http://smugglerscovesf.com; 650 Gough St; 5pm-2am; M Van Ness)

Hemlock Tavern

DIVE BAR

18 Map p108, F1

When you wake up tomorrow with peanut shells in your hair and someone else's mascara on your sleeve, you'll know it was another successful, near-lethal night at the Hemlock. Blame it on cheap drink at the oval bar, pogo-worthy punk rock in the back room, and free peanuts in the shell to eat or throw at infamously difficult Trivia Nights. (www.hemlocktavern.com; 1131 Polk St; 4pm-2am; Van Ness)

Rebel Bar

GAY CLUB

19 Map p108, A5

Funhouse southern biker bar disco, complete with antique mirrored walls, exposed pipes and signature Hell's Angel cocktail (Bulleit bourbon, Chartreuse and OJ). Rebel only looks tough; bartenders are flirty, there's vinegary Carolina-style BBQ, and everyone bounces to Gaga. The crowd is mostly 30-something, gay and tribally tattooed, but you can bring anyone who's not easily scandalized. (1760 Market St; admission varies; 5pm-3am Mon-Thu, to 4am Fri, 11am-4am Sat-Sun; M Market St)

Rye

COCKTAIL BAR

20 Map p108, G3

Polished cocktails with herb-infused spirits and fresh-squeezed juice in a sleek sunken lounge. Come early to settle into leather sofas, drink something challenging involving dark rum or juniper gin, and leave before the smoking cage overflows. (www.ryesf.com; 688 Geary St; 5:30pm-2am Mon-Fri, 7pm-2am Sat & Sun; Geary St, Powell-Mason)

Local Life

Heart of the City Farmers Market

The savviest wheeler-dealers aren't in City Hall – they're out front at the farmers market (Map p108, E4; United Nations Plaza; 7am-5pm Sun & Wed year-round; M S Civic Center), where California producers set up shop in UN Plaza amid the usual skateboarders, Scientologists and raving self-talkers. These stands yield heirloom organic raspberries for $1.99/pint and cold-filtered virgin olive oil for $8/bottle. Food trucks pull up alongside, selling roast chicken with lavender salt and warm maple-bacon doughnuts.

Two Sisters Bar & Books
BAR, BOOKSHOP

21 Map p108, B3

Gimlets in warehouses work for club nights, but for actual conversation, go for $8 glasses of wine in this cozy nook lined with bookshelves and Victorian wallpaper. Trade your *Thomas the Tank Engine* for *Fahrenheit 451* – there's a take-one, leave-one honor system – and savor 4pm–6pm weeknight specials like $5 cheese plates and the Port of SF, a seaworthy IPA/sherry concoction. (www.2sistersbarandbooks.com; 579 Hayes St; 4-11pm Tue-Thu, 4pm-midnight Fri, 1pm-midnight Sat, noon-8pm Sun; Hayes St)

Bourbon & Branch
BAR

22 Map p108, G3

'Don't even think of asking for a cosmo' reads one of many House Rules at this revived speakeasy, complete with secret exits from its Prohibition-era heyday. For top-shelf gin and bourbon cocktails in the library, give the bouncer the password ('books') and you'll be led through a bookcase secret passage. Reservations are required for front-room booths, and worth it for chats minus the usual bar din. (415-346-1735; www.bourbonandbranch.com; 501 Jones St; Wed-Sat by reservation; Geary St)

Edinburgh Castle
BAR

23 Map p108, F2

Photos of bagpipers, the *Trainspotting* soundtrack on the jukebox, dart boards and a service delivering vinegary fish and chips in newspaper provide all the Scottish authenticity you could ask for, short of haggis. The town's finest battlement of drink comes complete with dart boards, pool tables, rock bands and raucous literary readings. (www.castlenews.com; 950 Geary St; nightly; Geary St)

Rickshaw Stop
LIVE MUSIC

24 Map p108, C4

Red-velvet curtains line the black-box walls of this former TV studio, where the scene is flavored like a wilder, weirder MTV reality-show party. Crafty DJs cross-pollinate music and hemispheres to offer something for everyone: bad-ass banghra nights, Latin explosion bands, lesbian disco, and mainstay Thursday Popscene (18+). (www.rickshawstop.com; 155 Fell St; tickets $5-35; 6pm-2am Wed-Sat; Van Ness Ave)

Jones
LOUNGE

25 Map p108, H3

Bucolic splendor and top-shelf drinks where you least expect them: on a grassy rooftop patio lounge just above the urban fray and fragrance of Tenderloin streets. Their Bloody Mary makes Sunday brunches seem sunnier, but be warned: the Patty Hearst (vodka, lemon and rose jam) may induce Stockholm Syndrome, and decadent bar bites like parmesan and truffle fries will leave you Jonesing for more. (http://620-jones.com; 620 Jones St;

Martinis at the Edinburgh Castle

5pm-midnight Tue-Wed, 5pm-2am Thu-Sat, 11am-3pm Sun; Geary St)

Hôtel Biron

WINE BAR

26 Map p108, B5

A wine-lover's dream, this walk-in closet-cellar doubles as a wine bar, with standout Californian, Provencale and Tuscan vintages and a ceiling made of corks. The vibe is French underground, with exposed-brick walls, surreally romantic art, a leather couch and just a few tables for two. Barkeeps let you keep tasting until you find what you like; pair with decadent cheese plates. (www.hotelbiron.com; 45 Rose St; 5pm-2am; M Market St)

Entertainment

San Francisco Symphony

CLASSICAL

27 Map p108, C4

SF Symphony has won more Grammys than Lady Gaga, and you can see why: Michael Tilson Thomas conducts on the tips of his toes, keeping audiences on the edge of (comfy) seats through Beethoven, Mahler, and experimental modern music. Don't miss pre-show talks, where 'MTT' explains exactly what makes each piece exciting and relevant. During special programs, summer festivals and holidays, look out for stars like Joshua Bell, Pink Martini and (believe it) Metallica. (415-864-6000, rush tickets 415-503-5577;

Understand

Earthquakes & Opera

At the turn of the 20th century, San Francisco had a reputation for scandal, sleaze and great singers. The city commissioned a beaux-arts Civic Center to rival Parisian plazas, including a grand opera. The plan had just been finalized by April 18, 1906, when disaster struck – twice.

A quake estimated at a teeth-rattling 7.8 to 8.3 on today's Richter scale struck the city. In 47 seconds, San Franciscans discovered just how many corners had been cut on government contracts. Unreinforced civic structures – even City Hall – collapsed in ruins. Brick buildings crumbled and toppled chimneys set fires. Since city maintenance funds had been pocketed by unscrupulous officials, fire hydrants didn't work, and there was no way to contain fires downtown. The sole functioning water source was a fountain donated to the city by hometown opera prodigy Lotta Crabtree.

Fire-fighters couldn't haul equipment through the rubble-choked streets, so in a city surrounded by water on three sides, fires raged. Firebreaks were created by dynamiting a trough along Van Ness Ave – setting off new fires. Citizens fled to Potrero Hill and Buena Vista Park, and for three days watched their city and its dreams of grandeur go up in smoke. The death toll topped 3000, and 100,000-plus city residents were left homeless.

With politicians suddenly scarce, San Francisco's entertainers staged the city's comeback. All but one of the city's 20 historic theaters had been destroyed by the earthquake and fire, but theater tents were set up amid still-smoking rubble.

Opera divas sang their hearts out to San Francisco gratis – though the world's most famous tenor, Enrico Caruso, vowed never to return to the city after the quake jolted him out of bed. Soprano Luisa Tetrazzini ditched New York's Metropolitan Opera to return to San Francisco, and sang on Market St to an audience of 250,000 – virtually every surviving San Franciscan.

While singers gave marathon performances, San Francisco hummed along. The city was rebuilt at the astounding rate of 15 buildings a day. In a show of popular priorities, San Francisco's theaters were rebuilt long before City Hall. Free summer opera concerts are still held at **Golden Gate Park's Stern Grove Festival** (www.sterngrove.org).

www.sfsymphony.org; Davies Symphony Hall, 201 Van Ness Ave; tickets $30-125; season Sep-May; M Van Ness; S Civic Center)

San Francisco Opera

OPERA

28 Map p108, C3

For over a century, SF has been obsessed with opera – and in 2008 a stockbroker donated $40 million to keep the SF Opera in good voice. Don't miss original operas like *Dead Man Walking* and modern revivals like Puccini's *Girl of the Golden West* under acclaimed Tuscan director Nicola Luisotti. Book ahead, or score standing-room tickets two hours before performances.
(415-864-3330; www.sfopera.com; War Memorial Opera House, 301 Van Ness Ave; tickets $10-350; box office 10am-6pm Mon-Fri; M Van Ness; S Civic Center)

San Francisco Ballet

BALLET

29 Map p108, C3

The United State's oldest ballet company remains exceedingly sprightly for its advanced age, performing over 100 shows annually, nationally and abroad, from the classic *Nutcracker* (the US premiere was here) to modern Mark Morris. The company performs mostly at the War Memorial Opera House January–May, with occasional shows at Yerba Buena Center for the Arts. Check online for discounted senior, military and student tickets.
(415-861-5600, tickets 415-865-2000; www.sfballet.org; War Memorial Opera House, 301 Van Ness Ave; tickets $10-120; M Van Ness; S Civic Center)

Great American Music Hall

LIVE MUSIC

30 Map p108, F2

This opulent former bordello on a sketchy block is full of surprises: rockers Black Rebel Motorcycle Club playing acoustic, Nick Lowe jamming with Ry Cooder, and even the bouncers bopping to Ra Ra Riot's infectious baroque pop. Arrive early to claim front-row balcony seats with a pint and a passable burger, or find standing room downstairs by the stage.
(415-885-0750; www.gamh.com; 859 O'Farrell St; admission $12-35; box office 10:30am-6pm Mon-Fri & on show nights; Van Ness)

Warfield

LIVE MUSIC & COMEDY

31 Map p108, G5

Big acts with an international following play this old vaudeville theater, with balcony-shakers ranging from Iggy and the Stooges to Feist and Wilco, and the occasional comedy act like hometown favorite Margaret Cho, but motley lines wrap around the block for shows by Furthur (formerly the Grateful Dead). Hit the bar early for whiskey, beer and sustainable sausages at fair prices. (800-745-3000; thewarfieldtheatre.com; 982 Market St; prices vary; box office 10am-4pm Sun, and 90min before curtain on show nights; M S Powell St)

Dancers from the San Francisco Ballet (p119)

Aunt Charlie's
GAY BAR

32 Map p108, G4

Vintage pulp-fiction covers leap to life on one of Downtown's worst blocks during the Hot Boxxx Girls, the city's best classic drag show, Friday and Saturday nights at 10pm (make reservations). Thursday is Tubesteak Connection, when bathhouse anthems and '80s retro techno draw throngs of art-school gays. Other nights bring minor mayhem, with seedy glamour guaranteed. (415-441-2922; www.auntcharlieslounge.com; 133 Turk St; admission free-$5; M S Powell St)

Café Royale
LOUNGE

33 Map p108, G2

Velvet fainting couches, French tiled floors and rotating art shows lend Paris-in-the-1920s atmosphere to this lounge, but the eclectic bill is SF all the way: live Brazilian jazz, Ishmael Reed hip-hop poetry readings, electronic chamber music and eccentric pop by the Feral Cats. Serves food till 7pm. (www.caferoyale-sf.com; 800 Post St; admission free; 3pm-midnight Sun-Thu, to 2am Fri & Sat; M 2, 3, 27, 38)

Shopping

Reliquary
CLOTHING & ACCESSORIES

34 Map p108, B3

Owner Leah Bershad was once a designer for the Gap, but the folksy jet-set aesthetic here is the exact opposite of khaki-and-fleece global domination. Half the stock is well-travelled vintage (ikat silk kimonos, Santa Fe blankets, silver jewelry banged together by Humboldt hippies) and the rest are cult American designs like Court denim, Majestic tissue-tees and Claire Vivier pebble-leather clutches. (http://reliquarysf.com; 537 Octavia Blvd; 11am-7pm Tue-Sat, noon-6pm Sun; M Hayes St)

Nancy Boy

BEAUTY

35 Map p108, C4

All you closet pomaders and after-sun balmers: wear those products with pride, all locally made with plant oils. Clever Nancy Boy knows you'd rather pay for quality ingredients than for cheesy advertising campaigns, and supplies well-priced premium products tested for effectiveness on boyfriends, never animals. (www.nancyboy.com; 347 Hayes St; 11am-7pm Mon-Fri, to 6pm Sat & Sun; Hayes St)

MAC

CLOTHING & ACCESSORIES

36 Map p108, C3

'Modern Appealing Clothing' is what they promise, and what they deliver with two-tone Dries Van Noten jackets, local-designer frocks with New Wave graphics and art-collector tees designed by Oakland's Creative Growth arts nonprofit. Trust staff to style you, point out 40% to 75% off sales rack steals, and get any purchase tailored impeccably. Their second location showcases California designers on Dogpatch's artisan shopping strip (1003 Minnesota). (http://modernappealingclothing.com; 387 Grove St; 11am-7pm Mon-Sat, noon-6pm Sun; Van Ness)

Triple Aught Design

CLOTHING

37 Map p108, B3

Whether you're a social-media millionaire who runs parkour or just rock that look, this SF designer has your back with zip-up paramilitary sweaters and multi-function pants entirely too stylish to be considered cargo. Key design features include hidden pockets for business models on bar napkins, and unisex favorites include the sleek Stealth Hoodie, which transitions from TED conferences to off-the-grid weekends. (www.tripleaughtdesign.com; 551 Hayes St; 11am-7pm Tue-Sun; Hayes St)

Gimme Shoes

SHOES

38 Map p108, B3

Don't let SF hills become your arch-rivals: get your kicks at Gimme Shoes instead. Chie Mihara's oxblood ankle

Local Life

Kayo Books

Juvenile delinquents will find an entire section dedicated to their life stories at Kayo (Map p108, G2; www.kayobooks.com; 814 Post St; Thu-Sat; Geary St), where vintage pulp fiction titles ending in exclamation points (including the succinct *Wench!*) earned regular John Waters' endorsement on NPR. Digging may yield 1940s Dashiell Hammet whodunnits, a wayward nun's tale filed under Catholic Guilt, or *Women's Medical Problems* in Bizarre Nonfiction.

boots are worthy of cult worship and surprisingly sturdy, and stylish flats are not an oxymoron when it comes to Costume National's minimalist slip-ons. Men have their pick of high tops by Alexander McQueen for Puma or John Varvatos' foggy-grey oxfords. Don't miss the 40–60% off rack. (www.gimmeshoes.com; 416 & 381 Hayes St; 11am-7pm Mon-Sat, noon-6pm Sun; M Hayes St)

Isotope

BOOKSTORE

39 Map p108, B4

The toilet seats signed by famous cartoonists over the front counter show just how seriously Isotope takes comics. Newbies tentatively flip through Daniel Clowes and Chris Ware in the graphic-novel section, while fanboys load up on Berkeley's Adrian Tomine or the latest from SF's Last Gasp Publishing, and head upstairs to lounge with local cartoonists. (www.isotopecomics.com; 326 Fell St; 11am-7pm Tue-Fri, to 6pm Sat & Sun; Hayes St;)

Local Life

Gangs of San Francisco T-shirts

Watch out, because Laureano Faedi's about to get all historical on your T-shirt. The Brazil-born SF silkscreener has unearthed insignia for every thuggish clique to claim an SF street corner, from the San Francisco Vigilance Committee – known for kangaroo trials and hasty hangings during SF's Gold Rush era – to the Richmond Beer Town Brawlers, who malingered near Golden Gate Park c 1875 to 1896. (Map p108, B5; www.gangsofsanfrancisco.com; 66 Gough St; noon-6pm Sat-Sun, 4-9pm Wed; Hayes St).

Flight 001

ACCESSORIES

40 Map p108, B3

Having a nice flight in the zero-legroom era is actually a possibility with the in-flight assistance of Flight 001. Their Jet Comfort Kit is first class all the way, with earplugs, sleep mask, booties, neck rest, candy and cards. For jet-set friends, pick up a rubber alarm clock, travel Scrabble or pop-art luggage tags that stand out at baggage claim. (www.flight001.com; 525 Hayes St; 11am-7pm Mon-Sat, to 6pm Sun; Hayes St)

Miette

FOOD & DRINK

41 Map p108, B3

You die and go straight to pure candy heaven when you walk in the door here: racks of licorice twists, a table of artisan chocolate bars and a fully stocked cupcake counter. Tots load up on Pixie Stix and chocolate fire trucks, while adults ogle salty French caramels and dark chocolates spiked with chili. Ask for help first, so you don't get caught with your hand in the candy jar. (www.miettecakes.com; 449 Octavia Blvd; noon-7pm Sun-Fri, 11am-7pm Sat; Hayes St)

RICK GERHARTER/LONELY PLANET IMAGES ©

Browsing the aisles in Flight 001

Lotus Bleu HOUSEWARES, LOCAL DESIGNER

42 Map p108, C4

French whimsy, Vietnamese design and San Franciscan psychedelic color pack a punch in this compact design boutique, piled with fuchsia felt bulls-eye pillows, French laminated-canvas totes in spring green, and orange lacquer breakfast trays. (www.lotusbleudesign.com; 325 Hayes St; 11am-6pm Tue-Fri, to 7pm Sat, noon-5pm Sun; Hayes St)

Residents Apparel Gallery CLOTHING & ACCESSORIES

43 Map p108, B3

Local designers make eclectic SF chic easy at this certified-green cooperative boutique. Take your pick of limited-edition screen-printed tees, locally made dark denim (no sweatshops here, thank you), reconstructed vintage dresses and one-of-a-kind jewelry in silver, gemstones and found feathers – all at art-school prices. (www.ragsf.com; 541 Octavia Blvd; noon-7pm; Hayes St;)

Local Life
Shops, Sushi & Shows in Japantown

Waving *maneki neko* (ceramic cats) greet your arrival in Japantown at sushi bars, spas and boutiques. But Japantown is more than *kawaii* (cute); this pioneering community challenged WWII Japanese American internment orders to establish key US civil rights precedents. Japantown continues to innovate, premiering international films, launching jazz legends and setting style trends.

Getting There

Japantown is 1 mile south of the Marina

Bus 1, 2, 3, and 38 buses connect Fillmore St to downtown; 22 connects with the Mission.

Parking Fillmore St (at Post) and Post St (at Webster).

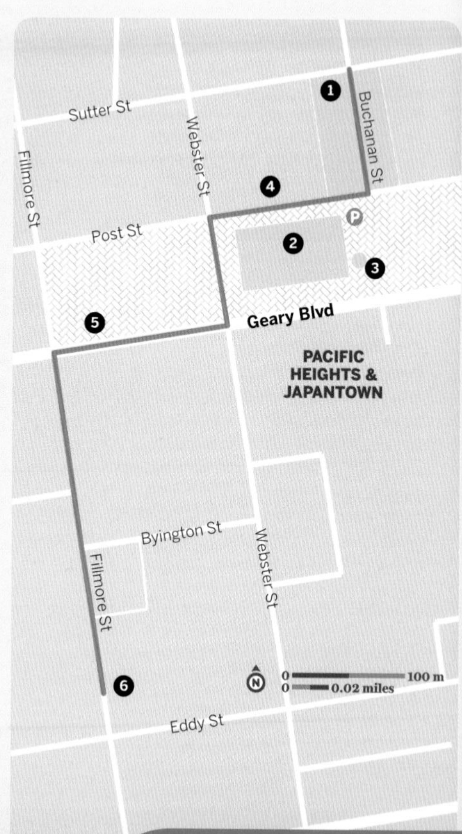

❶ Mochi at Benkyodo

Pass bronze origami-dandelion fountains by celebrated sculptor and former WWII internee Ruth Asawa on pedestrian Buchanan St, and you're in for a treat at **Benkyodo** (www.benkyodocompany.com; 1747 Buchanan St; ⏲8am-5pm Mon-Sat). This picture-perfect retro lunch counter cheerfully serves $4 sandwiches, followed by $1 *mochi* (rice cakes) made in-house daily. Come early for popular varieties of green tea and chocolate-filled strawberry, and don't miss nutty lima-bean *mochi*.

❷ Pop-Culture Immersion

Retro **Japan Center** (www.sfjapantown.org; ⏲10am-midnight) looks like a 1960s Tokyo movie set, with indoor pedestrian bridges, rock gardens and curtained restaurant entryways intact since the mall's grand opening in 1968. But Japan Center stays current, with anime photo-booths downstairs, Lolita Goths studying Harajuku fashion at **Kinokuniya Books & Stationery** (1581 Webster St), and spiky flowers gracing the windows of **Ikenobo Ikebana Society** (385 Kineketsu Bldg).

❸ Meditation at Peace Pagoda

Near Japan Center is Japantown's signature monument: Yoshiro Taniguchi's minimalist **Peace Pagoda** (Peace Plaza), a gift from SF's sister city of Osaka, Japan, in 1968. Similar stupas exist in India to commemorate Gandhi's peace efforts and in Hiroshima to remember victims of the atom bomb. Hewn-rock benches beneath plaza cherry trees offer prime perspectives on this 100ft structure and its lofty aspirations.

❹ Future Fashion & Film

Glimpse ahead of the curve at **New People** (☎415-525-8654; www.newpeopleworld. com; 1746 Post St), a three-story emporium of novelty. San Francisco International Film Festival prescreens unreleased international films year-round at New People Cinema. Upstairs, explore contemporary art installations at Superfrog Gallery, try on Lolita costumes (picture Alice in Wonderland on acid) at Baby the Stars Shine Bright and load up on MP3 lollipop speakers and Mt Fuji-shaped beer pint-glasses at New People Shop.

❺ Bathtime at Kabuki Springs

Unwind in communal baths at **Kabuki Springs & Spa** (1750 Geary Blvd; admission $22-25; ⏲10am-9:45pm, co-ed Tue, women only Sun, Wed & Fri, men only Mon, Thu & Sat). Scrub down with salt, soak in the hot pool, take a cold plunge and repeat as necessary. Bathing suits are required on co-ed Tuesdays.

❻ Jazz & Sushi at Yoshi's

The Fillmore St Jazz District was the 'Harlem of the West' back in the '40s and '50s, and **Yoshi's** (www.yoshis.com; 1300 Fillmore St; ⏲shows 8pm & sometimes 10pm) still draws the world's top talent, and serves a mean sushi roll besides. Bone up on your jazz legends in the lobby and next door at the **Jazz Heritage Center** (www.jazzheritagecenter.org; 1320 Fillmore St).

Explore

The Mission

San Francisco's original neighborhood was built around an 18th-century Spanish mission where nothing seemed to grow, until the gold rush brought boatloads of adventurers, and wild speculation took root. The Mission remains fertile ground for vivid imaginations and tall tales told over strong drink – hence mural-lined streets, pirate supply shops and margarita-fueled readings from teenage diaries.

The Sights in a Day

Walk 24th St past mural-covered bodegas to **Balmy Alley** (p129; pictured left), where the Mission muralist movement began in the 1970s. Stop for a decadent 'secret breakfast' (bourbon and cornflake) ice cream sundae at **Humphry Slocombe** (p138), then head up Valencia to another food-cult favorite, **Ritual Coffee Roasters** (p138). Pause for pirate supplies and watch ichthyoid antics in the Fish Theater at **826 Valencia** (p133), and duck into **Clarion Alley** (p129) to see the Mission's ongoing outdoor art show.

Pass the muraled **Women's Building** (p129), on your way to **Pizzeria Delfina** (p135) for lunch, and enjoy sun and downtown panoramas on the upper slopes of **Dolores Park** (p132). See San Francisco's first building, Spanish adobe **Mission Dolores** (p132), and visit the memorial to native Ohlone who built it. Head up 16th St to check out art shows at **Needles & Pens** (p142) and **Adobe Books & Backroom Gallery** (p141).

Snag an early seating at **Frances** (p135) and catch an indie movie at the **Roxie** (p139), topped with a toast **Elixir** (p137).

For a local's day in the Mission, see p128.

Local Life

Mission Murals (p128)

Best of San Francisco

Entertainment

Roxie Cinema (p139)

ODC (p139)

Intersection for the Arts (p139)

Drinks

Zeitgeist (p137)

Elixir (p137)

Heart (p137)

Ritual Coffee Roasters (p138)

Bargain Gourmet

Mr Pollo (p134)

La Taqueria (p133)

Udupi Palace (p135)

Getting There

BART Stations at 16th and 24th Sts.

Bus Line 14 runs through SoMa to the Mission; 33 links to the Castro; 22 connects to the Haight.

M Streetcar The J Church heads from downtown through the Mission.

Local Life
Mission Murals

Diego Rivera has no idea what he started. Inspired by the Mexican muralist's 1930s masterpieces in SF, generations of Mission muralists have covered alleys and institutions with 400 murals to show political dissent, community pride and bravado. These galleries are exposed to the elements and rival graffiti artists, not to mention incontinent barflies – but when historic Balmy Alley works are damaged, muralists lovingly restore them.

❶ Muralist-Led Precita Eyes Mural Walking Tours

Pack in the sights on two-hour mural tours led by local artists and organized by nonprofit **Precita Eyes** (☎415-285-2287; www.precitaeyes.org; Alabama & 24th Sts, adult $12-15, child $5; ⏲11am, noon, 1:30pm Sat & Sun; 🚇 S 24th St Mission). Tours cover 50 to 70 murals within a six to 10 block radius of mural-bedecked Balmy Alley. Proceeds fund mural upkeep. It's a good idea to make reservations.

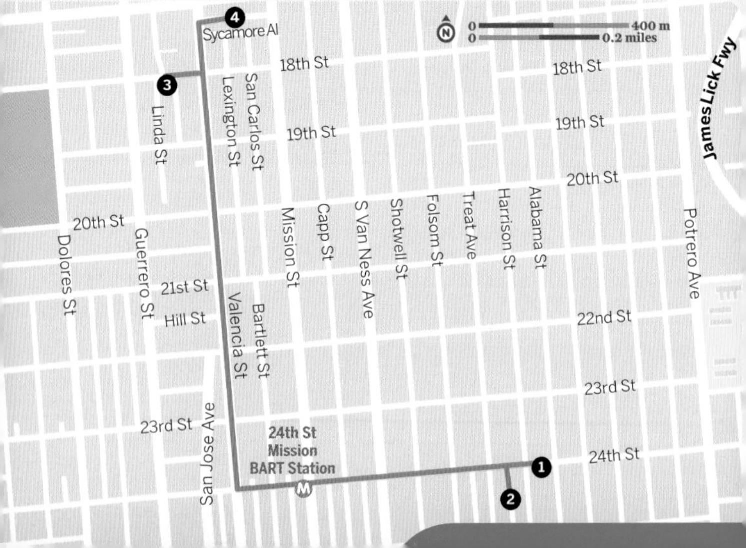

2 Historic Balmy Alley Murals

Without a platform to address US foreign policy in Central America in the 1970s, Mission activist-artists Mujeres Muralistas (Women Muralists) and Placa (meaning 'mark-making') transformed the political landscape one mural-covered garage door at a time along **Balmy Alley** (www.balmyalley.com; btwn Treat Ave & Harrison St, 24th & 25th Sts). One block covers three decades of iconic Mission murals, from the memorial to murdered El Salvador activist Archbishop Óscar Romero to an homage to silver-screen Mexican cinema.

3 Wrap-Around Women's Building Murals

The nation's first female-owned-and-operated community center has quietly done good work with 170 women's organizations since 1979 – but the 1994 *Maestrapeace* mural showed the **Women's Building** (www.womensbuilding.org; 3543 18th St; M18th St; S16th St Mission) for the landmark it truly is. An all-star team of seven muralistas covered the building on two sides with women trailblazers, including Nobel Prize–winner Rigoberta Menchu, poet Audre Lorde and former US surgeon-general Dr Jocelyn Elders.

4 Ground-Breaking Graffiti Art in Clarion Alley

Before Barry McGee, Chris Johansen and Alicia McCarthy headlined museum shows, they could be found in **Clarion Alley** (btwn 17th & 18th Sts, off Valencia St; 18th St; S16th St Mission), gripping spray-paint cans. Only the strongest street art survives here without getting peed on or painted over, such as Andrew Schoultz's mural of gentrifying elephants displacing scraggly birds. The alley is loosely curated, with topical murals like the one honoring the Arab Spring on the less-fragrant west end.

A
B
C
D
E
1
2
3
4
400 m
0.2 miles
0
0
Franklin Square
York St
Bryant St
Florida St
Alabama St
Harrison St
Treat Ave
Folsom St
Shotwell St
S Van Ness Ave
Capp St
Natoma St
Minna St
Otis St
Hoff St
Rondel Pl
Clarion Al
San Carlos St
Lexington St
Lapidge St
Dearborn St
Valencia St
Albion St
Guerrero St
Dolores St
Abbey St
Dolores Tce
Dorland St
Oakwood St
Camp St
Gaiser Ct
Adair St
Erie St
Clinton Park
Brosnan St
Duboce Ave
Market St
Central Fwy
13th St
14th St
15th St
16th St
17th St
Mariposa St
18th St
19th St
16th St Mission BART Station
THE MISSION
Creativity Explored
Mission Dolores
1
4
7
8
10
12
15
16
17
18
19
21
23
24
28
29
30
31
36
37
39
40
41
43
45
46

Mission Dolores Park
Dolores Park
826 Valencia
Cumberland St
20th St
Valencia St
Lexington St
San Carlos St
Liberty St
21st St
Chattanooga St
Guerrero St
Hill St
Ames St
22nd St
Alvarado St
Bartlett St
Mission St
Capp St
S Van Ness Ave
Shotwell St
Folsom St
Treat Ave
Harrison St
Alabama St
Florida St
Bryant St
23rd St
Quane St
Fair Oaks St
Elizabeth St
24th St Mission BART Station
NOE VALLEY
24th St
San Jose Ave
Poplar St
Orange Al
Cypress St
Lucky St
Treat Ave
Balmy Al
Harrison St
25th St
Garfield Square
Osage St
Lilac St
Capp St
Virgil St
Horace St
Folsom St
26th St
For reviews see
Sights p132
Eating p133
Drinking p137
Entertainment p139
Shopping p141
A
B
C
D
E
5
6
7
8

Sights

Mission Dolores

CHURCH

1 Map p130, A3

The city's oldest building and its namesake, the Mission (originally named Misión San Francisco de Asís) was founded in 1776 and rebuilt in 1782 with conscripted Native American labor – hence the graveyard Native memorial hut commemorating 5000 laborers who died in measles epidemics. Today, the original adobe is overshadowed by the adjoining 1913 basilica, featuring stained-glass windows of California's 21 missions. (www.missiondolores.org; 3321 16th St; adult/senior & child $5/3; 9am-4pm Nov-Apr, to 4:30pm May-Oct; S 16th St Mission, M Church St)

Mission Dolores Park

PARK

2 Map p130, A5

The site of quasi-professional tanning, a small children's playground (currently undergoing some reconstruction) and free movies on summer nights, this sloping park is also beloved for its year-round political protests and other favorite local sports. Join serious soccer games and lazy Frisbee sessions on flat patches; tennis courts and basketball hoops are open to anyone who is up for a game. Don't miss out on getting an eyeful of the panoramic views of downtown from southwest corner benches. (Dolores St, btwn 18th & 20th Sts; M Church St; 18th St;)

Understand

San Francisco's Original Mission

When Captain Juan Bautista de Anza and Father Francisco Palou brought 340 horses, 302 head of cattle and 160 mules to settle Mission San Francisco in 1776, there was a slight hitch: the area had already been settled by Native Americans for some 14,300 years. To build their mission, the new arrivals conscripted local Ohlone People. In exchange, Native laborers were allowed one scant meal a day and a place in God's kingdom – which came much sooner than expected. Measles and other introduced diseases reduced the Ohlone population by almost three-quarters during the 50 years of Spanish rule in California.

The mission settlement never really prospered. The sandy fields were difficult to farm, fleas were a constant irritation, and Spanish soldiers sent to retrieve runaway laborers went AWOL themselves. Spain readily handed off the colony to newly independent Mexico in 1821, which ceded California to the USA in 1848. Within months, gold was found near San Francisco, and leased mission property proved fertile ground for saloons and music-halls – as the Mission remains today.

826 Valencia

CULTURAL BUILDING

3 Map p130, B5

Avast, ye scurvy scalawags! If ye be shipwrecked without yer eye patch or yer McSweeney's literary anthology, lay down yer doubloons and claim yer booty at this here nonprofit Pirate Store. Below decks, kids be writing tall tales for dark nights asea – and ye can study making magazines and video games and suchlike, if that be yer dastardly inclination…arr! (www.826valencia.com; 826 Valencia St; noon-6pm; 18th St;)

Creativity Explored

ART GALLERY

4 Map p130, A3

Brave new worlds are captured in celebrated artworks that regularly make the New York art scene – all by local developmentally disabled artists. Intriguing themed shows at the nonprofit gallery reveal fresh perspectives on subjects ranging from love to politics, and openings are joyous celebrations with the artists, their families and rock-star fan base. (www.creativityexplored.org; 3245 16th St; donations welcome; 10am-3pm Mon-Fri, to 7pm Thu, 1-6pm Sat; S 16th St Mission)

La Raza Skatepark

OUTDOORS

5 Map p130, E8

An isolated, scrubby park, once abandoned to gangs, is now an urban-legendary skatepark, with city support. *Thrasher* magazine founders and fearless tweens alike blast ollies off these concrete bowls, though graffiti

RICK GERHARTER/LONELY PLANET IMAGES ©

Cemetery at Mission Dolores

on the concrete can make for a slippery ride. Wait for a clean area of the bowl to bust big moves, and yield to little skaters. For gear, hit up Mission Skateboards (p143). (www.sfgov.org; cnr 25th & Utah Sts; S 24th St Mission)

Eating

La Taqueria

MEXICAN $

6 Map p130, C8

Pure burrito bliss. There's no debatable saffron rice, spinach tortilla or mango salsa here – just perfectly grilled meats, flavorful beans and classic tomatillo or mesquite salsa wrapped in a flour tortilla. They're purists at La Taqueria – if you don't

Local Life

Galería de la Raza

Art flows from Mission streets and across the Americas into **Galería de la Raza** (Map p130; E7; www.galeriadelaraza.org; 2857 24th St; donations welcome; noon-6pm Wed-Sat, to 7pm Tue; S 24th St Mission), the non-profit Latino art showcase since 1970. Culture and community are constantly redefined here, by works like Sayuri Guzman's group portrait of Latinas connected by their braided hair, a group show exploring SF's Latin gay culture, and Enrique Chagoya's post-9/11 dinosaurs escaping the TV to rampage through suburban living rooms. Outside, the Galería has reserved billboard space for its Digital Mural Project, broadcasting such provocative messages as 'Trust Your Struggle' instead of the usual cigarette ads.

want beans, you'll pay extra, because they pack in more meat – but spicy pickled vegetables and *crema* (crème fraîche) are inspired additions. (2889 Mission St; burritos $6-8; 11am-9pm Mon-Sat, to 8pm Sun; S 24th St Mission;)

Commonwealth

CALIFORNIAN $$

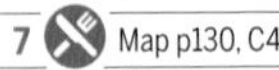

California's most imaginative farm-to-table dining isn't found in some quaint barn, but in the converted cinderblock Mission dive where chef Jason Fox serves crispy hen with toy-box carrots cooked in hay (yes, hay), and sea urchin floating on a bed of farm egg and organic asparagus that looks like a tide pool and tastes like a dream. Savor the $65 prix-fixe knowing $10 is donated to charity. (415-355-1500; www.commonwealthsf.com; 2224 Mission St; small plates $5-16; 5:30-10pm Tue-Thu & Sun, to 11pm Fri-Sat; S 16th St Mission;)

Locanda

ITALIAN $$

8 Map p130, B3

As the vintage Duran Duran Rome-concert poster in the bathroom hints, Locanda is all about cheeky, streetwise Roman fare. Scrumptious tripe melting into rich tomato-mint sauce is a must, *pizza bianco* with figs and prosciutto creates obsessions, and Roman fried artichokes and sweetbreads deliver authenticity minus the airfare. (www.locandasf.com; 557 Valencia St; share plates $10-24; 5:30pm-midnight; M S 16th St Mission)

Mr Pollo

CALIFORNIAN, VENEZUELAN $$

9 Map p130, C7

Mission-Mex devotees experience culinary awakenings at chef/owner Manny Torres Gimenez' outpost of market-fresh, Venezuelan-inspired cuisine. Currently this bolt hole seats 15, so arrive early for the bargain set-price menu – recent highlights include golden beets with pomegranate seeds and Douglas fir reduction, crispy wild salmon with yucca, salt-pork *arepas* (cornbread pockets), and housemade lychee ice cream. BYO; free corkage. (2823 Mission St; 3-4-dish tasting menu $15-20; dinner; M S 24th St Mission;)

Pizzeria Delfina

PIZZA **$$**

10 Map p130, A4

One single bite explains why San Francisco is so totally obsessed with pizza lately: Delfina's thin crust heroically supports the weight of fennel sausage and fresh mozzarella without drooping or cracking, while white pizzas let chefs freestyle with Cali-foodie ingredients such as maitake mushrooms, broccoli rabe and artisan cheese. You can't make reservations; just sign up on the chalkboard and wait with a glass of wine (or two, if it's busy) at Delfina bar next door. (www.delfinasf.com; 3611 18th St; pizzas $11-17; 11:30am-10pm Tue-Thu, to 11pm Fri, noon-11pm Sat-Sun, 5:30-10pm Mon; 18th St, M Church St;)

Ichi Sushi

SUSHI **$$**

11 Map p130, C8

Alluring on the plate, and positively obscene on the tongue, Ichi Sushi is a sharp cut above other fish food thanks to some very clever culinary engineering. Silky, sustainably sourced fish is sliced with a jeweler's precision, balanced atop well-packed rice, and topped with tiny but powerfully tangy dabs of gelled *yuzu* and microscopic *brunoise* of spring onion and chili daikon that make the addition of a single drop of soy sauce absolutely unthinkable. (3369 Mission St; www.ichisushi.com; 11:30am-10pm Tue-Thu, to 11pm Fri, 5:30-11pm Sun, 5:30-10pm Mon; Mission St, S 24th St Mission)

Frances

CALIFORNIAN **$$**

12 Map p130, A3

After chef/owner Melissa Perello earned a Michelin star for creative fine dining, she ditched downtown to reinvent neighborhood bistro dining at Frances. Daily menus showcase bright, seasonal flavors and luxurious textures: cloud-like sheep's-milk-ricotta gnocchi with crunchy breadcrumbs and broccolini, grilled calamari with preserved Meyer lemon, and artisan wine served by the ounce, directly from Wine Country. James Beard Award nominations and Michelin stars keep rolling in, so reserve ahead. (415-621-3870; www.frances-sf.com; 3870 17th St; mains $14-27; 5-10:30pm Tue-Sun)

Range

CALIFORNIAN, NEW AMERICAN **$$$**

13 Map p130, B5

Inspired American dining is alive and well within Range. The menu is seasonal Californian, prices reasonable, and style cleverly repurposed industrial chic – think coffee-rubbed pork shoulder served with micro-brewed beer from the repurposed medical supply cabinet. (415-282-8283; www.rangesf.com; 842 Valencia St; mains $20-28; 5:30-10pm Sun-Thu, to 11pm Fri-Sat; 18th St, S 16th St Mission;)

Udupi Palace

INDIAN **$**

14 Map p130, B6

Tandoori in the Tenderloin is for novices – seasoned San Francisco foodies head here for the bright, clean

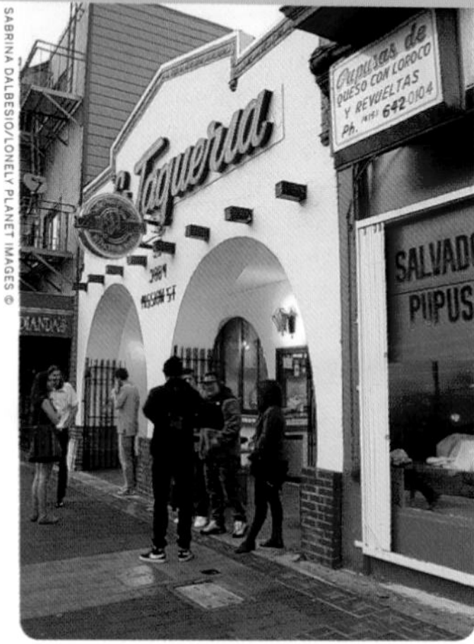

La Taqueria (p133)

flavors of South Indian *dosa*, a light, crispy lentil-flour pancake dipped in mildly spicy vegetable *sambar* (soup) and coconut chutney. Don't miss *medhu vada* (savory lentil donuts with *sambar* and chutney) or *bagala bhath* (yogurt rice with cucumber and nutty toasted mustard seeds). (www.udupipalaceca.com; 1007 Valencia St; mains $8-10; ⌚11am-10pm Mon-Thu, to 10:30pm Fri-Sun; 🚍Valencia St; S24th St Mission)

Maverick NEW AMERICAN, CALIFORNIAN $$

15 Map p130, C3

Cowboys start California dreaming at this tiny Mission bistro, where pasture-raised meats are spruced up with sensational California-grown sides. Enjoy Southern fried chicken with pan-seared broccoli rabe and whiskey gravy, sweetbreads with pickled cherries and edible nasturtium flowers, and terrific locals-only vintages – all at casual-dining prices. (www.sfmaverick.com; 3316 17th St; share plates $12-25; ⌚5:30-10pm Mon-Thu, to 11pm Fri-Sat, 5-9pm Sun, brunch 10:30am-2:30pm Sat & Sun; 🚍S16th St)

Radish CALIFORNIAN CREOLE $

16 Map p130, B4

Hedonists and food revolutionaries converge at Radish, where decadent Southern-inspired food is made with lavish helpings of organic Californian produce and sustainable meats. Mission barflies come here to recover with eggs and house-cured bacon in homemade biscuits and bottomless mimosas, while N'Orleans transplants get catfish po'boy sandwiches piled with tangy slaw, and vegetarians revel in roasted beets with candied pecans and sheep's feta. (www.radishsf.com; 3465 19th St; mains $8-16; ⌚5-10pm Mon-Tue, 10am-10pm Wed-Thu, 10am-11pm Fri-Sat, 9am-9pm Sun; 🚍18th St, S16th St Mission)

Bi-Rite Creamery ICE CREAM $

17 Map p130, A4

Across the street from Bi-Rite Market (p142), Bi-Rite Creamery is the only place in town where velvet ropes seem sensible rather than pretentious, keeping crowds waiting for organic salted caramel ice-cream smothered in housemade hot fudge from shoving. (3692 18th St; ⌚11am-10pm Sun-Thu, 11am-11pm Fri & Sat; MChurch St, S16th St Mission)

Drinking

Zeitgeist

BAR

18 Map p130, B1

On balmy Mission nights, all of alternative SF converges here for pitchers at communal picnic tables in the gravel-covered beer garden. Tough lady bartenders dish out sass to bikers who hesitate over the choice of 30 draft beers, and the Tamale Lady usually shows up around 10pm or 11pm to cure stoners' late-night munchies. (www.zeitgeistsf.com; 199 Valencia St; 9am-2am; 14th St, S 16th St Mission)

Elixir

BAR

19 Map p130, A3

Do the planet a favor and have another drink at SF's first certified-green bar, in an authentic 1858 Wild West saloon. Enjoy knockout cocktails made with seasonal organic fruit juices and local, organic, even biodynamic spirits – *ayiyi,* those peach margaritas with ancho-chili-infused tequila – and mingle over darts and a killer jukebox. Drink-for-a-cause nights encourage imbibing, with proceeds supporting local charities. (www.elixirsf.com; 3200 16th St; 3pm-2am Mon-Fri, noon-2am Sat & Sun; S 16th St Mission)

El Rio

NIGHTCLUB, GAY CLUB

20 Map p130, C8

The DJ mix takes its cue from El Rio regulars: eclectic, funky and internationally sexy, no matter your orientation. The club rightly boasts about the back garden, its 'Totally Fabulous Happy Hour' (5pm to 9pm Tuesday to Friday), and free oysters on Fridays at 5:30pm. Sunday afternoons are busiest, especially when salsa bands rock (dance lessons at 3pm); check calendar for Saturday night events. (www.elriosf.com; 3158 Mission St; admission $3-8; 5pm-2am Mon-Thu, 4pm-2am Fri, noon-2am Sun; S 24th St Mission)

Homestead

BAR

21 Map p130, D4

Your friendly corner dive c 1893, complete with carved-wood bar, roast peanuts in the shell, cheap draft beer and Victorian tin-stamped ceiling. On any given night, SF's creative contingent pack the place to celebrate an art opening, dance show or fashion launch – and when Iggy Pop or David Bowie hits the jukebox, watch out. (2301 Folsom St; 5pm-1am; 18th St, S 16th St Mission)

Heart

WINE BAR

22 Map p130, B7

Friendly, arty, gourmet – this wine bar is all Heart. Check the website for Kitchenette's pop-up nights, serving five-star organic, seasonal meals (share plates $4 to $12). Heart's pinot noir is entirely too good for dribbly Mason jars, but the wine menu descriptions are ingenious: one malbec is 'for kids who ate dirt' and a French white shows 'more soul than Marvin Gaye.' (www.heartsf.com; 1270 Valencia St;

Local Life

Humphry Slocombe

Indie-rock organic ice cream may permanently spoil you for Top 40 flavors: once Thai curry peanut butter and strawberry goat cheese have rocked your taste buds, cookie dough seems so obvious. And neither sundaes nor salads can compare to the Sonoma olive-oil ice cream drizzled with 20-year aged balsamic at **Humphry Slocombe** (Map p130; E7; www.humphryslocombe.com; 2790 Harrison St; ice cream $2.75-5; noon-9pm Mon-Thu, to 10pm Fri-Sun; S 24th St Mission)

5pm-11pm Sun, Mon & Wed, to midnight Thu-Sat; M S 24th St Mission)

Lexington Club — LESBIAN BAR

23 Map p130, B4

Also known as the Hex, because the odds are eerily high that you'll develop a crush on your girlfriend's ex-girlfriend here over $4 beer, pool marathons, pinball and tattoo comparisons. Go on, live dangerously at SF's most famous/notorious full-time lesbian bar. Women only...obviously. (www.lexingtonclub.com; 3464 19th St; 5pm-2am Mon-Thu, 3pm-2am Fri-Sun; Mission St)

Mission Cheese — WINE BAR

24 Map p130, B4

Smile and say wine at this cheese bar, serving up sublime pairings with expert advice and zero pretension. The all-domestic cheese menu ranges from triple-creamy to extra-stinky, raw cow's milk to sheep's milk, and California wines reign supreme. When in dairy doubt, try 'mongers choice' surprise-cheese platters with Sonoma wines by the glass. Order at the bar; note early closing. (missioncheese.net; 736 Valencia St; 11am-8pm Tue-Sun; 18th St, S 16th St Mission)

Amnesia — DIVE BAR

25  Map p130, B5

A teensy bar featuring nightly local music acts that may be playing in public for the first time, so cheer on hardworking bands and shy rappers. Check online for open-mic nights, when you too can take the world – or at least this postage-stamp stage – by storm. (www.amnesiathebar.com; 853 Valencia St; 6pm-2am; 18th St, S 16th St Mission)

Ritual Coffee Roasters — CAFE

26  Map p130, B6

Cults wish they inspired the same devotion as Ritual, where lines head out the door for house-roasted cappuccino with ferns in organic foam and specialty drip coffees with genuinely bizarre flavor profiles – believe the whiteboard descriptions of beans with grapefruit or blackberry notes. Electrical outlets are deliberately limited to encourage conversation; it works. (www.ritualroasters.com; 1026 Valencia St; 6am-10pm Mon-Fri, 7am-10pm Sat, 7am-9pm Sun; M S 24th St Mission; Wi-Fi)

Latin American Club
BAR

27 Map p130, B6

Margaritas go the distance here – just don't stand up too fast. Ninja piñatas and *papel picado* (cut-paper banners) add a festive atmosphere, and rosy lighting and generous pours enable shameless flirting outside your age range. Arrive early for window seats, and bring friends who still understand you when you slur. (3286 22nd St; 6pm-2am Mon-Fri, 2pm-2am Sat-Sun; M S 24th St Mission)

Entertainment

Roxie Cinema
CINEMA

28 Map p130, B3

A little neighborhood nonprofit cinema with international clout for distributing and launching indie films Stateside, and for showing controversial films and documentaries banned elsewhere. Film buffs, watch this space – film festival premieres, rare revivals and raucous Oscars telecasts sell out fast. When main attractions are packed, check out documentaries in teensy Little Roxy next door. No ads; personal introductions to every film. (www.roxie.com; 3117 16th St; admission $6-10; S 16th St Mission)

ODC
DANCE

29 Map p130, C3

ODC has produced risky, raw performances for nearly 40 years, captivating audiences' body and soul. The season runs September–December, and its stage presents year-round shows featuring local and international artists. ODC's Dance Commons is a hub and hangout for the dance community, and offers 200 classes a week; all ages and all levels are welcome. (415-863-9834; www.odctheater.org; 3153 17th St; admission & shows vary; S 16th St Mission)

Intersection For The Arts
LIVE MUSIC, THEATER, ART

30 Map p130, B2

SF's favorite interdisciplinary art space since 1965 works on many levels, including career-launching art installations upstairs, sizzling backroom improvisational jam sessions, and a tiny downstairs theater featuring premieres by huge talents: Pulitzer Prize winner Junot Diaz, National Book Award winner Denis Johnson, and American Book Award–winning poet Jessican Hagedorn, Between shows, check out workshops and open rehearsals (see website). (415-626-2787; www.theintersection.org; 446 Valencia St; admission $5-20; S 16th St Mission)

Elbo Room
LIVE MUSIC

31  Map p130, B4

Funny name, because there isn't much room to speak of upstairs on show nights with crowd-favorite funk, dancehall dub DJs, and offbeat local indie bands like Uni and Her Ukelele. Come any night for $2 pints from 5pm to 9pm at the chill downstairs bar (admission free). (www.elbo.com; 647 Valencia St; admission $5-15; 5pm-2am; S 16th St Mission)

Marsh

Marsh

THEATER, COMEDY

32 Map p130, B6

Choose your seat wisely: you may spend the evening on the edge of it at one-acts and comedy nights. The audience encircles the performers, so come early for frontal views; a few reserved seats are sometimes available ($50 per ticket). The sliding-scale pricing structure welcomes all to participate. Check website for show schedule, workshops and readings. (415-826-5750; www.themarsh.org; 1062 Valencia St; tickets $15-35; varies; S 24th St Mission)

Make-out Room

LIVE MUSIC, COMEDY

33 Map p130, C6

Velvet curtains and round booths help you settle in for the evening's entertainment, which ranges from punk-rock fiddle to '80s one-hit-wonder DJ mashups and painfully funny Mortified readings, when the power of margaritas convinces grown men to read aloud from their own lovelorn teenage journals. Booze is a bargain, but the bar is cash-only. (www.makeoutroom.com; 3225 22nd St; cover free-$10; 6pm-2am; S 24th St Mission)

Viracocha

LIVE MUSIC, SPOKEN WORD

34 Map p130, B5

Shotgun-shack Western home decor boutique by day, Viracocha hosts oddball songwriters, shy poets and occasional foraged-food events by night in its downstairs gallery and back-room vintage library (see website calendar). Bang away on the badly tuned piano if you like – it's that kind of place – but try not to dribble foraged-mushroom pastries onto the 1920s typewriters or driftwood sculpture. (www.viracochasf.com; 998 Valencia St; ⌚noon-6pm Wed-Fri, to 7pm Sat & Sun; 🚌18th St, S 24th St Mission)

Mission Cultural Center for Latino Arts
CLASSES

35 ★ Map p130, C8

Take a class in Afro-Peruvian dance, learn to make authentic *mole* (spice mix), or create a silkscreened protest poster at this happening cultural center. Teachers are friendly and multilingual, and participants range from *niños* to *abuelos* (kids to grand-parents). Check the online calendar for upcoming events; don't miss Day of the Dead altar displays in November or Christmas *posadas* (parties). (☎415-643-5001; www.missionculturalcenter.org; 2868 Mission St; ⌚10am-10pm Tue-Fri, Mon 5pm-10pm, Sat 10am-5:30pm; 🚌 S 24th St Mission; 👪)

18 Reasons
CLASSES

36 ★ Map p130, B4

Go gourmet at this local community food organization affiliated with Bi-Rite (p142) offering artisan cheese and wine tastings, knife-skills and edible perfume workshops and more – check the website for upcoming classes and frequent family friendly gourmet events. (☎415-252-9816; www.18reasons.org; 3674 18th St; ⌚events 7-9pm; M Church St, 🚌18th St; 👪)

Shopping

Adobe Books & BackRoom Gallery
BOOKS, ART

37 🔒 Map p130, B3

Find every book you never knew you needed to own, used and cheap, and stumble into 'zine launch parties, poetry readings and art openings. To reach the BackRoom gallery, first you have to navigate the obstacle course of sofas, cats, art books and tomes of German philosophy. But it's worth it; artists who debut here tend to pop up at international art fairs and Whitney Biennials. (http://adobebooksbackroomgallery.blogspot.com; 3166 16th St; ⌚11am-midnight; 🚌 S 16th St Mission)

Gravel & Gold
HOUSEWARES, GIFTS

38 🔒 Map p130, B5

The 1960s and 1970s NorCal hippie homesteader movement is making a comeback in today's off-the-grid movement and organic design trends, but here you'll find the original article: hand-hammered silver necklaces, Mendocino shingle-shack architecture books and vintage silkscreened Osborne Woods peace postcards. Try on organic cotton striped shirts and hand-dyed smocked dresses behind a patched curtain, surrounded by psychedelic murals. (gravelandgold.com; 3266 21st St; ⌚noon-7pm Tue-Sat, noon-5pm Sun; 🚌 S 24th St Mission)

Top Tip

Mission Street Smarts

Bars and restaurants make Mission a key nightlife destination, but it's not always the safest area to walk alone at night. Recruit a friend and be alert in the Mission east of Valencia, especially around 19th St gang-turf boundaries. Don't bring the bling – this isn't LA – or dawdle around BART stations. You should be fine in the daytime, but don't leave items like laptops and phones unattended at cafes.

Needles & Pens

BOOKS, ART

39 Map p130, A3

Do it yourself with style. This scrappy zine/craft/how-to/art gallery delivers the inspiration to create your own magazines, rehabbed T-shirts or album covers. Nab an issue of *Crap Hound*, or find lucky symbols intended for collages; check out Nigel Peake's pen-and-ink aerial views of patch-worked farmland, and buy alphabet buttons to pin your own credo onto a handmade messenger bag. (www.needles-pens.com; 3253 16th St; noon-7pm; S 16th St Mission)

Bi-Rite Market

FOOD & DRINK $

40 Map p130, A4

The Tiffany's of groceries, with spotlights trained on dazzling local artisan cheeses, chocolates, organic fruit, sustainable meats and the city's best-curated wine selection. (www.biritemarket.com; 3639 18th St; 9am-9pm; M Church St, S 16th St Mission)

Community Thrift

VINTAGE CLOTHING, ACCESSORIES

41 Map p130, B3

Go ahead and gloat over scoring major vintage pieces and new items by local designers, because every purchase supports local charities. Price tags induce double-takes: $4 totem-pole teacups, $7 '80s secretary blouses, even a $35 art-deco cigar humidor. Donate your own unwanted stuff to benefit your choice of 50 nonprofits, and show some love to the Community. (www.communitythriftsf.org; 623 Valencia St; 10am-6:30pm; 18th St; S 16th St Mission)

Aquarius Records

MUSIC

42 Map p130, B6

When pop seems played out, this is the dawning of the age of Aquarius Records, featuring Armenian blues, Oakland warehouse-party bands, and rare Japanese releases. Recent staff favorites include *Sounds of North American Frogs*, groovy '60 Brazilian tropicalia from Os Mutantes, woozy folk from New Zealand's Torlesse Super Group and SF's own Prizehog, enthusiastically described as 'dirgey doom pop slowcore!' (www.aquariusrecords.org; 1055 Valencia St; 10am-9pm Mon-Wed, to 10pm Thu-Sun; 18th St; S 16th St Mission)

NooWorks
CLOTHING

43 Map p130, B2

Artist-designed graphic prints make NooWorks the cream of the Mission's new crop of designers. A 1930s Mayan print adds a Mission edge to easygoing cotton minis, buttery-soft teal leather hobo bags hold the obligatory sweater for SF club nights, and surreal men's tees featuring a bewigged Bach cat are good to go to any gallery. (www.nooworks.com; 395 Valencia St; 11am-5pm Sun-Mon, 11am-7pm Sat; S 16th St Mission)

Mission Skateboards
CLOTHING & ACCESSORIES, SPORTING GOODS

44 Map p130, D7

Street creds come easy with locally designed Mission decks, custom tees to kick-flip over, and cult shoes at this shop owned by SF street-skate legend Scot Thompson. This shop is handy to La Raza Skatepark (p133) – and for newbies too cool for kneepads, SF General. Check their website for events, including street races and documentary premieres. (www.missionsk8boards.com; 3045 24th St; 11am-7pm; S 24th St Mission)

Accident & Artifact
GIFTS, ACCESSORIES

45 Map p130, B2

A most curious curiosity shop, even by Mission standards. Decorative dried fungi and redwood burls make regular appearances on farm-table displays, alongside patched Okinawan indigo textiles, cast-iron factory molds, sketches on topographical maps and the odd antler-topped taxidermied TV. Better curated than most galleries, and priced accordingly. (www.accidentandartifact.com; 381 Valencia St; noon-6pm Thu-Sun; S 16th St Mission)

Voyager
GIFTS, ACCESSORIES

46 Map p130, B2

Post-apocalyptic art-school surf-shack is the general vibe at this art-installation storefront gallery. The communal love-child of Revolver (p158) and Mollusk (p176) plus sundry Mission bookstores and galleries, items for sale range from 1970s rough leather belts and cultish Dutch Scotch and Soda jeans to surfboards and some 5000 art books. (http://thevoyagershop.com; 365 Valencia St; noon-7pm Sun-Fri, to 10pm Fri-Sat; S 16th St Mission)

Dema
CLOTHING, LOCAL DESIGNER

47 Map p130, B6

BART from Downtown lunches to Mission art openings in vintage-inspired chic by San Francisco's own Dema Grimm. House specialties are flattering bias-cut dresses and floaty silk blouses in original prints, with buttons that look like gumdrops. Like any original designs, Dema's limited editions aren't dirt-cheap – but check bins and sales racks for deals up to 80% off. (www.godemago.com; 1038 Valencia St; 11am-7pm Mon-Fri, noon-7pm Sat, noon-6pm Sun; S 24th St Mission)

Local Life
The History-Making Castro

Within a few years of moving into this quaint Victorian neighborhood in the 1970s, the Castro's out-and-proud community elected Harvey Milk as the nation's first gay official. When AIDS hit, the Castro wiped its tears and got to work, advocating interventions that saved lives worldwide. Today the little neighborhood under the giant rainbow flag is a global symbol of freedom; come out and see for yourself.

Getting There

The Castro is a couple of blocks west of the Mission between 15th and 18th Sts.

M Streetcar Take the scenic above-ground F line from downtown, or underground K, L, and M lines.

Bus No 33 connects to the upper Haight; 24 runs up Divisadero St to the Haight.

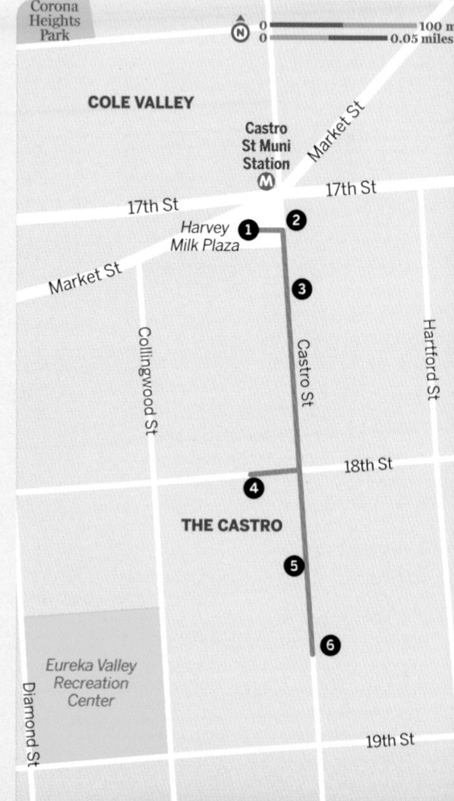

❶ Harvey Milk Plaza

A huge, irrepressibly cheerful rainbow flag greets arrivals on Muni to this **plaza** (Market & Castro Sts), named for the camera-store owner who became the nation's first openly gay official. Across Castro St, the public seating by the F-train terminus is a good place take in local color – including the occasional spray-tanned local nudists. Welcome to the Castro.

❷ Twin Peaks Tavern

Somewhere over the giant neon rainbow is **Twin Peaks** (www.twinpeakstavern.com; 401 Castro St; ⏲noon-2am Mon-Fri, 8am-2am Sat & Sun), the first gay bar in the world with windows opening to the street. Raise a toast to freedom, watch the gay world go by, and join the inevitable sing-a-long whenever an '80s anthem hits the jukebox.

❸ Castro Theatre

At the deco-fabulous **Castro Theatre** (www.thecastrotheatre.com; 429 Castro St; adult/child $10/7.50), show tunes on a Wurlitzer are overtures to independent cinema, silver-screen classics and unstoppable audience participation. Everyone cheers as the organist plays the city's anthem, *San Francisco Open Your Golden Gate* – (sing along, now): 'San Francisco open your Golden Gate/You let no stranger wait outside your door...' – written by Bronislaw Kaper, Walter Jurmann and Gus Kahn for the 1936 film *San Francisco*

❹ GLBT History Museum

America's first gay-history museum, **GLBT History Museum** (www.glbthistory.org/museum; 4127 18th St; admission $5, free 1st Wed of month; ⏲11am-7pm Tue-Sat, noon-5pm Sun-Mon) captures proud moments and historic challenges: Harvey Milk's campaign literature, interviews with trailblazing bisexual author Gore Vidal, matchbooks from long-gone bathhouses and 1950s penal codes banning homosexuality.

❺ Under One Roof

All the fabulous gifts at **Under One Roof** (www.underoneroof.org; 518a Castro St) are donated by local designers and businesses, so AIDS service organizations get 100% of the proceeds from your etched San Francisco–skyline martini glasses and adorable Jonathan Adler vase. Those sweet sales clerks are volunteers, so show them some love for raising – get this – $11 million to date.

❻ Human Rights Campaign Action Center & Store

If the storefront home of the **Human Rights Campaign** (www.hrc.org; 575 Castro St) seems familiar, there's a reason: this was once Harvey Milk's camera shop, as featured in the Academy Award–winning movie *Milk*. The civil rights advocacy outpost features a stunning mural, plus marriage-equality petitions and 'Equality' statement tees by Marc Jacobs for HRC.

Explore

The Haight

Was it the fall of 1966 or the winter of '67? As the Haight saying goes, if you can remember the Summer of Love, man, you probably weren't here. But it's not too late to join the revolution at radical cafes and bookstores, or make the scene at Haight and Ashbury Sts – the street corner that became the turning point of a generation.

The Sights in a Day

Start with an eye-opening, rabble-rousing mocha at **Coffee to the People** (p153) before taking on the **walking tour** (p180) to spot landmarks from the Haight's hippie heyday, including the heart of the Summer of Love: **Haight & Ashbury** (p150).

After restorative organic pub fare and a homebrew sampler at **Magnolia Brewpub** (p152), try on a few new alter egos for size on Haight Street: bejeweled Victorian Goth at **Loved to Death** (p158), wet-suited SF surfer at **Aqua Surf Shop** (p158), feather-boa drag diva at **Piedmont Boutique** (p157; pictured left), manifesto-wielding radical at **Bound Together Anarchist Book Collective** (p156), decked-out skater at **SFO Snowboarding & FTC Skateboarding** (p159), or fedora-wearing jazz bassist at **Goorin Brothers Hats** (p157). Troll Divisadero boutiques on the way up to **Alamo Square** (p150) for a breather, golden views of downtown behind a jagged Victorian roofline and a visit to the shoe-planter garden.

Head downhill to the lower Haight for sausages from **Rosamunde** (p150) to be enjoyed with a microbrew at **Toronado** (p154) – just try not to let the 400-beer selection distract you from showtime at the **Independent** (p156).

Best of San Francisco

Drinks

Toronado (p154)

Alembic (p154)

Aub Zam Zam (p154)

Coffee to the People (p153)

Shopping

Amoeba (p157)

Piedmont (p157)

Wasteland (p156)

Architecture

Alamo Square (p150)

Freebies

Concerts at Amoeba (p157)

Live Music

Independent (p156)

Getting There

Bus Buses 6 and 71 run up Haight St; 22 links to the Mission and Marina; 24 to the Castro; 43 to the Marina; 33 to Castro and Golden Gate Park.

Streetcar N Judah runs through the Haight.

A
B
C
D
1
2
3
4
5
Turk Blvd
Golden Gate Ave
McAllister St
Fulton St
Grove St
Hayes St
Fell St
Oak St
Page St
Waller St
Beulah St
Frederick St
Java St
Baker St
Parker Ave
Shrader St
Cole St
Clayton St
Ashbury St
Central Ave
Lyon St
Masonic Ave
Downey St
Belvedere St
Buena Vista Ave W
University of San Francisco
University of San Francisco
UPPER HAIGHT
The Panhandle
Haight & Ashbury
Grateful Dead House
COLE VALLEY
1
3
8
12
13
15
18
19
23
25
26
27
28
29
30
32
35
36
37

E
F
G
H
0 400 m
0 0.2 miles
1
2
3
4
5
McAllister St
Fulton St
Grove St
Broderick St
Divisadero St
Scott St
Alamo Square
2 Alamo Square
Grove St
Hayes St
6
24
11
21
Fell St
LOWER HAIGHT
Oak St
Broderick St
20
10
14
Page St
Pierce St
Steiner St
Fillmore St
9
31
16
22
17
5
7
33
Haight St
Laussat St
Waller St
34
Baker St
Buena Vista Park
Buena Vista Ave E
Castro St
Scott St
Hermann St
Duboce Park
Duboce Ave
4 Buena Vista Park
Alpine Tce
Divisadero St
Park Hill Ave
14th St
Noe St
Henry St
15th St
For reviews see
Sights p150
Eating p150
Drinking p153
Entertainment p156
Shopping p156

Sights

Haight & Ashbury LANDMARK

1 Map p148, C4

This legendary intersection was the epicenter of the psychedelic '60s and remains a counterculture magnet. On average Saturdays here you can sign Green Party petitions, commission a poem, hear Hare Krishna on keyboards and Bob Dylan on banjo. The clock overhead always reads 4:20 – better known in herbal circles as International Bong-Hit Time. A local clockmaker recently fixed it; within a week it was stuck at 4:20. (Haight St)

Alamo Square PARK

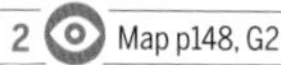

2 Map p148, G2

Weather-beaten picnic tables provide sweeping panoramas of City Hall's gilded dome and Postcard Row, a line-up of Victorian 'Painted Lady' houses on Steiner St with gingerbread detailing and frosting flourishes. Below windswept pines at the crest of the hill is a neighborhood art project: old shoes creatively reused as planters, including silver platforms sprouting succulents and ferns in work boots. (Cnr Hayes & Scott Sts; Hayes St)

Grateful Dead House HISTORIC BUILDING

3 Map p148, C4

Hippies may dimly recognize this candy-colored Victorian from the 1960s, when it was a flophouse where the Grateful Dead blew minds, amps and brain cells until the cops raided the place. The new owners would be most Grateful if everyone paid their respects with the silence of the Dead instead of singing, but commemorative dancing bears chalked on the sidewalk are fine. (710 Ashbury St; Haight St)

Buena Vista Park PARK

4 Map p148, E4

True to its name, this park – founded in 1867 – offers sweeping views of the city and the Golden Gate Bridge framed by century-old cypresses as a reward for hiking all the way up the steep hill. Hanging around after the park closes at sunset for boozing or cruising is risky, however, given recent criminal activity at night. (Haight St btwn Central Ave & Baker St; sunrise-sunset; Haight St)

Eating

Rosamunde Sausage Grill SAUSAGES $

5 Map p148, H3

Impress a dinner date on the cheap – load up classic Brats or duck-fig links with complimentary roasted peppers, grilled onions, whole-grain mustard and mango chutney, and wash it all down with your choice of 200 microbrews next door at Toronado (p154). (545 Haight St; sausages $4-6; 11:30am-10pm; Fillmore St)

Understand

Flower Power

The flower power movement kicked off in San Francisco with two critical miscalculations by Joe McCarthy and the CIA. McCarthy chose San Francisco City Hall as the location to expose alleged communists in 1960. UC Berkeley students organized a disruptive, sing-along sit-in on City Hall steps, and police turned fire hoses on them. Thousands rallied in outrage, and when McCarthy left town in a hurry, it marked the beginning of the end of the repressive McCarthy era.

In a pronounced lapse in screening judgment, the CIA hired local writer Ken Kesey to test psychoactive drugs intended to create the ultimate soldier. Instead, they unwittingly inspired Kesey to write the novel *One Flew Over the Cuckoo's Nest,* drive psychedelic busloads of Merry Pranksters across country, and introduce San Francisco to LSD and the Grateful Dead. Another LSD tester hired by the CIA, Stewart Brand, proposed an outrageous idea inspired by his LSD experiments: the complex technology governments used could empower ordinary people. The machines would be called 'personal computers.'

With free-thinking and futuristic visions, San Francisco seemed the obvious place to begin the Civil Rights era, build a new society and end the Vietnam War. At the January 14, 1967 Human Be-In in Golden Gate Park, trip-master Timothy Leary urged a crowd of 20,000 to 'turn on, tune in, drop out.' Free music filled Haight St, free food was distributed by the Diggers, free LSD supplied by Owsley Stanley, and free love transpired on dubious free mattresses at free Haight crash-pads.

A chill settled over San Francisco when civil rights hero Martin Luther King Jr was assassinated on April 8, 1968, an event followed by the fatal shooting of Robert Kennedy on June 5. Radicals worldwide called for revolution, and Oakland's Black Panther Party for Self-Defense took up arms. Meanwhile, recreational drug-taking was turning into a thankless career for many and a distinct itch in the nether regions made the rounds. By the time Owsley Stanley was released from a three-year jail term in 1970, the party seemed to be over – but many idealists headed 'back to the land' to found California's organic farm movement.

Bar Crudo

SEAFOOD $$

6 Map p148, F2

An international idea that's pure California: choice morsels of fresh seafood served raw Italian-style, with pan-Asian condiments and East-West beers. Start with Japanese Hitachino white ale and raw fluke with coconut milk and grapefruit, and graduate to potent Belgian Tripel ales with wasabi-spiked Arctic char. Don't miss Tuesday–Sunday happy hour from 5pm to 6:30pm, when specials include such treats as $1 local oysters. (www.barcrudo.com; 655 Divisadero St; small plates $10-14; 5-11pm Mon-Sat, to 10pm Sun; Divisidero St)

Three Twins

ICE CREAM $

7 Map p148, H3

Lower Haight's kids, locavores and pot-club regulars agree: Three Twins makes the creamiest organic ice creams around. Fall means Cardamom, winter is an excuse for Meyer Lemon Cookie, spring brings Honey Orange Blossom, and summer is Strawberry Je Ne Sais Quoi, with a dash of balsamic vinegar. For a taste sensation, get bittersweet chocolate drizzled with Sonoma olive oil and sea salt. At the time of research Three Twins was closed due to a building fire, but they plan to reopen in 2012. (www.threetwinsicecream.com; 254 Fillmore St; cone $2.25-3.25; noon-10:30pm Mon-Thu, 11am-11pm Fri-Sat, 11am-10:30pm Sun; Haight St)

Magnolia Brewpub

CALIFORNIAN, AMERICAN $$

8  Map p148, C4

Organic pub grub, homebrews and an easygoing attitude warms the hippie heart of the Haight. Join the communal table, try beer samplers and consult your neighbors on the all-local menu – bet they'll recommend grass-fed Prather Ranch burgers. Magnolia smells vaguely like a brewery because it is one, which can be off-putting at brunch – until you've tried the micro-brewed ales and wheat beer. (www.magnoliapub.com; 1398 Haight St; mains $11-20; noon-midnight Mon-Thu, to 1am Fri, 10am-1am Sat, 10am-midnight Sun; Haight St)

Axum

ETHIOPIAN $

9  Map p148, G3

When you've got SF surfer munchies or a hot date with a vegan, Axum's vegetarian platter for two is your saving grace; generous dollops of lip-tingling red lentils, fiery mushrooms and mellow yellow chickpeas, scooped up with spongy *injera* bread. (www.axumcafe.com; 698 Haight St; mains $7-14; 5:30-10pm Mon-Fri, 12:30-10pm Sat-Sun; Haight St;)

Ragazza

PIZZA $$

10  Map p148, F3

'Girl' is what the name means, as in, 'Oooh, *girl*, did you try the nettle pizza?!' Since it comes with local Boccalone pancetta, Portobello mushrooms and nutty provolone, you definitely should. Squash blossom pizza with truffle cheese keeps vegetarians happy, though a glass of Greco di Tufo couldn't hurt. (www.ragazzasf.com; 311 Divisadero St; pizza $13-18; 5-10pm Mon-Thu, to 10:30 Fri-Sat; Divisadero St;)

Ziryab
MIDDLE EASTERN $$

11 Map p148, F2

Replace all your old traumatic memories of dry chicken *shwarmas* with a new taste of juicy organic poultry rolled in flatbread and sealed by hummus with a tantalizing whiff of curry. The vegan lentil soup is so robust it'll make your voice drop an octave, and the hookahs on the front porch provide solace to smokers made fugitives by SF's antismoking laws. (www.ziryabgrill.com; 528 Divisadero St; mains $10-16; 4-11:30pm Mon-Thu, noon-12:30am Fri & Sat, noon-11pm Sun; Divisadero St;)

Cole Valley Cafe
SANDWICHES, SNACKS $

12 Map p148, A4

Restore your Haight St shopping stamina – and quite possibly your faith in humanity – with powerful coffee and chai, chocolate-chip pumpkin cake, fast free wi-fi, and bargain hot gourmet sandwiches – go with lip-smacking thyme-marinated chicken with lemony avocado spread, or smoky roasted eggplant with peppers and pesto. (www.colevalleycafe.com; 701 Cole St; sandwiches $5-6; 6:30am-8:30pm Mon-Fri, 6:30am-8pm Sat-Sun; Haight St, M Cole St;)

Escape from New York Pizza
PIZZA $

13 Map p148, A4

The Haight's obligatory mid-bender stop for a hot slice. Pesto with roasted garlic and potato will send you blissfully off to carbo-loaded sleep, but the sundried tomato with goat cheese, artichoke hearts and spinach will recharge you to go another round. (www.escapefromnewyorkpizza.com; 1737 Haight St; slices $3-4; 11:30am-midnight Sun-Thu, to 2am Fri & Sat; Haight St;)

Little Chihuahua
MEXICAN $

14 Map p148, F3

Who says sustainable, organic food has to be expensive or French? Charbroiled tomatillos, sustainable fish, Niman Ranch meats and organic veggies make these NorCal tacos, washed down with $3 draft beer or housemade, organic *agua fresca* (fruit drink). (www.thelittlechihuahua.com; 292 Divisadero St; tacos $4, burritos $7; 11am-11pm Mon-Fri, 10am-11pm Sat-Sun; Divisadero St)

Drinking

Coffee to the People
CAFE

15 Map p148, C4

The people, united, will never be decaffeinated at this utopian coffee shop with macramé on the walls, leftist bumper stickers covering tables, a social-change reading library, and 5% of your vegan muffin purchase pledged to community organizations – plus enough fair-trade coffee to revive the Sandinista movement. (1206 Masonic Ave; 6am-8pm Mon-Fri, 6am-9pm Sat & Sun; Haight St;)

Noc Noc

BAR

16 Map p148, H3

Who's there? Dreadlocked graffiti artists, electronica DJs and Mad Max–inspired fashion designers, that's who. This place looks like a post-apocalyptic cave dwelling designed by Tim Burton, and serves a sake cocktail that'll keep you buzzed until the next Burning Man. Beer and sake drinks only; bring cash. (www.nocnocs.com; 557 Haight St; 5pm-2am; Haight St)

Toronado

PUB

17 Map p148, H3

Glory hallelujah! Beer lovers, your prayers have been heard. Be humbled before the chalkboard altar, which lists 50-plus beers on tap and hundreds more bottled, including spectacular seasonal microbrews. Bring cash, come early and stay late, with a sausage from Rosamunde (p150) next door to accompany ale made by Trappist monks. (www.toronado.com; 547 Haight St; 11:30am-2am; Fillmore St)

Top Tip

Doctors & Dope

Medical marijuana use is legal in California – and common around Haight St – but only with a doctor's prescription and mandatory waiting period (sorry, dude).

Alembic

BAR

18 Map p148, A4

Haight St's spiffiest, tiniest bar has hammered tin ceilings, rough-hewn wood floors and 250 choices of specialty hooch – plus throngs of artisan bourbon drinkers and cocktail research historians proudly standing behind the 'No Red Bull/No Jagermeister' sign. Bar snacks here aren't elementary peanuts, but advanced-degree artisan cheeses, pickled quail eggs and iced duck hearts. (www.alembicbar.com; 1725 Haight St; noon-2am; Haight St)

Aub Zam Zam

LOUNGE

19 Map p148, B4

Arabesque arches, an *Arabian Nights*–style mural, 1930s jazz on the jukebox and top-shelf cocktails at low-shelf prices keep restless romantics coming back to this Haight St mainstay. Legendary founder Bruno was a character who'd throw you out for ordering a vodka martini, but he was a softie in the end, bequeathing his beloved bar to regulars who had become friends. Cash only. (1633 Haight St; 3pm-2am; Haight St)

Vinyl Wine Bar

WINE BAR

20 Map p148, F3

Combine three food trends – gourmet food trucks, wine on tap, and pop-up restaurants – swirl vigorously, and

Toronado

voilà: Vinyl Wine Bar. By day it's a cafe, but at night trucked-in culinary options ranging from fresh pasta to soul food present pairing possibilities: try Austrian Grüner Veltliner with grits, or invent your own Sangiovese blend to accompany asparagus ravioli. Check Vinyl's Facebook page for featured foods. (www.facebook.com/vinylwinebar; 359 Divisadero St; 5:30-11pm Mon-Thu, to midnight Fri-Sun; Divisadero St)

Madrone

LOUNGE

21 Map p148, F2

A changing roster of DJs and giggling cuties come as a surprise in a Victorian bar decorated with rotating art installations and a tree-trunk bar, complete with a bomb-shaped disco ball and an absinthe fountain, but nothing tops the jaw-dropping mashups at the monthly Prince vs Michael Jackson party, when the place packs. (www.madronelounge.com; 500 Divisadero St; 5pm-2am Tue-Sat, 6pm-2am Sun-Mon; Divisadero St)

Uva Enoteca

WINE BAR

22 Map p148, H3

Boys with shags and girls with bangs discover the joys of Bardolino and Barbera by the tasting glass, served with inventive small plates of local veggies, cheese and charcuterie boards by a staff of tattooed Lower Haight hotties. (www.uvaenoteca.com; 568 Haight St; 5-11pm Mon-Thu, 5-11:30pm Fri, 11am-2:30pm & 5-11:30pm Sat, 11am-2:30pm & 5-10pm Sun; Fillmore St)

Entertainment

Booksmith

LITERARY EVENTS

23 Map p148, B4

SF is one of America's top three book markets, and authors who swing through town on tours make Booksmith's Author Series a literary destination. Recent readings include *Sandman* and *Coraline* author Neil Gaiman, legendary rock critic Greil Marcus and controversial 'tiger mother' Amy Chua. Check the online calendar for book swaps and Saturday morning kids' story hour. (www.booksmith.com; 1644 Haight St; 10am-10pm Mon-Sat, to 8pm Sun; Haight St;)

Independent

LIVE MUSIC

24 Map p148, F2

One of the city's coolest live-music venues, the Independent showcases funky soul acts (Nikka Costa, Sergent Garcia), indie dreamers (Kimya Dawson, Blonde Redhead), and cult rock (Meat Puppets, Ted Nugent), plus such wacky events as the US Air Guitar Championships. Ventilation is poor, but drinks are cheap. (www.theindependentsf.com; 628 Divisadero St; tickets $13-20; box office 11am-6pm Mon-Fri, to 9:30pm show nights, doors 7:30pm or 8:30pm; Divisadero St)

Top Tip

Highs & Lows

The Lower Haight has better bars than Upper Haight, more economic and ethnic diversity, and a pot-club mellow occasionally disrupted by gang activity northeast of Fillmore and Haight Sts.

Shopping

Bound Together Anarchist Book Collective

BOOKS

25 Map p148, C4

You don't have to be a lifetime subscriber to *Eat the State* to be awed by this vast selection of free speech, from off-the-grid homesteading manuals to radical comics. Since 1976, this volunteer-run nonprofit bookstore has kept regular hours, coordinated the Anarchist Book Fair and expanded its 'Anarchists of the Americas' storefront mural – makes us tools of the state look like slackers. (http://boundtogetherbookstore.com; 1369 Haight St; 11:30am-7:30pm; Haight St)

Wasteland

CLOTHING

26 Map p148, B4

Flashbacks come with the territory at Wasteland, a cinema converted into a vintage emporium of trippy '60s maxi-dresses, '70s Frye boots, '80s extra-wide belts, and '90s grunge rock T-shirts. Hip occasionally verges on hideous with fringed vests and pirate shirts, but at these prices, you can afford to take fashion risks. (www.wastelandclothing.com; 1660 Haight St; 11am-8pm Mon-Sat, noon-7pm Sun; Haight St)

Amoeba Records

MUSIC

27 Map p148, A4

Enticements are hardly necessary to lure the masses to the West Coast's most eclectic collection of new and used music and video, but Amoeba offers listening stations, a free music zine with uncannily accurate reviews, a free concert series that recently starred Elvis Costello and Shonen Knife, and a foundation that's saved over 1000 acres of rainforest. (www.amoeba.com; 1855 Haight St; 10:30am-10pm Mon-Sat, 11am-9pm Sun; Haight St)

Piedmont Boutique

CLOTHING, ACCESSORIES

28 Map p148, C4

Glam up or get out at this supplier of drag fabulousness: faux-fur hot pants, airplane earrings and a wall of feather boas. These getups aren't cheap, honey, because they're custom-designed in-house, built to last and in demand by cabaret singers, cross-dressers, Burning Man devotees, strippers and people who take Halloween very seriously – in other words, everyone in SF. (www.piedmontsf.com; 1452 Haight St; 11am-7pm; Haight St)

Loyal Army Clothing

CLOTHING, ACCESSORIES

29 Map p148, A4

Food with high self-esteem is a recurring theme on this San Francisco designer's cartoon-cute tees, totes and baby clothes: a bag of chips says, 'All that and me!' while California sushi rolls brag, 'That's how we roll!' But the most popular character is the San Francisco fogbank: most clouds are silver and smiling, but there's always one that has fangs. (www.loyalarmy.com; 1728 Haight St; 11am-7pm Mon-Sat, 11:30am-7pm Sun; Haight St;)

Goorin Brothers Hats

ACCESSORIES

30 Map p148, C4

Peacock feathers, high crowns and local-artist-designed embellishments make it easy for SF hipsters to withstand the fog while standing out in a crowd. Straw fedoras with striped tie-silk bands throw shade in style, and flat-brim baseball caps have an added edge with warrior embroidery by Hawaiian San Franciscan tattoo artist Orly Lacquiao. (www.goorin.com; 1446 Haight St; 11am-7pm Sun-Fri, to 8pm Sat; Haight St)

Xapno

GIFTS

31 Map p148, G3

Antique typewriter ribbon tins, clove cigarette perfume, succulents dripping from hanging nautilus shells: such unusual gifts lead grateful recipients to believe you've spent weeks and small fortunes in San Francisco curiosity shops. But Xapno regularly stocks rare finds at reasonable prices, and will wrap them for you too. Hours are erratic. (www.xapno.com; 678 Haight St; 11am-7pm Tue-Thu & Sun, Fri-Sat 10am-9pm; Haight St)

Understand

Street Scene on Haight

Ever since the 1960s, America's youth have headed to the Haight as a place to fit in, no questions asked. Yet in 2010, San Francisco passed the controversial Sit/Lie Law, making daytime sidewalk loitering punishable by $50 to $100 fines. Critics claim the law targets vulnerable homeless teens in the Haight – with 1300 shelter beds to accommodate 6500 to 13,000 city homeless, many youth have no place to go. Spare change is a short-term fix; for sustained support, consider donations to youth-service nonprofits.

Loved to Death — GIFTS

32 Map p148, B4

Herds of dead deer stare from the walls alongside *ex voto* miniatures and a rusty saw – the signs at this ghoulish gallery are definitely ominous. And the Victorian hair lockets and beetle brooches are not for the faint of heart, or vegans – though as proprietors point out, no animal has been killed specifically for these designs. (www.lovedtodeath.net; 1681 Haight St; 11:30-7pm Mon-Sat, noon-7 Sun; Haight St)

Upper Playground — CLOTHING, LOCAL DESIGNER

33 Map p148, H3

Score instant street cred at this local designer of San Francisco skater chic with 'Left Coast' hoodies, Muni stocking caps, and collegiate pennants for city neighborhoods (the Tenderloin totally needs a cheering section). Men's gear dominates, but there are women's tees and children's tees out in the back room, and you'll find slick graffiti art in Fifty24SF Gallery next door. (www.upperplayground.com; 220 Fillmore St; noon-7pm; Haight St)

Revolver — CLOTHING, ACCESSORIES

34 Map p148, H3

Entering this boutique is a little like wandering into the bedroom of some stoner-dandy Wild Western novelist, with piles of raw denim and organic cotton cowboy shirts strewn all across wooden crates. The rear gallery is wallpapered with maps, strung with feisty air plants in glass terrariums, and stocked with American-made suede saddle shoes and Japanese linen sundresses. (www.bluebirdcollection.com; 136 Fillmore St; noon-8pm; Haight St)

Aqua Surf Shop — SURF GEAR

35 Map p148, A4

You will find no locals-only attitude here; this laid-back, tiki-themed surf shop has sex wax for your board, reversible polka-dot bikinis, and signature hoodies for you to wear whilst braving chilly Ocean Beach. Even kooks (newbies) become mavericks with Aqua's wetsuit rentals, tide updates and lesson referrals. (www.aquasurfshop.com; 1742 Haight St; board/wetsuit rental per day $25/15; 11am-7pm; Haight St)

Loyal Army Clothing (p157)

Braindrops

TATTOOS & BODY JEWELRY

36  Map p148, D4

New Yorkers and Berliners fly in for original custom designs by top tattoo artists here – bring design ideas to your consultant, or trust them to make suggestions. Piercings are done here gently without a gun, with body jewelry ranging from pop-star opal belly-button studs to mondo jade ear spools. (www.braindrops.net; 1324 Haight St; noon-7pm Sun-Thu, to 8pm Fri & Sat; Haight St)

SFO Snowboarding & FTC Skateboarding

OUTDOOR GEAR

37 Map p148, B4

Big moves and big style are the tip at this local snowboard and skateboard outfitter. Show some local flair as you grab air on a Western Edition deck with drawings of ramshackle Victorians, or hit the slopes with Tahoe-tested gear (mostly for dudes, some unisex). Ask skater/boarder staff about upcoming SF street games and Tahoe snow conditions. (www.sfosnow.com; 1630-32 Haight St; 11am-7pm; Haight St)

Explore

Golden Gate Park & the Avenues

When other Americans want an extreme experience, they head to San Francisco – but when San Franciscans go to extremes, they end up here. Surfers brave walls of water on blustery Ocean Beach, runners try to keep pace with the stampeding bison in Golden Gate Park and dim sum gluttons have one more round of dumplings in Sunset or Richmond, the family-friendly neighborhoods along the park.

The Sights in a Day

Head out to **Ocean Beach** (p168) early to catch SF's daredevil surfers, then join wet-suited mavericks at **Trouble Coffee** (p174). Pick up a local-designer hoodie at **Mollusk** (p176) before hopping the N Judah to 9th Ave to **Strybing Arboretum** (p168). Hang out with blue butterflies in the rainforest dome at the **California Academy of Sciences** (p162), and visit outer space in the **Morrison Planetarium** (p163) before a sustainable dim sum lunch in the **Academy Cafe** (p163).

Globe-trot from Egyptian goddesses to James Turrell light installations in **MH de Young Memorial Museum** (p164), then enjoy a Zen moment in the **Japanese Tea Garden** (p168). Summit Strawberry Hill for views over **Stow Lake** (p170) to the Pacific. Next, hop bus 44 to browse books at **Green Apple** (p177) and gifts at **Park Life** (p176), and get the 2 Clement bus to see sculpture and radical comics at the **Legion of Honor** (p168). If you've still got stretch in those legs, follow the trailhead from the Legion to end-of-the-world sunsets at **Sutro Baths** (p170).

As the evening fog rolls in, hop the 38 Geary bus to tropical cocktails at **Trad'r Sam's** (p175) and organic Moroccan-Californian feasts at **Aziza** (p170).

Top Sights

California Academy Of Sciences (p162)

MH de Young Memorial Museum (p164)

Best of San Francisco

Outdoors

Golden Gate Park (p169, pictured left)

Ocean Beach (p168)

Coastal Trail (p177)

Stow Lake (p170)

Strybing Arboretum & Botanical Gardens (p168)

Bargain Gourmet

Outerlands (p171)

Namu (p171)

Spices (p173)

Academy Cafe (p162)

Getting There

Bus Nos 1 and 38 run from Downtown. Buses 5 and 21 head along the north edge of the park. Bus 2 runs along Clement St. Bus 71 follows alongside the park to the south.

M Streetcar The N train runs from Downtown.

Top Sights

California Academy of Sciences

Leave it to San Francisco to dedicate a glorious four-story monument entirely to freaks of nature. Architect Renzo Piano's 2008 landmark Platinum LEED-certified green building houses 38,000 weird and wonderful animals, with a four-story rainforest and underground aquarium under a 'living roof' of California wildflowers.

Map p166, G3

www.calacademy.org

55 Music Concourse Dr, inside Golden Gate Park

adult/child $29.95/24.95

9:30am-5pm Mon-Sat, 11am-5pm Sat

M 9th Ave

Displays inside the California Academy of Sciences

Don't Miss

Collections

The Academy's tradition of weird science dates from 1853 and has expanded to include thousands of live animals. Butterflies flutter through the glass Rainforest Dome, a rare white alligator stalks a swamp and Pierre the Penguin paddles the tank in the African Hall.

Steinhart Aquarium

In the basement aquarium kids duck inside a glass bubble to enter an eel forest, find Nemos in the tropical-fish tanks and befriend starfish in the aquatic petting zoo. Premier attractions include the California aquaculture wall, the walk-in tropical fish theatre, columns of golden sea dragons and the shy giant pink Pacific octopus.

Architecture

To make the Academy the world's greenest museum, Pritzker Prize–winning architect Renzo Piano creatively repurposed the original neoclassical facade while adding a 2.5 acre wildflower-covered roof, polka-dotted with solar panels and air vents.

Morrison Planetarium

Glimpse into infinity under the massive digital projection dome and take a half-hour virtual journey through ancient forests and billions of years to explore the earliest signs of life in the universe.

Wild Nights at the Academy

After the penguins nod off to sleep, the wild rumpus starts at kids-only Academy Sleepovers. At over-21 NightLife Thursdays, rainforest-themed cocktails are served. Book ahead online.

Top Tips

- Crowds are biggest on weekends, at 21+ Thursday NightLife events (admission $10; 6–10pm) and Academy sleepovers. Weekday afternoons are quieter.
- Download the free *The Academy Insider* iPhone app for a self-guided tour of the Academy's collections.
- Take public transportation to the Academy and get $3 off admission by showing your Muni ticket.
- Avoid the $5 surcharge applied during holidays and other peak periods by pre-ordering tickets online.

Take a Break

Academy Cafe features treats made with local, organically grown ingredients by award-winning SF chefs Loretta Keller and Charles Phan.

The Academy's **Moss Room** (www.themossroom.com; 11am-3pm daily & 5-9pm Thu-Sun) offers sustainable fine dining from chef Loretta Keller.

Top Sights
MH de Young Memorial Museum

Follow sculptor Andy Goldsworthy's artificial fault-line in the sidewalk into Herzog & de Meuron's faultlessly sleek, copper-clad building that's oxidizing green to blend into the park. But don't be fooled by the de Young's camouflaged exterior: the global art and fine craft shows boldly broaden artistic horizons, from Oceanic ceremonial masks to California sculptor Al Farrow's cathedrals built from bullets.

Map p166, F3

www.famsf.org/deyoung

50 Hagiwara Tea Garden Dr

adult/child under 12yr $10/free

9:30am–5:15pm Tue–Sun, to 8:45pm Fri

M 9th Ave

View from the Hamon Tower in the MH de Young Memorial Museum

Don't Miss

Collection

You can see all the way from contemporary California to ancient Egypt at the globally eclectic de Young, and you might spot uncanny similarities between Gerhard Richter's radical squeegee paintings and traditional Afghani rugs from the textile collection's 11,000-plus works. Upstairs, don't miss excellent modern photography and 19th-century Oceanic ceremonial oars, alongside African masks, Meso-American sculpture and meticulous California crafts.

Blockbuster Shows

The de Young's blockbuster basement shows range from Queen Nefertiti's treasures to Jean Paul Gaultier's sculptural chic. Traveling exhibits of fashion and ancient treasures are sometimes criticized as pandering to popular demand, but they're consistent with the de Young's mission to showcase global arts and crafts – and art shows here are also world-class, from scandalously sensual Venetian Renaissance paintings to Hiroshi Sugimoto's haunting time-lapse photographs.

Architecture

The oxidizing copper building keeps a deliberately low profile, but there's no denying that the new home of the MH de Young Museum by Swiss architects Herzog & de Meuron (of Tate Modern fame) is San Francisco's star architectural attraction – rivaled only by Renzo Piano's Academy of Sciences (p162), right across the Music Concourse. The seemingly abstract pattern of the de Young's perforated copper cladding is actually drawn from aerial photography of the park. Indoors, clever lightwells illuminate surprises around every corner.

☑ Top Tips

- The de Young offers exceptional freebies: free admission the first Tuesday of each month, children under 12 admitted free always, and admission to the tower viewing platform gratis for all.
- Take public transit and keep your Muni ticket for $2 off admission.
- Fridays are an arty party with live music, performances, film premieres and artists-in-residence mingling over cocktails. All events are free; admission applies to gallery access.
- The de Young bookstore has a well-curated selection of one-of-a-kind jewelry, home decor and fashion.

Take a Break

Take a breather with locally roasted coffee, California wine and creative menu items themed to match traveling shows in the **museum cafe** (9:30am-4:30pm Tue-Sun, to 8pm Fri), adjoining the sculpture garden.

A
B
C
D
1
2
3
4
5
PACIFIC OCEAN
Land's End
Deadman's Point
China Beach
Uncle Wish Mem Rd
Coastal Trail
Point Lobos
Lincoln Park
7
Legion of Honor
1
El Camino del Mar
Lincoln Park Golf Course
34th Ave
Fort Miley
Lincoln Park
Sutro Baths
8
Clement St
Point Lobos Ave
Geary Blvd
Lake St
California St
32nd Ave
30th Ave
29th Ave
28th Ave
27th Ave
25th Ave
24th Ave
25
28
THE RICHMOND
Anza St
Sutro Heights Park
48th Ave
47th Ave
46th Ave
45th Ave
44th Ave
43rd Ave
42nd Ave
41st Ave
40th Ave
39th Ave
38th Ave
37th Ave
36th Ave
35th Ave
34th Ave
33rd Ave
32nd Ave
31st Ave
Upper Great Hwy
La Playa St
Fulton St
North Lake
Spreckels Lake
John F Kennedy Dr
19
Golden Gate Municipal Golf Course
Golden Gate Park Equestrian Center & Stadium
Middle Dr W
Metson Lake
2
OCEAN BEACH
Ocean Beach
Great Hwy
Middle Lake
Martin Luther King Dr
Mallard Lake
South Lake
Lincoln Way
30
Irving St
29th Ave
28th Ave
27th Ave
26th Ave
25th Ave
Judah St
15
21
11
31
Sunset Blvd
THE SUNSET
Sunset Recreation Center
Lawton St

E
F
G
H
0 1 km
0 0.5 miles
Pacific Ave
Washington St
Clay St
Sacramento St
California St
Mountain Lake Park
Lake St
Iris Ave
Clement St
Arguello Blvd
Palm Ave
Jordan Ave
Parker Ave
Spruce St
Cook St
Geary Blvd
21st Ave
20th Ave
19th Ave
18th Ave
17th Ave
16th Ave
15th Ave
14th Ave
Funston Ave
12th Ave
11th Ave
10th Ave
6th Ave
5th Ave
4th Ave
3rd Ave
2nd Ave
Rossi Playground
University of San Francisco
Anza St
Park Presidio Blvd
Turk Blvd
Balboa St
Cabrillo St
9th Ave
8th Ave
7th Ave
Fulton St
Stanyan St
Conservatory Dr
MH de Young Memorial Museum
California Academy of Sciences
Conservatory of Flowers
Lily Pond
Oak St
Page St
Lloyd Lake
John F Kennedy Dr
Golden Gate Park
Japanese Tea Garden
Middle Dr E
Stow Lake
Stow Lake Dr
San Francisco Botanical Garden & Strybing Arboretum
Elk Glen Lake
Strybing Arboretum & Botanical Gardens
Bowling Green Dr
Kezar Dr
Lincoln Way
Frederick St
Hugo St
Carl St
Irving St
Parnassus Ave
Lawton St
24th Ave
23rd Ave
22nd Ave
For reviews see
Top Sights p162
Sights p168
Eating p170
Drinking p173
Entertainment p175
Shopping p176

Sights

Legion of Honor MUSEUM

1 Map p166, B1

A nude sculptor's model who married well and collected art with a passion, 'Big Alma' de Bretteville Spreckels gifted this museum to San Francisco as a tribute to Californians killed in France in WWI. Featured artworks range from Monet water lilies to John Cage soundscapes, Iraqi ivories to R Crumb comics – part of the Legion's Achenbach collection of 90,000 modern graphic artworks. (http://legionofhonor.famsf.org; 100 34th Ave; adult/child $10/6, $2 discount with Muni ticket, 1st Tue of month free; 9:30am-5:15pm Tue-Sun; Clement St)

Ocean Beach BEACH

2 Map p166, A4

The park ends in this blustery beach, too chilly for bikini-clad clambakes but ideal for wet-suited pro surfers braving rip tides (casual swimmers beware). Bonfires are permitted in artist-designed fire-pits only; no alcohol allowed. At the south end of the beach, beachcombers may spot sand dollars and the remains of a 19th century shipwreck. (www.parksconservancy.org; sunrise-sunset; M 48th Ave)

Strybing Arboretum & Botanical Gardens GARDEN

3 Map p166, F4

Sniff your way around the world inside this 70-acre garden, where there's always something blooming. The Garden of Fragrance is designed for the visually impaired, and the California native plant section explodes with color when native wildflowers bloom in early spring, right off the redwood trail. Free tours take place daily; for details, stop by the bookstore inside the entrance. (www.strybing.org; 1199 9th Ave; admission $7; 9am-6pm Apr-Oct, 10am-5pm Nov-Mar; M 9th Ave)

Japanese Tea Garden GARDEN

4 Map p166, F3

Mellow out in the Zen Garden, sip toasted-rice green tea overlooking a waterfall, and admire doll-sized trees that are pushing 100 years old. These bonsai are a credit to the Hagiwara family gardeners, who returned from WWII Japanese American internment camps to discover their bonsai were sold. The Hagiwaras spent the next two decades tracking down the trees and returning them to their rightful home. (http://japaneseteagardensf.com; Hagiwara Tea Garden Dr; adult/child $7/5, free Mon, Wed, Fri before 10am; 9am-6pm; Lincoln Blvd/9th Ave;)

Conservatory of Flowers GARDEN, HISTORIC BUILDING

5 Map p166, G3

Flower power is alive inside the newly restored 1878 Victorian conservatory, where orchids sprawl out like Bohemian divas, lilies float contemplatively and carnivorous plants reek of insect belches. (www.conservatoryofflowers.org; Conservatory Dr West; adult/child $7/2; sunrise-sunset; 10am-4pm Tue-Sun; Stanyan St)

Understand

Golden Gate Park

Everything that San Franciscans hold dear is in Golden Gate Park: free spirits, free music, redwoods, Frisbee, protests, fine art, bonsai and buffalo. On the northeast end of the park, you'll find Dahlia Garden, Conservatory of Flowers and the sheltered, contemplative valley of the AIDS Memorial Grove. On the southeast corner is a children's playground, while further west is a baseball diamond, pagan altars on the hill behind and the Shakespeare Garden, featuring 150 plants mentioned in Shakespeare's writings. To the west around Martin Luther King Jr Dr are the Polo Fields, where the 1967 Human Be-In took place and free concerts are still held. At the park's wild western edge, quixotic bison stampede in their paddock towards windmills and Ocean Beach sunsets.

History

In 1866, San Franciscans petitioned City Hall with an impossible demand: to transform 1017 acres of sand dunes into the world's largest developed park. The task scared off even Frederick Law Olmstead, who built New York's Central Park. Instead, San Francisco's green scheme was handed to 24-year-old San Franciscan engineer William Hammond Hall, who proved to be no pushover with casino developers, theme-park boosters and slippery politicians. During the 20-year park construction effort, he quit twice to protest schemes for racetracks, hotels and an igloo village, preserving precious parkland for botanical gardens, the Japanese Tea Garden and boating on scenic Stow Lake (p170). Though a local newspaper cautioned that its scenic benches led to 'excess hugging,' San Franciscans immediately flocked to the new park. On a single sunny day in 1886, almost a fifth of the city's entire population made the trip to the park.

Information

Today, free park walking tours are organized by Friends of Recreation & Parks (p211), and park information is available from McLaren Lodge (p211), under the splendid cypress that's the city's official tree.

Japanese Tea Garden (p168)

Stow Lake LAKE

6 Map p166, E4

Red-tailed hawks circle overhead as Huntington Falls tumbles down steep 400ft Strawberry Hill into the lake, near a romantic Chinese pavilion and a 1946 boathouse offering boat and bike rentals. (http://sfrecpark.org/StowLake.aspx; per hr paddleboats/canoes/rowboats/tandem bikes/bikes $24/20/19/15/8; sunrise-sunset, rentals 10am-4pm; M 9th Ave)

Lincoln Park PARK

7 Map p166, B1

The official western terminus of the cross-country Lincoln Highway is the beginning of the 9-mile Coastal Trail, with a trailhead north of the Legion of Honor. A partially paved path covers wooded coastline around Land's End, with views of Golden Gate Bridge and low-tide sightings of coastal shipwrecks along the 45-minute hike to Sutro Baths. (Clement St; admission free; sunrise-sunset; Clement St)

Sutro Baths PARK

8 Map p166, A2

Hard to imagine from these ruins, but Victorian dandies and working stiffs converged here for bracing baths and workouts in itchy wool rental swimsuits. Millionaire Adolph Sutro built indoor hot and cold pools to accommodate 10,000 unwashed masses c1896, but the masses apparently preferred dirt – the baths closed in 1952. Head through the sea-cave archway at low tide for end-of-the-world views of Marin Headlands. (sunrise-sunset; www.nps.gov/prsf; 48th Ave)

Eating

Aziza CALIFORNIAN, MOROCCAN $$

9 Map p166, E2

Mourad Lahlou's inspiration is Moroccan and his produce organic Californian, but his flavors are out of this world: Sonoma duck confit melts into caramelized onion in flaky pastry *basteeya* (chicken pie), while sour cherries rouse slow-cooked local lamb shank from its barley bed – and pastry chef Melissa Chou's Moroccan-mint-tea Bavarian deserves its own landmark. (www.azizasf.com; 5800 Geary Blvd; mains $16-29; 5:30-10:30pm Wed-Mon; Geary Blvd;)

Namu

KOREAN/CALIFORNIAN $$

10 Map p166, G2

Organic ingredients, Silicon Valley inventiveness and Pacific Rim roots are showcased in Korean-inspired soul food, including housemade kimchee, umami-rich shitake mushroom dumplings and NorCal's original farm-to-table *bibimbap:* organic vegetables, grass-fed steak and Sonoma farm egg served in a sizzling stone pot. The drink menu stresses soju, but try Natural Process Alliance's organic Napa Sauvignon Blanc wine, dispensed from a metal canteen. (www.namusf.com; 439 Balboa St; small plates $8-16; 6-10:30pm Sun-Tue, 6pm-midnight Wed-Sat, 10:30am-3pm Sat-Sun; Balboa St)

Outerlands

CALIFORNIAN $$

11 Map p166, B5

When windy Ocean Beach leaves you feeling shipwrecked, drift into this beach-shack bistro for organic California comfort food. Lunch means a $9 grilled artisan cheese combo with seasonal housemade soup, and dinner brings slow-cooked pork shoulder slouching into green-garlic risotto. Arrive early and sip wine outside until seats open up indoors. (http://outerlandssf.com; 4001 Judah St; sandwiches & small plates $8-9; 11am-3pm & 6-10pm Tue-Sat, 10am-2:30pm Sun; M Judah St).

Ton Kiang

DIM SUM $$

12 Map p166, E2

Don't bother asking what's in those bamboo steamers loaded onto carts: choose some by aroma alone, and ask for legendary *gao choy gat* (shrimp and chive dumplings), *dao miu gao* (pea tendril and shrimp dumplings) and *jin doy* (sesame balls). A tally is kept at your table, so you could quit while it's under $20 – but wait, here comes another cart… (www.tonkiang.net; 5821 Geary Blvd; dim sum $3-7; 10am-9pm Mon-Thu, 10am-9:30pm Fri, 9:30am-9:30pm Sat, 9am-9pm Sun; Geary Blvd;)

Local Life

Freewheeling through the Park

To cover the entire 48-block stretch of the park, rent your own two wheels (bike helmet included) at the eastern edge of the park at **Avenue Cyclery** (Map p166, H3; 415-387-3155; www.avenuecyclery.com; 756 Stanyan St; per hr/day $8/30; 10am-6pm Mon-Sat, to 5pm Sun). Sundays year-round and Saturdays June to October, Golden Gate Park's JFK Drive is closed to traffic east of Crossover Dr (around 8th Ave), and wide open to walkers, cyclists and skaters. Join the weekend disco-skate derby off JFK Drive at 7th Ave with skate rentals from **Golden Gate Park Bike & Skate** (Map p166, G3; 415-668-1117; www.goldengatepark-bikeandskate.com; 3038 Fulton St; skates per hr/day $5-6/20-24, bikes $3-5/15-25, tandem bikes $15/75, discs $6/25; 10am-6pm;), which also rents disc golf equipment. Call ahead weekdays to make sure they're open if the weather's dismal.

Beach Chalet Brewery

Kabuto

CALIFORNIAN, SUSHI $$

13 Map p166, F2

Innovative sushi served in a converted hot-dog drive-in. Sit at the bar to witness seaweed wrapped around sushi rice with foie gras and ollalieberry reduction, *hamachi* (yellowtail) topped with pear and wasabi mustard, and – eureka! – the '49er oyster, piled with sea urchin, caviar, a quail's egg and gold leaf. Reserve ahead; seats groups up to four. (415-752-5652; www.kabutosushi.com; 5121 Geary Blvd; sushi $6-10; 11:30am-2:30pm & 5:30-10:30pm Tue-Sat, 5:30-10:30pm Sun; Geary Blvd)

Spruce

CALIFORNIAN $$$

14 Map p166, H1

VIP all the way. Baccarat crystal chandeliers, tawny leather chairs and an 1000-wine menu. Ladies who lunch dispense with polite conversation, tearing into grass-fed burgers on house-baked English muffins loaded with pickled onions, zucchini grown on the restaurant's own organic farm, and optional foie gras. Want fries with that? Oh yes you do – Spruce's are cooked in duck fat. (415-931-5100; www.sprucesf.com; 3640 Sacramento St; mains $14-30; 11:30am-2:30pm Mon-Fri, 5-10pm Mon-Sun, 5-11pm Fri-Sat; California St)

Thanh Long

VIETNAMESE $$

15 Map p166, B5

Since 1971, San Franciscans have lingered in the Sunset after sunset for two main reasons, both found at Thanh Long: roast pepper crab and garlic noodles. One crab serves two (market price runs $34–$40) with noodles ($9), but shaking beef and mussels make a proper feast. The wine list offers good-value local pairings, especially Navarro's dry Gewurztraminer. (www.anfamily.com/Restaurants/thanhlong_restaurant; 4101 Judah St; mains $10-18; 5-9:30pm Tue-Thu & Sun, to 10pm Fri-Sat; M Judah St;)

Spices

CHINESE $

 Map p166, G2

The menu reads like an oddly dubbed Hong Kong action flick, with dishes labeled 'explosive!!' and 'stinky!', but the chefs can call zesty pickled Napa cabbage, silky ma-po tofu and brain-curdling spicy chicken whatever they want – they're all worthy of exclamation. Cash only. (http://spicesrestaurantonline.com; 294 8th Ave; mains $6.95-12.95; lunch & dinner; Geary Blvd)

Halu

JAPANESE $$

 Map p166, G2

Dinner at this surreal, snug *yakitori* joint covered with Beatles memorabilia feels like stowing away on the Yellow Submarine. Small bites are crammed onto sticks and barbecued, including bacon-wrapped scallops, quail eggs and mochi – and if you're up for offal, have a heart. (312 8th Ave; yakitori $2.50-4, $10-11 ramen; 5-10pm Tue-Sat)

Genki

DESSERT, GROCERIES, JAPANESE $

18 Map p166, G1

A teen mob scene for French crepes by way of Tokyo, with green-tea ice cream and Nutella, plus tropical fruit tapioca bubble tea. Stock up in the beauty supply and Pocky aisle to satisfy any sudden snack or hair-dye cravings. (www.genkicrepes.com; 330 Clement St; crepes $5; 2-10:30pm Mon, 10:30am-10:30pm Tue-Thu & Sun, 10am-11:30pm Fri-Sat; Geary Blvd)

Drinking

Beach Chalet Brewery

BREWERY

 Map p166, A4

Microbrews with views: sunsets over the Pacific upstairs, a backyard bar, and Lucien Labaudt's recently restored 1930s WPA frescoes downstairs showing a condensed history of San Francisco. BYO blanket to outdoor Friday movie nights in the Beach Chalet's backyard, where admission is free with your purchase of house-brewed beer. (www.beachchalet.com; 1000 Great Hwy; 9am-10pm Sun-Thu, to 11pm Fri & Sat; 48th Ave)

Hollow

CAFE

 Map p166, F4

Between simple explanations and Golden Gate Park, there's Hollow: cultish Ritual coffee and Guinness cupcakes served amid art-installation displays of magnifying glasses, tin pails, and monster etchings. There are only a couple of marble tables, so expect a wait among like-minded eccentrics. (http://hollowsf.com; 1493 Irving St; 8am-5pm Mon-Fri, 9am-5pm Sat-Sun; M Irving St).

Trouble Coffee

CAFE

21 Map p166, B5

Coconuts are unlikely near blustery Ocean Beach, but here comes Trouble with the 'Build Your Own Damn House' $8 breakfast special: coffee, thick-cut cinnamon-laced toast, and an entire young coconut. The hewn-wood bench out front is permanently damp from surfers' rears, but house-roasted 'The Hammer' espresso at the reclaimed wood counter indoors breaks through any morning fog. (www.troublecoffee.com; 4033 Judah St; 7am-8pm Mon-Fri, 8am-8pm Sat, 8am-5pm Sun; M Judah St)

540 Club

BAR

22 Map p166, G2

Unless you're a master criminal, this is the most fun you'll ever have inside a bank. Enter the converted savings and loan office to find minor mayhem already in progress, thanks to absinthe, $2 PBR, Punk Rock BBQ and Catholic School Karaoke (see website for events). A dozen brews on tap fuel marathons of darts or pool. (www.540-club.com; 540 Clement St; 11am-2am; Geary St)

Social

BREWERY

23 Map p166, G4

In every Social situation, there are a couple of troublemakers – here it's L'Enfant Terrible, a dark Belgian ale with an attitude, and bitter but golden Rapscallion. This snazzy, skylit modern building looks like an architect's office but tastes like a neighborhood brewpub, which just happens to serve addictive lime-laced Brussels-sprout chips – but hey, hogging the bowl is anti-Social. (http://socialkitchenandbrew ery.com; 1326 9th Ave; 5pm-midnight Mon-

Understand

The Fog Belt

Not sure how to dress for the weather? Join the club. San Francisco is notorious for its unpredictable microclimates. Downtown may be sunny and hot, while the Avenues are blanketed in coastal fog and 20°F (10°C) colder. You might need to wear a coat in July. Why is it so foggy? The vast agricultural region in the state's interior, the Central Valley, is ringed by mountains, like a giant bathtub. As this inland valley heats up and the warm air rises, it creates a deficit of air at surface level, generating wind that gets sucked through the only opening it can find: the Golden Gate. Suddenly the misty air hovering over the chilly Pacific gets pulled into the bay, and ta-da! The city disappears behind a misty veil. Thanks to satellite imagery, you can see if clouds are hugging the shoreline. Go to the National Oceanic and Atmospheric Administration (NOAA) website for San Francisco (www.wrh.noaa.gov/mtr), navigate to the 'satellite imagery' page, and click on the '1km visible satellite' for Monterey, California.

Thu, to 2am Fri, 11:30am-2am Sat, 11:30am-midnight Sun; M Irving St)

Bitter End PUB

24  Map p166, G2

Don't be bitter if tricky Tuesday-night trivia ends in near-victory – it's a fine excuse for another beer or hard pear cider at this local haunt with proper creaky wood floors, Irish bartenders and passable pub grub. Sore losers can always challenge trivia champs to a friendly grudge match at the pool tables and dartboard on the balcony. (441 Clement St; 4pm-2am Mon-Fri, 11am-2am Sat & Sun; Geary Blvd)

Trad'r Sam's TIKI BAR

25 Map p166, D2

Island getaways in rattan booths at this threadbare tiki lounge will cure that Ocean Beach chill. You won't find beer on tap, but you may discover an ice-cream island in your cocktail. Classic-kitsch lovers order the Hurricane, which comes with two straws to share for a reason: drink it by yourself and it'll blow you away. (6150 Geary Blvd; 11am-2am; M Geary Blvd)

Entertainment

Plough & Stars LIVE MUSIC

26  Map p166, G2

The Emerald Isle by the Golden Gate. Bluegrass and Celtic bands who sell out shows from Ireland to Appalachia turn up to jam on weeknights, taking breaks to clink pint glasses at long union-hall style tables. Mondays they compensate for no live music with an all-day happy hour, plus free pool and blarney from regulars. Expect a modest cover charges Friday–Saturday. (www.theploughandstars.com; 116 Clement St; 3pm-2am Mon-Thu, 2pm-2am Fri-Sun, showtime 9pm; Geary Blvd)

Bridge Theater CINEMA

27  Map p166, H2

One of SF's last single-screen theaters, the Bridge screens international indie films from yakuza gangster thrillers to film-festival sensations. Weekends in summer, the Bridge hosts Midnight Mass ($13; open midnight), featuring camp, horror and B-grade movies such as *Showgirls* and *Mommie Dearest*, with screenings preceded by a drag show spoofing the film. Drag diva Peaches Christ wrangles the always-raucous crowd; reserve ahead. (415-267-4893; www.landmarktheatres.com; 3010 Geary Blvd; adult/child & matinee $10.50/8; Geary St)

Four Star Theatre CINEMA

28  Map p166, D2

Long before John Woo, Ang Lee and Wong Kar Wai hit multiplex marquees, they brought down the house with international indie double features in the Four Star's postage stamp-sized screening rooms – directors have even shown up to do Q&A for a full house of 25. (www.lntsf.com; 2200 Clement St; double features evening/matinee $10/8; Geary St)

Shopping

Park Life
ART, BOOKS, ACCESSORIES

29 Map p166, G2

The Swiss Army knife of hip SF stores: design store, indie publisher and art gallery all in one. Park Life is exceptionally gifted – tees with drawn-on pockets, Park Life's catalog of graffiti artist Andrew Schoultz, and Ian Johnson's portrait of Miles Davis radiating prismatic thought waves all make presents too good to wait for a birthday. (www.parklifestore.com; 220 Clement St; 11am-8pm; Geary Blvd;)

Local Life

Great Park Pastimes

Whether you're looking for a game or are content to watch, Golden Gate Park has baseball and softball diamonds, four soccer fields and 21 tennis courts – but atypical athletes also find their niches here. At the park's vintage-1901 **Lawn Bowling Club** (Map p166, G4; 415-487-8787; http://sflb.filesforfriends.com; Bowling Green Dr, Golden Gate Park; M Stanyan St), free lessons are available at noon on Wednesday and Saturdays; call to confirm and wear flat-soled shoes. Sundays swing at **Lindy in the Park** (Map p166, F4; www.lindyinthepark.com; Music Concourse Dr, Golden Gate Park; admission free; 11am-2pm Sun, weather permitting; M 9th Ave;), the free, all-ages lindy-hopping dance party held at the outdoor bandshell, preceded by free half-hour lessons at noon. Across from the buffalo paddock in Golden Gate Park, anglers fish in casting pools open to the public at the **Flycasting Club** (Map p166; B4; www.ggacc.org; John F Kennedy Dr, Golden Gate Park; M Fulton St;) – check the website for free lessons.

Mollusk
SURF GEAR

30 Map p166, B4

Back home no one can bite your SF style, with boards by celebrity shapers and local artist-designed Mollusk hoodies to warm up in style after a gnarly session. Surf books, locally designed skate decks and collages by local surfer/international art-fair sensation Thomas Campbell provide SF surf-subculture thrills without the damp wetsuit. (www.mollusksurfshop.com; 4500 Irving St; 10am-6:30pm; M Judah St)

General Store
GIFTS & ACCESSORIES

31 Map p166, B5

Anyone born in the wrong place or time to be a NorCal hippie-architect can still look the part, thanks to a) beards and b) General Store. Pine-lined walls showcase handcrafted recycled-leather boots, antique turquoise necklaces, brass bicycle bells, egg-shaped terrariums and vintage how-to books. Don't miss art openings, when smokers flirt dangerously on hay bales out front and folkies strum in the backyard garden. (4035 Judah St; 11am-7pm Mon-Fri, 10am-7pm Sat-Sun; M Judah St)

Green Apple

BOOKS

32 Map p166, G2

The opium den of San Francisco's literary set, where readers lose track of untold hours spent poring over shelves of excellent staff picks, piles of bargain-priced remainders and displays of tantalizing new releases. And ust when you tear yourself away, you realize there is another whole floor of poetry and nonfiction...and, uh-oh, an annex of used fiction and CDs two doors down. (506 Clement St; 10am-10:30pm Sun-Thu, to 11:30pm Fri & Sat; Geary Blvd;)

Wishbone

GIFTS & TOYS

33 Map p166, G4

Certain gifts never fail to please: explode-in-your-mouth Pop Rocks candy, smiling toast coin-purses, and blue ribbons that proclaim 'Computer Whiz!' Gifts here will gratify hip parents, from a bath towel that doubles as a pirate's cape to the onesie silkscreened to look like a BART card. (www.wishbonesf.com; 601 Irving St; 11:30am-7pm Mon-Tue & Thu-Sat, to 6pm Sun; M Irving St;)

Local Life

Coasting the Coast

Hit your stride on the 9-mile **Coastal Trail** (Map p166, A1; sunrise-sunset; M Judah St), starting at Fort Funston and wrapping around the Presidio paralleling Lincoln Blvd to end at Fort Mason. The 4 miles of sandy Ocean Beach will definitely work those calves and numb your toes – yep, the water's about that cold year-round. Casual strollers will prefer to pick up the trail near Sutro Baths, head around Lands End for a peek at Golden Gate Bridge and then duck into the Legion of Honor (p168) at Lincoln Park.

Seedstore

CLOTHING

34 Map p166, G2

Less like entering a store than raiding the wardrobe of a modern spaghetti-Western star. The old-timey shingle hung over the door is misleading – no gardening supplies are sold here, but you will probably find Joe's Jeans, Superdry military-style jackets, BB Dakota riding pants, filmy Free People peasant blouses, and vintage Navajo-pattern cardigans. (www.seedstoresf.com; 212 Clement St; 11am-7pm Mon-Fri, to 8 Sat, to 6pm Sun; Geary St)

28

The Best of San Francisco

San Francisco's Best Walks

San Francisco's Best...

Cable car on Russian Hill, with Alcatraz in the background
LARRY MULVEHILL/CORBIS ©

Best Walks
Haight Flashback

The Walk

Whether you're a hippie born too late, punk born too early, or a weirdo who passes as normal, Haight St is here to claim you as its own. On this walk you'll cover 100 years of Haight history, starting in 1867 with the park that was San Francisco's saving grace in the disastrous 1906 earthquake and fire. Fog and grit come with the scenery, but there's no better place to break away from the everyday and find your nonconformist niche.

Start Buena Vista Park; Haight St

Finish Golden Pate Park; Stanyan St

Length 1.3 miles; one hour nonstop

Take a Break

What a long, strange trip it's been – refuel with a burger and beer at Magnolia (p152), the corner microbrewery and organic eatery named after a Grateful Dead song.

Shopfront on Haight St

1 Buena Vista Park

Start your trip back in time in **Buena Vista Park** (p150), where San Franciscans found refuge from the earthquake and fire of 1906, and watched their town burn for days.

2 Bound Together Anarchist Book Collective

Heading west up Haight St, you may recognize Emma Goldman and Sacco and Vanzetti in the *Anarchists of Americas* mural at **Bound Together Anarchist Book Collective** (p156); if you don't, staff can provide you with some biographical comics by way of introduction.

3 SLA Safehouse

At 1235 Masonic Ave, you might once have glimpsed the Simbionese Liberation Army. Apparently this was once a safehouse where the SLA is believed to have held Patty Hearst, the kidnapped heiress turned revolutionary bank robber.

❹ Grateful Dead House

Pay your respects to the former flophouse of Jerry Garcia, Bob Weir, Pigpen and sundry Deadheads at the **Grateful Dead House** (p150) at 710 Ashbury St. In October 1967, antidrug cops arrested everyone in it (Garcia wasn't home).

❺ Janis Joplin's Crash Pad

Down the block, 635 Ashbury St is one of many known Haight addresses for Janis Joplin, who had a hard time hanging onto leases in the 1960s – but as she sang, 'freedom's just another word for nothin' left to lose.'

❻ Haight & Ashbury

At the corner of Haight and Ashbury, the clock overhead always reads 4:20, better known in 'Hashbury' as International Bong Hit Time.

❼ Jimi's Jams

The Victorian at 1524 Haight St was one of the Haight's most notorious hippie flophouses, where Jimi Hendrix jammed and crashed in his 'Purple Haze' days. Fittingly, it is now a head shop; the next-door music store sells a lot of guitars.

❽ Hippie Hill

Follow the beat of your inner drummer to the drum circle at Hippie Hill in **Golden Gate Park** (p169) – 40 years since it all began, free spirits haven't entirely agreed on a rhythm. Notice the singular, shaggy 'Janis Joplin Tree' – squint hard, and it resembles the singer's wild-haired profile.

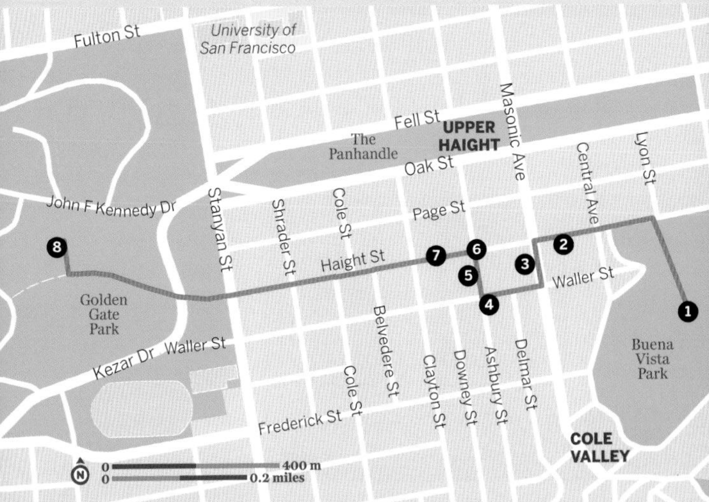

Best Walks Mission Gallery Hop

The Walk

The underground art scene surfaces in Mission galleries and art nonprofits, where you'll find artworks more affordable than downtown galleries and more portable than Mission murals (p128). Respected area art schools keep fresh talent coming, yet next-generation 'Mission School' artists remain streetwise and dreamy. Homegrown traditions of '50s Beat collage, '60s psychedelia, '70s beautiful-mess punk, '80s graffiti and '90s skater-graphics keep the art scene down to earth – and deeply rooted.

Start Ratio 3; M S 16th St Mission

Finish Eleanor Harwood Gallery; S 24th St Mission

Length 2.3 miles; three hours

Take a Break

Join starving artists in line at La Taqueria (p133).

SABRINA DALBESIO/LONELY PLANET IMAGES ©

Galería de la Raza

1 Ratio 3

Museum-worthy art isn't behind velvet ropes in the Mission, but in unfinished back-alley lofts like **Ratio 3** (415-821-3371; www.ratio3.org; 1447 Stevenson St; admission free; 11am-6pm Wed-Sat). Here Whitney Museum wunderkind Chris Perez mounts head-trippy shows such as Geof Oppenheimer's *Inside Us All There is a Part That Would Like to Burn Down Our Own House* and Takeshi Murata's alien/familiar life-form mashups in *Get Your Ass to Mars.*

2 Intersection for the Arts

Jazz musicians jam downstairs at **Intersection for the Arts** (p139), but the think pieces in the upstairs gallery raise an even bigger ruckus.

3 Creativity Explored

Creativity Explored (p133) showcases works by developmentally disabled artists, including John McKenzie's carefully inked word poems: 'war is weird/ war is pushy/war is old-fashioned.'

❹ Guerrero Gallery

Read between carefully drawn lines at **Guerrero Gallery** (☎415-400-5168; www.guerrerogallery.com; 2700 19th St; admission free; ⌚11am-7pm Tue-Sat), and you'll find wry, social critiques – such as Jovi Schnell's recent *Meme Decay*, which maps out what happens to internet memes when they fall off your Twitter feed.

❺ Southern Exposure

Southern Exposure (www.soex.org; 3030 20th St; donations welcome; ⌚noon-6pm Thu-Sat) pulls you into the action with community art pieces that invite your participation. For the recent 'Working Conditions' show, artists kept regular office hours and invited visitor 'interns' to join a makeshift Mayan claymation studio and immigrant-identity laboratory.

❻ Galería de la Raza

Works by Latino artists at **Galería de la Raza** (p134) show that it's possible to envision a different world without forgetting your roots, as in a recent show where 12 Latina artists reimagined the Mexican legend of La Llorona, the 'Weeping Woman'.

❼ Eleanor Harwood Gallery

Eleanor Harwood Gallery (www.eleanorharwood.com; 1295 Alabama St; admission free; ⌚11am-6pm Wed-Sat) is an escape hatch from reality into meticulous imaginary worlds, including Alika Cooper's charming folk-art quilts (that often require a double take).

Best Walks
North Beach Beat

The Walk

Poetry is in the air and on the sidewalk on this literary tour of North Beach, starting with legendary City Lights bookstore, home of Beat poetry and free speech. It's an easy walk, but you'll want at least a couple hours to see the neighborhood as *On the Road* author Jack Kerouac did – with drinks at the beginning, middle and end.

Start Bob Kaufman Alley; Columbus Ave

Finish Li Po; Kearny St

Length 1.5 miles; two hours

Take a Break

You may think the chef has lost the plot, but like its William S Burroughs' novel namesake, Naked Lunch (p63) makes its own perverse sense: fried pork rinds are the only way to accompany a foie gras sandwich...obviously.

Beat Museum

❶ Bob Kaufman Alley

This quiet alley is named for the spoken-word poet who co-founded *Beatitudes* magazine in 1959, but took a vow of silence after Kennedy's assassination. He didn't speak again until the Vietnam War ended, when he walked into a North Beach cafe and recited his poem, 'All Those Ships that Never Sailed', which includes the lines: 'Today I bring them back/Huge and transitory/And let them sail/Forever.'

❷ Caffe Trieste

Order a potent espresso, check out the opera on the jukebox and slide into the back booth under the Sicilian mural, where Francis Ford Coppola drafted *The Godfather*. **Caffe Trieste** (p65) has been a neighborhood institution since 1956, with the local characters and bathroom wall poetry to prove it.

❸ City Lights

'Abandon all despair, all ye who enter,' orders the sign by the door to **City**

Lights (p68), written by founder and San Francisco poet laureate Lawrence Ferlinghetti. This commandment is easy to follow upstairs in the sunny Poetry Room. Pick up some poetry to inspire your journey into the heart of literary North Beach, such as Allen Ginsberg's banned, beautiful *Howl*.

❹ Beat Museum

Don't be surprised to hear a Dylan jam session by the front door, or see Allen Ginsberg naked in documentary footage screened inside the **Beat Museum** (p58); the Beat goes on here in rare form.

❺ Specs Museum Café

Begin your literary bar crawl at **Specs** (p65) amid merchant-marine memorabilia, walrus parts behind the bar, choice words worthy of a sailor and a glass of Anchor Steam.

❻ Jack Kerouac Alley

The mural-covered byway **Jack Kerouac Alley** (p58) is aptly named for the Beat Generation's most famous author, since this is where he was tossed after raucous nights at Vesuvio. Kerouac's words embedded in the alley sum up North Beach nights: 'The air was soft, the stars so fine, and the promise of every cobbled alley so great...'

❼ Li Po Cocktails

Follow the literary lead of Kerouac and Ginsberg and end your night in a vinyl booth at **Li Po** (p67), with another beer beneath the gold Buddha's forgiving gaze.

Best
Fine Dining

Other US cities boast bigger monuments, but San Francisco packs more flavor. With more restaurants per capita than any other North American city (sorry, New York) San Francisco spoils diners for choice. Almost anything grows in California's fertile farmland, so SF's top chefs have an unfair advantage with local, organic and – oh yes – incredibly tasty ingredients.

Wild West Cuisine

Multi-ethnic San Francisco has been finessing fusion since the Gold Rush days, when miners exchanged nuggets for Wild West feasts of oysters, French champagne and Chinese noodles. SF's favorite flavors are still cross-cultural, but now highlight local ingredients – oysters sustainably farmed in Sonoma, bubbly from Napa, and noodles made with Mendocino seaweed. Forty years after Alice Waters started the local, organic food revolution in Berkeley, her influence is all over SF menus, from farm name-dropping in menu descriptions to footnotes defining humane ranching practices. Lately no local chef's tasting menu is complete without wild-crafted ingredients: chanterelles found beneath California oaks, miner's lettuce from Berkeley hillsides or SF-backyard nasturtium flowers. Eccentric? Absolutely – but it's hard to argue with your mouth full.

Etiquette

SF's top tables are mostly California casual; jeans are acceptable, welcomes warm rather than formal, and servers informative to the point of chatty. Budget an additional 9.5% for tax, tips ranging from 15% (faulty service) to 25% (extra attention), and an occasional 4% to 5% healthcare surcharge.

MICHAEL MACOR/CORBIS ©

Top Tips

- **Reservations** On weekends, reservations are mandatory, unless you want to eat before 6pm or after 9:30pm.
- **Online bookings** Most SF restaurants offer online reservations through **OpenTable** (www.opentable.com), but if the system shows no availability, call the restaurant directly. Some seats may be held for phone reservations and walk-ins.

Fusion Flair

Benu (p91) Fine dining meets DJ styling. Ingenious remixes of Eastern classics and the best ingredients in the West.

JUDY BELLAH/LONELY PLANET IMAGES ©

Aziza (p170) Sunny flavors evaporate Pacific fog in the Avenues, where California mysteriously bumps up against Morocco.

California's Wild Side

Coi (p61) Wild tasting menus featuring foraged morels, wildflowers and Pacific seafood are like licking the California coastline.

Sons & Daughters (p91) Urban-legendary, from ingredients grown in the restaurant's urban farm to the upstart co-chefs' irreverent takes on classics.

Commonwealth (p134) A disco ball still spins in this converted Mission dive, but the inventive Californian food dazzles.

Date-Night Favorites

Jardinière (p112) Behind the opera, chef Traci des Jardins hits all the right notes – decadent, smart, sustainable – with a slight Italian accent.

Gary Danko (p44) Escape from Alcatraz for romance served in three to five leisurely, luxuriant courses along Fisherman's Wharf.

Power Lunches

Boulevard (p92) Chef Nancy Oakes' hearty, unfussy Californian fare seals more downtown deals than Google.

Michael Mina (p92) Upbeat downtown dining from the master of high-low inventions, including the foie gras PB&J.

Worth a Trip

To appreciate the Bay Area's local, sustainable food obsessions, you could read *Slow Food Nation: Why Our Food Should Be Good, Clean and Fair*, by Carlo Petrini and Alice Waters – but it's a pure pleasure to eat her words at **Chez Panisse** (☎510-548-5525, cafe 510-548-5049; 1517 Shattuck, Berkeley; S Downtown Berkeley), the restaurant where she's cooked good, clean, fair, fabulous food since 1971. Book ahead.

Best Bargain Gourmet

Top Chefs for Less

Cotogna (p61) Rustic Italian from 2011 James Beard Award–winner Michael Tusk.

Mr Pollo (p134) Food Network–featured three-course, Cali culinary wonders under $20.

Academy Cafe (p162) Acclaimed chefs Charles Phan and Loretta Keller serve local, sustainable bites inside California Academy of Sciences.

Sentinel (p93) Chef Dennis Leary gets radical on American lunch classics downtown.

Food Trucks & Market Stalls

Off the Grid (p31) Up to 30 food trucks provide a movable feast, from curry to cupcakes.

Ferry Plaza Farmers Market (p79) Graze on organic peaches, Sonoma goat cheese, and Korean tacos.

Heart of the City Farmers Market (p115) DIY Lunches of roast chicken, heirloom tomatoes, organic berries and more.

Hot Deals

La Taqueria (p133) Where SF's most memorable meals come wrapped in foil and under $8 – including spicy pickles.

Lahore Karahi (p113) Classic tandoori dive – a crowd-pleaser in the dodgy theatre district.

Spices (p173) Whether you like your Szechuan lip-tingling or 'explosive' this hotspot delivers.

Brenda's French Soul Food (p112) Creole cures for what ails you the morning after, before Hayes Valley boutiques.

Udupi Palace (p135) South Indian in the Mission – SF's definitive *dosa* (lentil pancake).

Casual Dates

Namu (p171) Creative, Korean-inspired soul food sets the mood near Golden Gate Park.

Outerlands (p171) After long walks on Ocean Beach, share plates of heartwarming organic fare – this could be serious.

City View (p61) Carts zoom past piled with dim-sum possibilities – play the field, but commit to shrimp dumplings.

JUDY BELLAH/LONELY PLANET IMAGES ©

☑ Top Tips

- **Food trucks** See where your next meal is coming from on **Twitter** (@MobileCravings/sf-food-trucks, @streetfoodsf).
- **Coupons** Deals at top SF restaurants are available at **Blackbird Eats** (http://blackboardeats.com/san-francisco) and **OpenTable** (www.opentable.com).

Best Live Music

Classical & Opera

San Francisco Symphony (p117) Edge-of-your-seat, Grammy-winning performances.

San Francisco Opera (p119) Italian classic reinvented.

Bluegrass, Folk & Jazz

Plough & Stars (p175) Major bluegrass and Celtic bands pack Irish pub benches.

Yoshi's (p125) Top international names in jazz play this legendary Japantown joint – and eat at the sushi bar afterwards.

Rock, Pop & Hip-Hop

Great American Music Hall (p119) A former bordello now hosts red-hot acts, from alt-rock legends and baroque poppers to world music.

Slim's (p98) From punk to Prince, major acts pack the dance floor at this small, all-ages venue.

Bimbo's 365 Club (p68) Top 40 names and retro-rockers play a historic speakeasy.

Hotel Utah Saloon (p99) Underground bands rock this genuine-article Wild West saloon.

Warfield (p119) Marquee names from the Beastie Boys to Wilco raise the roof on this vaudeville theatre.

Independent (p156) True to its name, this place features up-and-comers and oddball acts like the National Air Guitar Championships.

Mezzanine (p98) Street creds and sound quality, together at last – West Coast rap and hip-hop.

Worth a Trip

The Fillmore (www.thefillmore.com; 1805 Geary Blvd; tickets from $20; ⌚shows nightly) Hendrix, Zeppelin, Janis – they all played the Fillmore. The legendary venue that launched the psychedelic era has the posters to prove it upstairs, and hosts arena acts in a 1250-seat venue where you can squeeze in next to the stage.

Bottom of the Hill (www.bottomofthehill.com; 1233 17th St; admission $5-12; ⌚shows 9pm Tue-Sat; M 16th St) Alt-rock legends start at this hidden hotspot (pictured above), with bargain admission and great beer.

SABRINA DALBESIO/LONELY PLANET IMAGES ©

☑ Top Tip

▶ Bargain tickets are sold on the day of the performance for cash only at **TIX Bay Area** (☎415-433-7827; 251 Stockton St; ⌚11am-6pm Tue-Thu, to 7pm Fri & Sat).

▶ Otherwise, try SF-based **Craig's List** (www.cragislist.org).

Best Drinks

Ban 'the usual' from your drinking vocabulary, and go for the extraordinary instead. The Gold Rush brought a rush on the bar; by 1850, San Francisco had one woman per 100 men, but 500 saloons shilling hooch. Today California's traditions of wine, beer and cocktails are converging in saloon revivals, wine-bar trends, and microbrewery booms – and, for the morning after, specialty coffee roasters.

SF Cocktails – History in the Making

In San Francisco's Barbary Coast days, cocktails were used to sedate sailors and shanghai them onto outbound ships. Now bartenders are researching local recipes and reviving old SF traditions, straining absinthe into cordial glasses of Sazerac, whipping egg whites into Pisco sours, and apparently still trying to knock sailors cold with combinations of tawny port and Nicaraguan rum served in punch bowls. If you order a martini, you may get the original, invented-in-SF version: vermouth, gin, bitters, lemon, maraschino cherry and ice. All that authenticity-tripping may sound self-conscious, but after strong pours at California's vintage saloons, consciousness is hardly an issue.

Museums after Hours

Museums offer some of SF's most eclectic nights out. NightLife at California Academy of Sciences (p163) has rainforest-themed cocktails every Thursday night. The Exploratorium After Dark (p28) offers such mad-scientist concoctions as glow-in-the-dark cocktails on first Thursdays, while the MH de Young Memorial Museum (p165) invites you to mingle with artists-in-residence over art-themed cocktails (first Fridays of alternate months).

SABRINA DALBESIO/LONELY PLANET IMAGES ©

Beer

Zeitgeist (p137) Beer garden with 30 brews on tap and sometimes tamales. Settle in for the duration.

Toronado (p154) More than 400 microbrewed beers, ales, meads and barley wines – plus sausages next door.

Beach Chalet Brewery (p173) Microbrews with views: Pacific Ocean out front, Works Project Administration (WPA) murals downstairs, Golden Gate Park backyard.

City Beer Store & Tasting Room (p95) Three hundred brews, salami platter pairings and home-brewing supplies.

Speakeasies

Smuggler's Cove (p115) Behind tinted doors lurks a triple-decker pirate shipwreck, with 70 historically researched cocktails and 200 rums.

Bourbon & Branch (p116) Prohibition-perfect cocktails in a secret backroom library bar.

Wine Bars

RN74 (p94) The best list in town, and possibly the west coast – plus a Michael Mina–designed bar menu.

Heart (p137) Wine in Mason jars, inspired small plates and warm welcomes. All Heart.

Two Sisters Bar & Books (p116) A bookish beauty with bargain happy hours.

Cafes

Caffe Trieste (p65) The soul of North Beach: poets, directors, accordion jams and espresso.

Ritual Coffee Roasters (p138) Cultish coffee roasted onsite and prepared by expert baristas.

Trouble Coffee (p174) Local roasts and breakfasts with the Ocean Beach surfer crowd.

Hollow (p173) Espresso inside an art installation off Golden Gate Park.

Coffee to the People (p153) Revolutionary cafe with espresso to match.

Saloons

Comstock Saloon (p65) Decadent, historically correct turn-of-the-century cocktails and bar bites.

Rickhouse (p96) Top-notch bourbon in a shotgun-shack setting downtown.

Drink Think Tanks

Bar Agricole (p94) Valedictorian cocktails, with a James Beard Award and double major in history and scotch.

Rye (p115) Alcohol alchemy: exact ratios of obscure bitters, small-batch liquor, fresh-squeezed juices.

Alembic (p154) Bourbon concoctions and gourmet bites for aficionados.

Elixir (p137) Organic, local drinks in a wild West, green-certified saloon.

Cantina (p95) Specialist in tequila, Pisco and other Latin liquors.

Epic Dives

Specs (p65) Drink like a sailor at this hideaway plastered with seven seas mementos.

Hemlock Tavern (p115) Peanuts and punk rock, plus near-impossible trivia nights.

Bloodhound (p94) Top-shelf booze in Mason jars by the pool table; food trucks out front.

Edinburgh Castle (p116) Literary pub with readings, darts, and a thick Scottish accent.

Lounges

Tosca (p65) Warm up from the inside out with jukebox opera and spiked espresso drinks.

Aub Zam Zam (p154) Persian jazz lounge with impeccable cocktails in the Haight.

Best Gay/Lesbian/Bi/ Trans SF

Doesn't matter where you're from, who you love or who's your daddy: if you're here, and queer, welcome home. Singling out the best places to be out in San Francisco is almost redundant. Though the Castro is a gay hub and the Mission is a magnet for lesbians, the entire city is gay-friendly – hence the number of out elected representatives in City Hall.

GLBT Nightlife Scene

New York Marys may label SF the retirement home of the young – the sidewalks do roll up early – but honey, SF's drag glitter nuns need some beauty rest between throwing Hunky Jesus contests and running for public office. Most thump-thump clubs are concentrated not in the lesbian-magnet Mission or historic gay Castro, but in SoMa warehouses, where dancing queens, playbois and leather scenesters can make some noise. In the 1950s, bars euphemistically designated Sunday afternoons as 'tea dances,' appealing to gay crowds to make money at an otherwise slow time – and the tradition sticks today, especially on packed, rare, sweaty hot days.

SF Pride Month

No one does Pride like San Francisco. Pride lasts all of June, including the **Gay and Lesbian Film Festival** (www.frameline.org) with 200 film screenings at the Castro Theatre. Around 50,000 women converge in Dolores Park at 7:30pm on the last Saturday in June for the **Dyke March & Pink Saturday** (www.dykemarch.org, www.sfpride.org). It all comes to a climax the next day with the **Lesbian, Gay, Bisexual and Transgender Pride Parade** (www.sfpride.org): 1.2 million people, seven stages, tons of glitter.

GLOWIMAGES/CORBIS ©

Top Tips

- Enjoy public spankings for local charities on the last Sunday in September at the **Folsom Street Fair** (www.folsomstreetfair.com), a clothing-optional leather fair.
- Check the **Sisters of Perpetual Indulgence** (☎415-820-9697; www.thesisters.org) calendar for costumed fundraising extravaganzas, including the Hunky Jesus contest on Easter Sunday.

Classic Bars

The Stud (p94) Leather bears, art drag, rocker-chick nights, and raunchy comedy showcases.

Upper Polk Street (p72) San Francisco's historic gay sailor–bar strip still has a few good dives left.

Twin Peaks Tavern (p145) The first gay bar with windows; now there's a neon rainbow. Toast to progress.

Women into Women

Lexington Club (p138) Full-time lesbian bar with the works: pool, pinball, tattoos, beer.

Cat Club (p85) Retro '90s, twisted Bondage a Go Go and totally rad '80s Thursdays.

El Rio (p137) Oyster happy hours, air hockey and *muy caliente* Salsa Sundays.

Harlot (p84) Bring your inner hussy to monthly Fem Bar parties.

DNA (p85) Drag king competitions and Goth nights are gender-ambiguous attractions.

Dance Clubs

EndUp (p85) Ride the beat from Ghettodisco Saturdays to Monday morning sunrises over the freeway.

Rebel Bar (p115) Southern hospitality behind the bar, and dance floor rebels everywhere.

Rickshaw Stop (p116) Something for everyone, SF-style: lesbian disco, Bollywood mashups, Latin spice.

Drag Cabaret & Disco

Aunt Charlie's (p120) Maximum freak-fabulous on the grittiest block in the city.

Beach Blanket Babylon (p67) Drag satire with giant hats and no mercy; the original San Francisco treat.

AsiaSF (p98) Are they or aren't they? You won't know until the disco after party downstairs.

By Day

Under One Roof (p145) Shop for a cause: designers donate new stuff and samples to raise $11 million for local HIV/AIDS organizations.

GLBT History Museum (p145) The first gay-history museum in America, right in the historic heart of the Castro.

Party Supplies

Madame S & Mr S (p100) Spiked dog collars, PVC, and oh yes, leather.

Piedmont Boutique (p157) Orange faux-fur hot pants, legwarmers and a boa...done!

Best Entertainment

Theater & Comedy

American Conservatory Theater (p97) Breakthrough premieres and controversial original plays, from Tony Kushner to David Mamet.

Intersection for the Arts (p139) Experimental works by distinguished playwrights and improvisational jazz on a postage-stamp stage.

Fort Mason (p28) Cutting-edge theater, improv comedy and art fairs at a creatively repurposed army base.

Cobb's Comedy Club (p68) HBO and NBC talents try their riskiest material here first.

Dance

Yerba Buena Center for the Arts (p97) Inspirations range from machinery to martial arts at this all-star performing arts showcase.

ODC (p139) Raw and risky performances September–December, and 200 dance classes a week all year-round.

San Francisco Ballet (p119) Classical elegance and gorgeous staging, with performances January–May.

Cinema

Castro Theatre (p145) Deco movie palace (pictured right) featuring silver-screen classics and cult hits for cinemaniac audiences.

Roxie Cinema (p139) Film festivals, documentaries and rare cult classics.

Drag

AsiaSF (p98) Hot Asian-inspired dishes – and the food's not bad either.

Beach Blanket Babylon (p67) SF's longest-running, sharpest-witted, biggest-wigged comedy cabaret.

Bridge Theater (p175) Midnight B-movies hosted by drag diva Peaches Christ – come as you are, or in costume

LEE FOSTER/LONELY PLANET IMAGES ©

Worth a Trip

Sundance Kabuki Cinema (www.sundancecinemas.com/kabuki.html; 1881 Post St; adult/child $14/10) Get eco-entertained at this green multiplex with GMO-free popcorn, reserved seating in recycled-fiber seats and the frankly brilliant Balcony Bar, where you can slurp seasonal cocktails during your movie.

San Francisco 49ers (☎415-656-4900; www.sf49ers.com; Monster Park; tickets $25-100 at www.ticketmaster.com; Ⓜ T) Shivering through foggy 'Niners football games is an SF bonding ritual. The 49ers were the National Football League dream team during the 1980s–'90s, and though they haven't made the playoffs lately, fan loyalty hasn't flagged.

Best Museums & Galleries

Museums

San Francisco Museum of Modern Art (p76; pictured right) Sculpture on the roof, photography and new media downstairs, and a new wing of modern masterpieces.

Asian Art Museum (p106) Trip through 6000 years and 4000 miles in an hour, with masterpieces from Mumbai to Tokyo.

MH de Young Memorial Museum (p164) Wonder at craftsmanship and artistic vision, from ancient Olmec heads to James Turrell light installations.

California Academy of Sciences (p162) Chase butterflies under the rainforest dome or hang with the penguins inside this living museum.

Cartoon Art Museum (p88) Better than the movie; original artwork from legendary comics, from Superman to Robert Crumb.

Contemporary Jewish Museum (p88) Artworks by Warhol, Houdini, Lou Reed and Gertrude Stein prove great minds don't always think alike.

Legion of Honor (p168) Eclectic collecting at its SF best: ancient Mesopotamian art, John Cage soundscapes and weekend organ recitals in the Rodin sculpture gallery.

History

Alcatraz (p50) Tour the notorious island and prison, from solitary cells to attempted escape routes.

USS Pampanito (p37) Dive into history on a WWII submarine.

Murals

Coit Tower (p54) Murals showing SF during the Great Depression got 27 artists labeled first communists, then national treasures.

Mission Murals (p128) Diego Rivera's influence is everywhere in 400 colorful, political, streetwise murals.

RICHARD CUMMINS/CORBIS ©

Contemporary Art Galleries

Catharine Clark Gallery (p88) Stealing SFMOMA's thunder with dangerous, moving, memorable shows from current and future museum-show headliners.

Gallery Paule Anglim (p88) Experimental works and conceptual art conundrums from established art stars.

49 Geary (p89) Four floors of galleries covering all media, from interactive environmental art to classic silver-gelatin photographs.

77 Geary (p90) Two floors of luscious painting and provocative ideas lift spirits and open minds.

Best Outdoors

If the climb doesn't take your breath away on hilltop parks, the scenery surely will. Nature has been kind to San Francisco, but it has taken generations of pioneering conservation efforts to preserve this splendor. Early champions include Sierra Club founder John Muir, Golden Gate Park planner William Hammond Hall, and ordinary San Franciscans who saw beauty and not just gold in these hills.

San Francisco's Green Outlook

Recent reports rank San Francisco the greenest city in North America – but you could probably guess that at a glance. All around you'll notice wild ideas at work, from mandatory citywide composting to Green Party politics (the sheriff was a founding Green Party member), freeway overpasses converted into urban farmland to Army airstrips reinvented as birdwatching preserves. This is one town where you can eat, sleep and cavort sustainably – and from the bottom of its heart to the top of its green hills, San Francisco thanks you.

Wheels & Waves

Daredevil hills and dazzling waters invite SF visitors to roll, surf and sail around town. Haight St is urban skating at its obstacle-course best. Inline skaters cover the bay waterfront every Friday night and disco-skate in Golden Gate Park on Sundays.

Bone-chilling Pacific surf is not for novices; check the **surf report** (☎415-273-1618) before you suit up. Sailing is best April through August, but whale-watching season peaks mid-October through December.

Hilltop Vistas

Alamo Square (p150) Sweeping downtown vistas (pictured above), plus a scene-stealing hilltop shoe garden.

Sterling Park (p41) The crowning glory of Lombard St; wind-sculpted pines frame Golden Gate Bridge panoramas.

Coit Tower (p54) Get parrot's eye views over the bay on the garden-lined climb to Coit Tower.

Beaches & Waterfront

Crissy Field (p28) The old Army airstrip is now patrolled by windsurfers, joggers and puppies.

Ocean Beach (p168) Beachcombers, surfers and serious sand-castle architects brave SF's blustery Pacific Ocean.

Coastal Trail

Baker Beach (p28) So San Fran: Golden Gate Bridge views, sustainable fishing, and clothing-optional sunbathing on a former Army base.

Coastal Trail (p177) Cover nine miles of waterfront from Fort Funston to Fort Mason, with sparkling Pacific and bay views.

San Francisco Maritime National Historic Park (p38) Tour 120-year-old boats bobbing like giant bath toys along Fisherman's Wharf.

Outdoor Activities

Golden Gate Park (p169) All of San Francisco's favorite pastimes in one place: baseball, skating, lawn bowling, lindy-hopping, drum-circling and general lollygagging.

La Raza Skatepark (p133) Where SF's urban skate legends blast off the bowl and kindergartners land their first kick-flips.

Mission Dolores Park (p132) Pick up games of soccer, Frisbee, basketball and tennis, plus protests, parades and free movies.

Stow Lake (p170) Paddle-boat to the pagoda and back around a picturesque island in Golden Gate Park.

Botanical Wonders

Strybing Arboretum & Botanical Gardens (p168) Everything grows in this Golden Gate Park corner, from South African savannahs and California redwoods to New Zealand cloud forests.

Japanese Tea Garden (p168) Contemplate priceless lost-and-found bonsai over iron pots of tea.

Urban Wildlife

Sea lions at Pier 39 (p37) This harem features more posturing, clowning and in-fighting than a reality show.

Hayes Valley Farm (p112) Bees are making honey on a freeway on-ramp at this unbelievable two-acre urban farm.

Jones (p116) Rise above the concrete jungle for captivating Patty Hearst cocktails in a rooftop forest.

Best Architecture

Superman wouldn't be so impressive in San Francisco, where most buildings are low enough for a middling superhero to leap in a single bound. But San Francisco's low-profile buildings are its highlights, from original adobe and gabled Victorians to flower-topped museums.

Iconic Landmarks

Golden Gate Bridge (p24) Orange deco span with the best disappearing act on the planet.

Transamerica Pyramid (p91; pictured right, next to the Sentinel Building) William Pereira's Egyptian space-age monument built atop whaling ships defines San Francisco.

Coit Tower (p54) The white exclamation point on SF's skyline is dedicated to firefighters and lined with murals.

Victorians

Alamo Square (p150) Picture-perfect snapshot of SF Victorian architecture, from Queen Annes to Sticks.

Haight Flashback Walking Tour (p180) The most colorful Victorians in town are also landmarks of hippie history.

Modern Marvels

California Academy of Sciences (p162) The world's first Platinum LEED–certified green museum by Renzo Piano, capped with a living wildflower roof.

MH de Young Memorial Museum (p164) Herzog & de Meuron's copper-clad building is oxidizing green, blending into the scenery.

San Francisco Museum of Modern Art (p76) Mario Botta's brick-boxed lightwell is getting a radical extension by Snøhetta architects.

RUDY SULGAN/CORBIS ©

Know Your Victorians

- **Stick** (1880s) Flat fronts and long, narrow windows; see the Haight.
- **Queen Anne** (1880s–1910) Exuberant turreted, gabled mansions; see Alamo Square.
- **Edwardian** (1901–1914) False gables and Arts & Crafts details; see the Avenues.

Best For Kids

San Francisco has the least kids per capita of any US city, and according to SFSPCA data, about 19,000 more dogs than children live here. Yet many locals make a living entertaining kids – from Pixar animators to video-game designers – and this town is packed with attractions for youngsters.

Junior Foodies

When spirits and feet begin to drag, there's plenty of ice cream and kid-friendly meals to pick them back up – look for the symbol throughout this book.

Major Thrills

Exploratorium (p28) Mind-bending technology and hands-on weird science exhibits that won a MacArthur genius grant.

Cable cars (p80) Look mom, no seat belt!

Musée Mecanique (p37) Saloon brawls, public executions, space invaders and other vintage arcade games.

La Raza Skatepark (p133) Even *Thrasher* pros yield to little ones in kneepads...awww.

San Francisco Carousel (p38) Hold on tight as vintage ponies gallop past San Francisco scenery.

Creative Kids

Children's Creativity Museum (p89) Live-action video games and kiddie claymation workshops taught by special-effects pros.

Cartoon Art Museum (p88) Wall-to-wall superheroes and graphic-novel antiheroes – brace for fanboy/girl freakouts.

826 Valencia (p133) Writing workshops, pirate supplies and fish theater fuel active imaginations.

Kids Go Wild

California Academy of Sciences (p162) Penguins, an eel forest, starfish petting zoos and sleepovers amid rare wildlife.

Aquarium of the Bay (p37) Walk underwater through glass tubes, as skates flutter past and sharks circle around.

Best Shopping

San Franciscans may claim they avoid chain stores for political reasons (supporting local designers, the economy, fellow workers of the world, etc) but individualist vanity drives the offbeat street fashion and trend-setting decor. Find your own signature SF style on the city's most boutique-studded streets: Haight, Valencia, Hayes, upper Grant, Fillmore, Union and Polk.

Pre-Shopping Planning

Before you browse, check **Urban Daddy** (www.urbandaddy.com) for store openings and events, **Thrillist** (www.thrillist.com) for guy gifts and gadgets, **Refinery 29** (www.refinery29.com) for sales and trends, and **Daily Candy** (www.dailycandy.com) for SF finds and deals. Factor non-refundable SF city and CA state sales taxes into your shopping budget – combined, they tack 9.5% onto purchase prices.

Further Adventures in Retail

Retail can get surreal in San Francisco, where stores tend to look more like natural history museums or pioneer farm sheds, and often pull double duty as nonprofits, event spaces and art galleries.

For even more adventurous retail, the city hosts regular only-in-San Francisco shopping experiences. In February **Noise Pop** (www.noisepop.com) features concerts and rock-star pop-up shops and **Monster Drawing Rally** (www.soex.org) finds artists scribbling furiously and audience members snapping up their work while still wet. At **LitQuake** (www.litquake.org) in September you can score signed books and grab drinks with authors afterwards. October's **Alternative Press Expo** (www.comic-con.org/ape) has comics, drawings, 'zines and crafts, plus workshops with comics artists.

SABRINA DALBESIO/LONELY PLANET IMAGES ©

SF Lifestyle

Gravel & Gold (p141) Head back to the land in style, with original hippie homesteader pottery, smock dresses and how-to manuals.

Park Life (p176) Instant street smarts, from local artist–designed tees to original works by SF's graffiti-art greats.

Local Maker

Heath Ceramics (p99) Pottery purveyor to star chefs since 1948.

Mollusk (p176) Surf legends shop here for artist-designed hoodies, T-shirts, skateboard decks and hand-shaped surfboards.

Needles & Pens (p142) Local art, 'zines and accessories for streetwise romantics.

Nancy Boy (p121) Overachieving beauty products, locally made with effective natural ingredients.

Triple Aught Design (p121) Clothes fit for inventors and supervillains serve more functions than a Swiss army knife.

Fashion Statements

Reliquary (p120) SF's signature bohemian chic, from cult denim to vintage hippie jewelry.

MAC (p121) Haute but never haughty: impeccable, easy pieces for trend-setting men and women.

Piedmont Boutique (p157) Cross-dress to impress with locally designed drag fabulousness.

Mingle (p32) Get the indie-rocker-plays-acoustic look with locally designed denim and swingy dresses.

Jeremys (p100) Hot-off-the-runway style and international designer samples at steep discounts.

Books & 'Zines

City Lights (p68) This little bookshop (pictured left) won a major free-speech lawsuit 50 years ago, and keeps publishing avant-garde literature.

Adobe Books & Back-Room Gallery (p141) Readers on sofas, cats atop philosophy and art wedged between history and religion.

Kayo Books (p121) Perfect vacation reads: vintage pulp fiction, original 1930s noir novels and juicy 1960s shock-lit paperbacks.

Green Apple (p177) A literary opium den, where bookish dreamers lose days browsing half-a-city-block of new and used titles.

Vintage, Antique & Repurposed

Community Thrift (p142) Vintage scores plus store-donated items, with all proceeds going to local charities.

Wasteland (p156) Fashion-forward, retro '40s to '80s clothes, plus recent designer scores.

Local Food & Drink

Recchiuti Chocolates (p100) Local artisan chocolates for every San Fran occasion, from gourmet brunches to beer tastings.

Bi-Rite Market (p142) Caution: gazing too long at Bi-Rite's dazzling wines, cheeses and sustainable meats may induce vows to relocate.

Golden Gate Fortune Cookie (p68) Make a fortune in San Francisco for 50¢: slip your secret message into a hot cookie here.

Music

101 Music (p69) Join DJs thumbing through milk-crates of rare, cheap LPs, and you might spot Carlos Santana browsing guitars.

Amoeba Records (p157) Free concerts and a store 'zine that outsmarts *Rolling Stone*, plus thousands of new and used CDs and DVDs.

Best Freebies

Free SF History

Rincon Annex Post Office (p90) Murals cover San Francisco history, from Native American oyster-gathering origins to McCarthy-era censorship.

Aquatic Park Bathhouse (p43) An old WPA project to convince sailors to bathe, covered with uplifting Depression-era public art.

San Francisco Main Library (p110) Volunteer-run neighborhood history walking tours (www.sfcityguides.org) and free onsite history exhibits.

City Hall tours (p110) See where the first sit-in happened (pictured above), and the first gay official was elected...and assassinated.

Free Art Shows

Mission Murals (p128) Mission alleys do double duty as open-air galleries, constantly showing new public artworks.

San Francisco Art Institute (p43) See a Diego Rivera masterpiece, avant-garde shows, and sweeping bay views, all gratis.

49 Geary (p89) Free contemporary art shows across four floors, plus free wine and pretzels on the first Thursday of each month, 5pm to 7:30pm.

77 Geary (p90) Two tiers of free contemporary art shows, plus drink and fabulousness on first Thursdays, 5pm to 7:30pm.

Catharine Clark Gallery (p88) Bold art banned elsewhere is shown here, and it's free for all.

Gallery Paule Anglim (p88) Museum-caliber shows minus the admission fee.

Electric Works (p88) Wild imaginings and friendly, food-filled openings – though the gallery store is tempting.

Free Entertainment

Concerts at Amoeba (p157) From Elvis Costello to Tenacious D, everyone plays free in the back of this music store.

Mission Dolores Park summer movies (p132) Family-friendly fare, especially movies set in SF – expect snark about Mrs Doubtfire's drag.

View of Giants games from Waterfront Promenade (p98) The local crowd may grant you a glimpse, especially if you bring beer.

Sea lions at Pier 39 (p37) Sea mammal slapstick on yacht marina docks.

Survival Guide

Survival Guide

Before You Go

When to Go

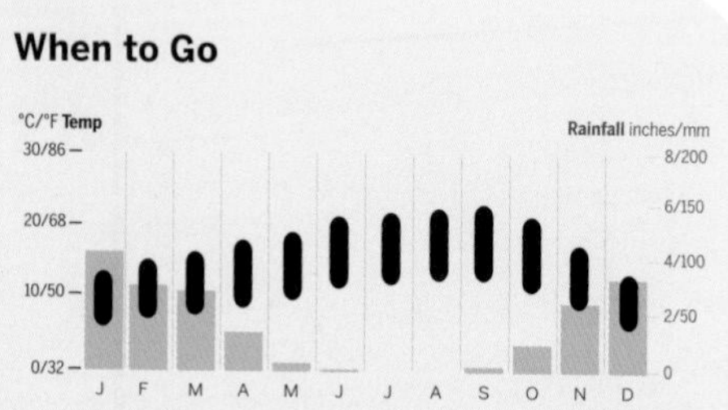

➡ **Winter (Dec–Feb)** Low-season rates, brisk but rarely cold days, and the colorful Lunar New Year parade.

➡ **Spring (Mar–Apr)** Film festivals, blooming parks and mid-season rates make the occasional wet day worthwhile.

➡ **Summer (May–Aug)** Street fairs, farmers markets and June Pride celebrations compensate for high-season rates and chilly afternoon fog.

➡ **Fall (Sep–Nov)** Prime time for blue skies, free concerts, bargain hotel rates and flavor-bursting harvest cuisine.

Book Your Stay

☑ **Top Tip** San Francisco's 15.5% hotel tax is not included in most quoted rates

➡ Downtown hotels offer bargain rates, but avoid the sketchy, depressing area west of Mason.

➡ Most motels offer free onsite parking. At downtown hotels, expect to pay $35–$50 for overnight parking.

Useful Websites

Bed & Breakfast SF (www.bbsf.com) Personable, non-chain local B&Bs and inns.

SF Visitor Information Center Reservations (www.onlyinsanfrancisco.com) Vacancies and deals; indispensible in high season and during conventions.

Lonely Planet (http://hotels.lonelyplanet.com) Expert author reviews, user feedback, booking engine.

Best Budget

San Remo Hotel (www.sanremohotel.com) Old-style North Beach charm, with antique furnishings and shared bathrooms.

Hayes Valley Inn (www.hayesvalleyinn.com) Simple but homey, with shared bathrooms and boutiques at your doorstep.

Fitzgerald Hotel (www.fitzgeraldhotel.com) Quirky, scuffed, downtown hotel with in-room fridges and microwaves; wine bar downstairs.

Marina Motel (www.marinainn.com) Bougainvillea-bedecked 1939 motel; optional kitchens, free parking.

Pacific Tradewinds Guest House (www.sanfranciscohostel.org) Cheerful 4th-floor hostel near North Beach; full kitchen, no elevator.

Best Midrange

Hotel Rex (www.jdvhotels.com) Cozy rooms with sumptuous beds and a downstairs literary lounge; off Union Square.

Hotel Bohème (www.hotelboheme.com) North Beach jazz-era gem; small, period-perfect rooms.

Orchard Garden Hotel (www.theorchardgardenhotel.com) LEED-certified green downtown hotel, with spa-luxe rooms.

Tuscan Inn (www.tuscaninn.com) Fashion-forward and kid-friendly; on Fisherman's Wharf.

Hotel des Arts (www.sfhoteldesarts.com) Art installations double as guestrooms downtown.

Hotel Del Sol (www.thehoteldelsol.com) Revamped, family-friendly 1950s Marina motel; heated outdoor pool.

Best Top End

Palace Hotel (www.sfpalace.com) Opulent 1906 downtown landmark; cushy rooms, onsite spa, indoor pool.

Hotel Palomar (www.hotelpalomar-sf.com) Contemporary lounge-chic that's smack downtown; soundproof windows.

Hotel Vitale (www.hotelvitale.com) Soothing bayside spa-hotel, across from the Ferry Building.

Argonaut Hotel(www.argonauthotel.com) Nautical-chic, converted 1908 wharf-side cannery, with bay views.

Arriving in San Francisco

☑ **Top Tip** To find out how best to get to your accommodations, see p17.

From San Francisco International Airport (SFO)

BART (Bay Area Rapid Transit; www.bart.gov; one-way $8.10) Direct 30-minute ride to/from downtown San Francisco; SFO BART station is outside the international terminal.

Door-to-door vans Share vans depart outside baggage claim; 45 minutes to most SF locations; fares $14–$17 one-way. Companies include: **SuperShuttle** (☎800-258-3826; www.supershuttle.com), **Quake City** (☎415-255-4899; www.quakecityshuttle.com), **Lorrie's** (☎415-334-9000; www.gosfovan.com) and **American Airporter Shuttle** (☎415-202-0733; www.americanairporter.com).

Green Tortoise

Green Tortoise (☎800-867-8647, 415-956-7500; www.greentortoise.com) offers quasi-organized, slow travel on biodiesel-fueled buses with built-in berths from San Francisco to West Coast destinations including Santa Cruz, Death Valley, Big Sur and LA.

Taxis Depart from outside baggage claim; $35–$50 to most SF destinations.

Driving It's a 20–60 minute, 14-mile trip north from SFO Airport, up Hwy 101, to get to downtown San Francisco.

From Oakland International Airport (OAK)

BART AirBART shuttle (adult/child $3/1) runs every 10–20 minutes to Coliseum station, where you catch BART to downtown SF ($3.80, 25 minutes).

Taxis Depart curbside; fares $50–$70 to SF.

Door-to-door vans Shared rides to SF run $25–$30 on SuperShuttle (p205).

From Norman Y Mineta San Jose International Airport (SJC)

Caltrain (www.caltrain.com) VTA Airport Flyer (bus 10; tickets $2; 5am-midnight) departs every 15–30 minutes to Santa Clara station, where trains depart to San Francisco. Caltrain terminal is at the corner of 4th and King Sts (one-way $8.75; 90 minutes).

Car Downtown San Francisco is 50 miles north of SJC, via Highway 101.

From Emeryville Amtrak Station (EMY)

Amtrak (www.amtrakcalifornia.com) serves San Francisco via Emeryville (near Oakland), and runs free shuttle buses from its Emeryville station to San Francisco's Ferry Building and Caltrain station.

Getting Around

BART

☑ **Best for**... travel between downtown and the Mission, East Bay and SFO.

Throughout this book, venues readily accessible by **BART** (Bay Area Rapid Transit; www.bart.gov; ⏲4am-midnight Mon-Fri, 6am-midnight Sat, 8am-midnight Sun) are denoted by **S** followed by the name of the nearest BART station.

Destinations Downtown, Mission District, SF & Oakland airports, Berkeley & Oakland.

Schedules Consult http://transit.511.org.

Tickets Sold in BART station machines; fares start at $1.75.

Bicycle

☑ **Best for**... sightseeing west of Van Ness Ave.

Rentals Near Golden Gate Park (p171) and Fisherman's Wharf (p44).

Bus

☑ **Best for**... travel to/from the Haight, Marina and Avenues.

Muni (Municipal Transit Agency; www.sfmuni.com) operates bus, streetcar and cable-car lines. Throughout this book, venues accessible by bus are denoted by 🚌 followed by the street where the nearest bus stop is located.

Tickets Standard fare $2; buy on board (exact change required) and at underground Muni stations. Keep ticket for transfers (good for 90 minutes on streetcars and buses), and to avoid a $100 fine.

Schedules On digital bus stop displays and maps, plus http://transit.511.org. Weekend and evening service is limited.

Night service Owl service (1am to 5am) offered on limited lines, with departures every 30–60 minutes; Late Night Transfers valid for travel 8:30pm–5:30am.

System map Available free online and at the Powell MUNI kiosk ($3).

Cable Car

☑ **Best for**... scenic routes and handling hills between downtown and Fisherman's Wharf and North Beach.

For more on cable car lines, service, and history, see p80.

Fares Tickets cost $6 per ride (no on/off privileges). Purchase on board from conductor or at cable-car turnaround kiosks.

Passes For multiple rides, get a Passport (p207).

Seating Each car seats about 30, plus standing passengers clinging to straps. To secure a seat, get on at cable-car turnarounds.

Car

☑ **Best for**... trips out of town

Avoid driving in San Francisco; traffic is constant, street parking scarce, hills tricky and meter readers ruthless.

Garages Around $2–$8 per hour ($25–$50 per day) downtown; for public parking garages, see www.sfmta.com. Inquire at hotels, restaurants and entertainment venues about validation.

Rentals Start at $50–$60 per day, $175–$300 per week, plus 9.5% sales tax and insurance.

Car share Prius Hybrids and Minis are rented by the hour by **Zipcar** (☎866-494-7227; www.zipcar.com) for flat rates

Transit Passes

➡ **Muni Passport** (1/3/7 days $14/21/27) Allows unlimited travel on all Muni transport, including cable cars; it's sold at the Muni kiosk at the Powell St cable-car turnaround on Market St, San Francisco Visitor Information Center (p211) and from a number of hotels. One-day passports can be purchased from cable car conductors.

➡ **Clipper Cards** Downtown Muni/BART stations issue the Clipper Card – a reloadable transit card with a $5 minimum valid for Muni, BART, Caltrain and Golden Gate Transit (not cable cars). Clipper cards automatically deduct fares and apply transfers – only one Muni fare is deducted in a 90-minute period.

(including gas and insurance) starting at $6.98 per hour ($69.30 per day); $25 application fee and $50 prepaid usage required in advance.

Rush hour Avoid peak traffic weekdays 7:30am–9:30am and 4:30pm–6:30pm; call ☎511 for traffic updates.

Towed cars Retrieve cars towed for parking violations at **Autoreturn** (www.autoreturn.com; 450 7th St; 24hr); fines run $73 plus towing and storage fee, starting at $392.75/first four hours.

Roadside assistance Members of the **American Automobile Association** (AAA; ☎800-222-4357; www.aaa.com; 160 Sutter St; 8:30am-5:30pm Mon-Fri) can call the 800 number any time for emergency road service and towing.

Parking Restrictions

Red	no parking/stopping
Blue	disabled only
Green	10 min 9am-6pm
White	pick-up/drop-off only
Yellow	loading zone 7am-6pm.

Streetcar

☑ **Best for**... travel to the Castro and Ocean Beach and along Market St.

Throughout this book, venues accessible by Muni Metro streetcar lines are denoted by M followed by the name of the nearest streetcar stop. The N Judah line goes through many key neighborhoods, from Downtown to Ocean Beach. It's a cheap way to get the lay of the land.

Tickets Standard fares $2; see p207 for passes.

Schedule 5am–midnight weekdays; limited schedules on weekends.

Night service L and N lines operate 24 hours, but above-ground 'Owl' buses replace streetcars between 12:30am and 5:30am.

Key Routes & Destinations

F	Fisherman's Wharf & Embarcadero to Castro
J	Downtown to Mission/Castro
K, L, M	Downtown to Castro
N	Caltrain and SBC Ballpark to Haight, Golden Gate Park & Ocean Beach
T	Embarcadero to Caltrain & Bayview

Taxi

☑ **Best for**... SoMa and Mission club nights.

Meters start at $3.50 plus about $2.25 per mile and 10% tip ($1 minimum).

Taxi companies with 24-hour dispatches:

Green Cab (☎415-626-4733; www.626green.com)

DeSoto Cab (☎415-970-1300)

Luxor (☎415-282-4141)

Yellow Cab (☎415-333-3333)

Essential Information

Business Hours

Nonstandard hours are listed in reviews; standard business hours are:

Banks 9am–4:30/5pm Monday to Friday (occasionally 9am–noon Saturday)

Offices 8:30am–5:30pm Monday to Friday

Restaurants Breakfast 8am–noon, lunch noon–3pm, dinner 5:30–10pm; Saturday and Sunday brunch 10am–2pm

Shops 9/10am–6/7pm Monday to Saturday and noon–6pm Sunday

Discount Cards

Go Card (www.gosanfranciscocard.com; adult/child 1-day $54.99/39.99, 2-day $75.99/54.99, 3-day $95.99/69.99) offers unlimited access to major attractions, cable cars, discounts on packaged tours and waterfront eateries.

Green Zebra guide (www.thegreenzebra.org) offers special discounts on Bay Area green-friendly businesses.

Electricity

120V/60Hz

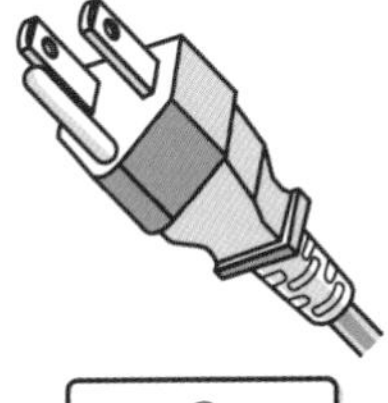

120V/60Hz

Emergency

Police, fire and ambulance (☎emergency 911, non-emergency 311)

San Francisco General Hospital (☎emergency room 415-206-8111, main hospital 415-206-8000; www.sfdph.org; 1001 Potrero Ave)

Drug & alcohol emergency treatment (☎415-362-3400)

Trauma Recovery & Rape Treatment Center (☎415-437-3000; http://traumarecoverycenter.org)

Money

☑ **Top Tip** Most banks have ATM machines open 24 hours; service charges may apply.

US dollars are the only accepted currency in San Francisco; debit/credit cards are accepted widely.

Changing Money

Exchange bureaus Located at airports, but most city banks offer better rates – try centrally located **Bank of America** (www.bankamerica.com; downstairs, 1 Powell St; 9am-6pm Mon-Fri, to 2pm Sat; M S Powell St)

Exchange rates Consult www.xe.com, a currency converter site.

Credit Cards

To report lost or stolen credit cards, contact:

American Express (☎800-992-3404)

Diners Club (☎800-234-6377)

Discover (☎800-347-2683)

MasterCard (☎800-622-7747)

Visa (☎800-847-2911)

Travelers Checks

Many establishments will accept travelers checks just like cash. For check purchase and exchange, visit **American Express** (AmEx; ☎415-536-2600; www.americanexpress.

Money-Saving Tips

- Make the most of Freebies (p202).
- First Tuesdays of each month are free at many museums; see individual listings.
- Hang on to your Muni ticket for discounted admission at key attractions, including California Academy of Sciences, Mh De Young Museum and Legion of Honor.

com/travel; 455 Market St; ⏰8:30am-5:30pm Mon-Fri, 9:30am-3:30pm Sat; M S Embarcadero).

Travelers checks in US dollars can be replaced if lost or stolen. Contact the following numbers:

- **American Express** (☎800-992-3404)
- **MasterCard** (☎800-622-7747)
- **Thomas Cook** (☎800-223-7373)
- **Visa** (☎800-227-6811)

Public Holidays

Holidays that may affect business hours and transit schedules include the following:

New Year's Day January 1

Martin Luther King Jr Day Third Monday in January

Presidents' Day Third Monday in February

Easter Sunday (and Good Friday and Easter Monday) in March or April

Memorial Day Last Monday in May

Independence Day July 4

Labor Day First Monday in September

Columbus Day Second Monday in October

Veterans Day November 11

Thanksgiving Fourth Thursday in November

Christmas Day December 25

Safe Travel

☑ **Top Tip** Keep your city smarts and wits about you, especially at night in the Tenderloin, SoMa and the Mission.

After dark, Dolores Park, Buena Vista Park and the entry to Golden Gate Park at Haight and Stanyan Sts can turn seedy, with occasional drug dealing.

Panhandlers and homeless people are a reality in San Francisco. People will probably ask you for spare change, but donations to local nonprofits stretch further. For safety, don't engage with panhandlers at night or around ATMs. Otherwise, a simple 'I'm sorry,' is a polite response.

Telephone

☑ **Top Tip** North American travelers can use their cell phones in San Francisco and the Bay Area, but should check with the carrier about roaming charges.

US country code ☎1

San Francisco area code ☎415

International calls From the Bay Area, call ☎011 + country code + area code + number; when calling Canada, skip the initial ☎011.

Calling other area codes The area code must be preceded by a ☎1.

Area Codes in the Bay Area

East Bay ☎510

Marin County ☎415

Peninsula ☎650

San Jose ☎408

Santa Cruz ☎831

Wine Country ☎707

Cell Phones

Most US cell phones – aside from iPhones – operate on CDMA, not the European standard GSM. Be sure to double check compatibility with your phone service provider.

Operator Services

International operator ☎00

Local directory ☎411

Long-distance directory information ☎1 + area code + 555-1212

Operator ☎0

Toll-free number information ☎800-555-1212

Toilets

☑ **Top Tip** Haight-Ashbury and the Mission District have a woeful lack of public toilets; you may have to buy coffee to access locked customer-only bathrooms.

➡ **Citywide** Self-cleaning, coin-operated outdoor kiosk commodes cost 25¢; there are 25 citywide, mostly located in North Beach, Fisherman's Wharf and downtown. Toilet paper not always available.

➡ **Downtown** Clean toilets and baby-changing tables can be found in Westfield San Francisco Centre (p102).

➡ **Civic Center** San Francisco Main Library (p110) has restrooms, as do public library branches and parks throughout the city.

Tourist Information

California Welcome Center (Map p42, D1; ☎415-981-1280; www.visitcwc.com; Pier 39, Bldg P, Suite 241b; ⏲10am-5pm) Supplies brochures, maps and help booking accommodations.

Friends of Recreation & Parks (☎415-263-0991) Organizes free tours of Golden Gate Park.

McLaren Lodge (Map p166, E4; ☎415-831-2700; cnr Fell & Stanyan Sts; ⏲8am-5pm Mon-Fri) Information on Golden Gate Park.

San Francisco Visitors Information Center (Map p86, D2; ☎415-391-2000; www.onlyinsanfrancisco.com; lower level, Hallidie Plaza; ⏲9am-5pm Mon-Fri, 9am-3pm Sat & Sun) Maps, guidebooks, brochures and help with accommodations.

Travelers with Disabilities

☑ **Top Tip** All Bay Area transit companies offer travel discounts for disabled travelers and wheelchair-accessible service.

Transit For services see **San Francisco Bay Area Regional Transit Guide** (http://transit.511.org/disabled/index.aspx).

Pedestrian crossings Major downtown crosswalks emit a chirping signal to indicate when it is safe for visually impaired pedestrians to cross the street.

Wheelchair accessibility Independent Living Resource Center of San Francisco (☎415-543-6222; www.ilrcsf.org; ⏲9am-4:30pm Mon-Thu, to 4pm Fri) covers Bay Area public transit, hotels and other facilities.

Dos & Don'ts

➡ **Fashion** Casual is the norm, but pretty much anything goes fashion-wise in San Francisco, from bird costumes to public nudity. But there is one rule: don't stare.

➡ **Food** Vegans, pescatarians, and allergies are accommodated at many restaurants – but do confirm when you call for reservations so the chef can adjust recipes as needed. Don't be shy about asking about food sourcing – many restaurants are proud to serve local, organic, humane, sustainable fare.

➡ **Politics** Leftist politics are mainstream in San Francisco, as is friendly debate. Don't be shy about sharing your views, and do hear out others.

Visas

☑ **Top Tip** Check the US Department of State (http://travel.state.gov/visa) for updates and details on the following requirements.

Canadians Proof of identity and citizenship required.

Visa Waiver Program (VWP) Allows nationals from 36 countries to enter the US without a visa. It requires a machine-readable passport issued after November 2006. Citizens of VWP countries need to register with the **US Department of Homeland Security** (http://esta.cbp.dhs.gov/) three days before their visit. There is a $14 fee for registration application; when approved, the registration is valid for two years.

Visa required For anyone staying longer than 90 days, or with plans to work or study in the US.

Behind the Scenes

Send Us Your Feedback

We love to hear from travelers – your comments help make our books better. We read every word, and we guarantee that your feedback goes straight to the authors. Visit **lonelyplanet.com/contact** to submit your updates and suggestions.

Note: We may edit, reproduce and incorporate your comments in Lonely Planet products such as guidebooks, websites and digital products, so let us know if you don't want your comments reproduced or your name acknowledged. For a copy of our privacy policy visit lonelyplanet.com/privacy.

Our Readers

Many thanks to the travelers who used the last edition and wrote to us with helpful hints, useful advice and interesting anecdotes:

Damian Ennis, Roe Cheung, Christine Dauer, T Hawkins, Kelvin Hayes, Bobbi Lee Hitchon.

Alison's Thanks

Many thanks and crushing California bear hugs to commissioning editor Suki Gear and editors Anna Metcalfe and Monique Perrin, but above all Marco Flavio Marinucci, who made waiting for a Muni bus the adventure of a lifetime.

Acknowledgments

Cover photograph: Cable car crossing California St, San Francisco; Danita Delimont/AWL. Many of the images in this guide are available for licensing from Lonely Planet Images: www.lonelyplanetimages.com.

This Book

This 3rd edition of *Pocket San Francisco* was written by Alison Bing. Previous editions were also researched and written by Alison. This guidebook was commissioned in Lonely Planet's Oakland office, and produced by the following: **Commissioning Editor** Suki Gear **Coordinating Editors** Pat Kinsella, Monique Perrin **Coordinating Cartographer** Xavier Di Toro **Coordinating Layout Designer** Mazzy Prinsep **Managing Editor** Anna Metcalfe **Senior Editors** Victoria Harrison, Susan Paterson, Angela Tinson **Managing Cartographers** Shahara Ahmed, Alison Lyall **Managing Layout Designer** Jane Hart **Assisting Editors** Alice Barker, Sophie Splatt **Assisting Cartographer** James Leversha **Cover Research** Naomi Parker **Internal Image Research** Rebecca Skinner **Thanks to** Lucy Birchley, Janine Eberle, Ryan Evans, Chris Girdler, Liz Heynes, Laura Jane, David Kemp, Trent Paton, Piers Pickard, Lachlan Ross, Michael Ruff, Julie Sheridan, Laura Stansfeld, John Taufa, John Vlahides, Gerard Walker, Clifton Wilkinson

Index

See also separate subindexes for:

Eating p220

Drinking p221

Entertainment p221

Shopping p222

Sights p000
Map Pages **p000**

Sights p000
Map Pages **p000**

Sights p000
Map Pages **p000**

Eating

Drinking

Entertainment

Sights p000
Map Pages **p000**